American Politicians and Journalists

American Politicians and Journalists

Charles Press
Michigan State University

Kenneth VerBurg
Michigan State University

Scott, Foresman/Little, Brown College Division
Scott, Foresman and Company
Glenview, Illinois   Boston   London

Library of Congress Cataloging-in-Publication Data

Press, Charles.
  American politicians and journalists.

  Includes index.
  1. Press and politics — United States.
  2. Journalists — United States.   I. VerBurg, Kenneth.
  II. Title.
  PN4751.P7   1988   302.2'34'0973   87-23321
  ISBN 0-673-39743-2

1   2   3   4   5   6   7   8   9   -   PAT   -   93   92   91   90   89   88   87

Printed in the United States of America

Acknowledgments

The authors wish to thank the following individuals and organizations for granting permission to use their cartoons and photographs in this text:

p. 3: The Lyndon Baines Johnson Library
pp. 16, 85, 152, 185: © 1979, 1981, 1984, 1986 by G. B. Trudeau. Reprinted by permission of Universal Press Syndicate. All rights reserved.
p. 31: Brown Brothers, Sterling, PA. 18463
p. 71: The Gerald R. Ford Library
p. 107: UPI/Bettmann Newsphotos
p. 141: Paul Schutzer, LIFE MAGAZINE © 1960 Time Inc.
p. 175: UPI/Bettmann Newsphotos
p. 209: © 1979, Robert Phillips from Black Star
p. 239: © 1979, Don Wright, Inc.
p. 265: UPI Photo by Thai Khac Chuong
p. 295: AP/Wide World Photos

Preface

In teaching a course on government and the media, we have found that our students are somewhat cynical about politicians. They are willing to believe that foremost in any politician's thinking is getting elected. Some would add, at whatever cost.

But these same students are usually less willing to recognize that career goals also motivate journalists. Once introduced to the idea, however, they begin to see its practical value in explaining journalists' behavior.

The way politicians and journalists interact — each seeking to advance their own careers — is the theme that ties together the topics we cover in this book.

Some presidents and some newspeople view this interaction as a zero-sum game — or equivalent to a military engagement. Our view differs. We suggest that the healthiest form of interaction for a democratic polity is a mixed-motive game, with elements of both cooperation and conflict. A stance of guarded cooperation generally promotes civility, tends to maximize news for the citizen consumers, and makes politics and journalism fascinating enterprises for practitioners and students.

While career advancement forms the integrating core of professional journalism and politics, we note here, as we do again in Chapter 1, that the practitioners in both have other, more altruistic goals as well.

We are indebted especially to the work of one former and one present colleague. Norton E. Long, in his classic article "The Local Community as an Ecology of Games," describes how the journalist seeks out the minister for a news item on his Sunday sermon. The ecclesiastic happily gives the reporter the details — a cooperative interaction that satisfies the career goals of each. Joseph A. Schlesinger in *Ambition and Politics* discusses in detail how career goals influence political behavior. To both authors we owe a great deal, academically and personally.

We are also indebted to our editor at Scott, Foresman/Little, Brown College Division, John Covell, as well as to our reviewers — Richard Hofstetter, San Diego State University; Michael Johnston, Colgate University; and Thomas Rochon, Princeton University — who helped us improve our manuscript and encouraged us to complete it.

And finally, for their help, and encouragement, we wish to thank Nancy Press and Esther VerBurg.

Charles Press
Kenneth VerBurg

Contents

3

☆ ──────────────────────────── ☆

The Journalists
Whom Politicians Face   70

4

☆ ──────────────────────────── ☆

The Politicians
Whom Journalists Face   105

5

☆ ──────────────────────────── ☆

The Presidency:
Getting Nominated and Elected   140

6

☆ ───────────────────────────── ☆

Governing in the
Television Age:
The President   173

7

☆ ───────────────────────────── ☆

Congress Meets the Press   207

8

☆ ───────────────────────────── ☆

Bureaucrats, Judges,
and Journalists   238

American Politicians and Journalists

1

Journalists and Politicians: A Star-Crossed Romance

Getting a start in politics is not always easy. Here is how former Vice President Hubert H. Humphrey got his.

Humphrey worked in his family's drugstore in Doland, South Dakota, for six years. Then his interest in politics drove him to study political science at the University of Minnesota. To support himself he taught part time at Macalester College in St. Paul. Midway through graduate school, impatient with his studies, he decided to become active in politics — as a candidate for mayor of Minneapolis.

But he had a problem — no one would take his campaign seriously. His public statements drew little attention. He challenged the incumbent to a debate. The mayor disdained even to answer the challenge. Hubert Humphrey's fledgling candidacy was walled in by silence and indifference.

Humphrey and his friends therefore devised a scheme. A fellow political science graduate student went to city hall and told the mayor's secretary that he wanted to become a volunteer in the mayor's reelection campaign. The message was relayed and the mayor, all smiles, marched out ready to greet this intelligent young man.

As soon as the mayor appeared, in came Hubert Humphrey with a *Minneapolis Star* reporter with camera in tow. The debate began. Humphrey put on a show — talking rapidly, shaking his finger in the mayor's face, and reeling off one charge after another.

That afternoon, Humphrey's staged event dominated page one of the *Star* and launched his political career. After that, what he did and said was news. Minnesotans became aware of his "percolate up" personality and continued reading about his doings. After serving as mayor, he moved on to become U.S. senator, vice president, and Democratic candidate for president. He was always at the center of Minnesota political news.

CHAPTER OVERVIEW

In this chapter we examine the relationship between politicians and journalists. We look first at the role of political journalists, and what we see suggests why politicians need journalists. We also note how politicians and journalists, often to the politicians' surprise and dismay, define political news differently. Next we consider the politician-journalist interaction from the journalist's point of view. We then discuss the guarded relationship in which politicians and journalists use each other to advance their own careers. We end by considering whether the by-products of these interactions are always beneficial to democratic governing.

WHAT POLITICAL JOURNALISTS DO

In the late 1960s, Delmar Dunn interviewed journalists in the Wisconsin legislature. He asked them to describe what they did, and they outlined four major aspects of the job.[1]

Report Events

All the reporters said reporting political events — "getting the facts" — was part of their job. Some insisted that reporters should do nothing more, but others argued that facts were not enough. President Franklin Roosevelt would have agreed with the first group. He claimed that when he retired he would publish a newspaper printing only facts. He said he would let people draw their own conclusions.

Interpret the News

But reporting only facts, most journalists now recognize, is an illusion. Space or time does not now allow them to report all details. In deciding what to include or leave out of their stories, they interpret for the readers and viewers and tell them which facts are important. Such screening may lead to a conclusion.

Journalists may highlight from a senator's speech his proposals on acid rain because he chairs a Senate subcommittee studying the problem.

They may completely ignore his comments on the Soviet Union, balancing the national budget, or the virtues of the red-bellied woodpecker. Inevitably, reporting facts requires reporters to give readers some idea of what is important and what the facts mean. Interpreting events, most journalists now agree, also goes with the job of being a good reporter.

Public Watchdogs

In addition to reporting events, some of Dunn's journalists added the "watchdog" function — investigative uncovering of buried information. These reporters, Dunn suggested, saw themselves as "representatives

President Lyndon B. Johnson (1963–69) reviews his daily collection of newspapers in the Oval Office. Presidents, as well as other politicians, regularly check the national media because they provide a variety of perspectives on how speeches or actions taken the day before are being presented to the reading or viewing public. The media may also supply information about problems that are not reported directly to the president.

of the public" looking out for the ordinary citizen's interests. They argued that they need to do more than report events. They must also dig out information, perhaps on matters that politicians would just as soon not have them report. Thus, they recognized that journalists sometimes create news. And by uncovering information they generally imply a point of view — "this needs reforming!"

Active Participants

But some reporters told Dunn the job involved even more — that occasionally they had to become active participants in the political process itself. They recognized that reporting facts, interpreting events, or digging out data often influenced political outcomes, as much, sometimes, as the actions of lobbyists, party leaders, or political officials themselves. The *Miami Herald* reporters who tracked Gary Hart and Donna Rice radically changed the 1988 presidential race. Some reporters told Dunn they participated reluctantly, others said they did so enthusiastically.

Journalistic participation in politics is a primary role and one we focus on throughout this book. Political scientists occasionally overlook the journalist's influence. Politicians, though, soon learn not to make that mistake!

POLITICIANS NEED JOURNALISTS

Political scientist Joseph A. Schlesinger argues that a great many actions of politicians can be explained by their career ambitions, their attempt to gain and hold public office. Some politicians, content with their present political success, have career motivations that Schlesinger calls "static": they want only to keep the office they hold. But others aspire to a higher office. They have "progressive" ambitions.

The out-of-office beginners such as young Humphrey have progressive ambitions, as does the state legislator who hopes someday to be governor or a member of Congress. Also holding progressive career ambitions are administrators who plan to head their own department in the future, or the county judge who hopes someday to be elected to the state supreme court or appointed to a federal judgeship. But the state legislator who wants only to be reelected, the federal district judge appointed for life, or the bureaucrat at the top of the classification system generally have static ambitions.[2]

Political Payoffs of News Coverage

Political ambitions, whether static or progressive, force politicians to communicate with the public. The public learns most of what it knows about them and what they are doing from news reports. Politicians find that what reporters write or say in interpretive or investigative stories can directly influence their political careers. It is not astonishing then to find that politicians seek to use journalists to help their political careers.

Getting Public Recognition. Trying to get elected or change a government policy often involves communicating your ideas to thousands of voters. Aspiring politicians usually have no more effective way of "talking" to voters than through newspapers, television, or radio.

The out-of-office politician or participant in social movements perhaps need news coverage most, but find it difficult to get journalists' attention. Humphrey could have campaigned door to door for months and not gained the name recognition he got through that page-one story in the *Star*.

Politicians already in office also use journalists to build their political careers. They know that news coverage is more effective than "tooting their own horns" — voters see news reports as coming from an independent source. Moreover, news stories reach more constituents than do the politician's newsletters. And people are more apt to read or listen to press reports. Those who do are more likely to think the politician deserves a little credit. Then too, of course, politicians do not have to pay for news coverage.

Politicians know that getting favorable news stories between elections is one of the best ways to campaign. Voters see the good work they are doing as public-spirited efforts rather than crass bids for votes. If a dam is to be opened in the district, the member of Congress likes to be in the news story carrying the announcement. If a tornado hits the state, the governor goes out to view the damage, and, incidentally, to edge into a newspaper or television picture.

Seeking Advice. Politicians sometimes also welcome the journalist's active help. They may use journalists to gauge the public's reaction to their proposals and decisions, as well as to "talk" to other public officials and learn what they think. Douglass Cater observed that Washington politicians seemed to talk to each other through the nation's prestige press — the Washington newspapers and *The New York Times*. They form, he says, a political community in microcosm — one that thrashes out political issues before the larger public.[3] Dunn saw the same thing as state politicians followed news reports in Wisconsin's major newspapers.

We find some politicians turning regularly to journalists for political advice. President Theodore Roosevelt institutionalized this method through a "reporter's cabinet," including journalists from the major New York and Washington papers and the wire services. Together they discussed with Roosevelt (off the record) how he might handle breaking political stories — unexpected political events that Roosevelt himself had not initiated. In his autobiography, Roosevelt wrote that he usually followed their advice.

Appointive Officials. Administrators are less in need of personal publicity. But they know how important "proper" media coverage is for their agency, its programs, and indirectly, their own careers. Most of all, appointive officeholders desire articles praising their agency. But short of that, they are pleased when journalists print their news releases. At a minimum, they want to avoid unfavorable publicity. And they find reporters useful for informing other elective or appointive officials of their agency's interests and programs.

Even judges, who generally avoid news coverage, don't enjoy reading news stories critical of themselves.

Coverage of "Worthwhile" Proposals

Do politicians seek publicity only out of self-serving career advancement? Not necessarily. Even when they work for idealistic ends, politicians recognize that favorable news coverage is necessary.

Officeholders — administrators and judges — and even politicians out of office, regard themselves as professionals. Most want to make their mark, to achieve something, a record of public service they can point to with pride. Their goals may be as modest as helping the department of natural resources pass a bill to stamp out "swimmer's itch" (a rash that lake snails cause). Or the goal may be as ambitious as crafting a law to eradicate a toxic waste dump in the district.

Journalists can help politicians get such pet projects moving or keep them alive when public interest wanes.

The Importance of Public Support

American public officials respond to public opinion. Abraham Lincoln described policy making in our decentralized, Madisonian system of government: "Public sentiment is everything. With public sentiment nothing can fail. Without it, nothing can succeed. *Consequently he who holds public sentiment goes deeper than he who enacts statutes or pronounces decisions.*" (Emphasis added).

Lincoln probably overstated reality. But most politicians would agree that demonstrating public backing is usually necessary to achieve anything that matters.

Once leaders lose that support, as Presidents Johnson, Nixon, Carter, and Reagan did during their terms, they have little chance to succeed, no matter what they try. That is why Washington politicos watch with interest the monthly Gallup poll on public support for the president. It is a significant index of presidential leadership in the short term.

Lincoln's comment may suggest that the powerful politician can bypass journalists by reaching out directly to citizens to create this valued public support. A number of presidents have tried it: Franklin D. Roosevelt did so most effectively with his radio "fireside chats." Few political leaders have been as successful. And Roosevelt was wise enough to use the technique sparingly, not more than once or twice a year.

Today's journalists are not easily bypassed. When the president wants to address the nation, he must request network time. Even then, some station managers decide to carry a basketball game or an old movie rather than the political speech. Moreover, the president depends on newspapers and the network newscasters to tell others how important his speech will be. Otherwise many people will not think it is worth listening to. And he knows he risks wearing out his welcome — citizens have loved, respected, and listened so intently to few presidents as they did to Roosevelt during the bleak days of the Great Depression or the tense times during World War II.

Contemporary presidents know that, unlike presidential broadcasts fifty years ago, theirs will get instantaneous reaction. As the Oval Office fades from the television screen, George Will, Jack Germond, or Ken Bode will come on to hash over what he said. Joining in the "analysis" will be economists, political scientists, or fellow news commentators. Not only will they review the high points of the speech, but they will tell viewers what it means, and sometimes whether the proposals make sense. Meanwhile dozens of other journalists begin tapping out "in-depth" analyses for tomorrow's newspaper columns.

Journalists May Sway Public Support

How much does journalistic coverage count in a politician's bid for public support? At times it seems to have little effect. Politicians somehow

Swaying public opinion

occasionally survive a steady flow of hostile news coverage. But the effect is not always minor.

Consider an event involving President Gerald Ford. In the heat and tension of a 1976 presidential debate with Jimmy Carter, President Ford doggedly insisted that Poland was not then under Russian domination, a major gaffe.

Pollsters interviewing a random sample of citizens immediately after the debate found that a majority believed President Ford had "won." The next day, news broadcasters and columnists played up Ford's statement and interpreted it as a major blunder. Public opinion shifted dramatically, pollsters now finding that the public believed challenger Carter was the debate winner. That was the opinion that held. The event led one social psychologist to suggest, somewhat in jest, that the public should elect newscasters also.[4] A week later President Ford weakly suggested he had misspoken. But some citizens, it seems, were left with the lingering feeling that the president was not well informed about what was happening outside his hometown, Grand Rapids, Michigan.

No doubt you have heard that politicians think bad publicity is better than none at all. They prefer good publicity, however, to either of the above. Politicians like journalists to report that they are on the job solving problems plaguing the public, not that they are making major mistakes.

Thus, whether politicians are selfishly interested in advancing their own political careers or idealistically seeking to influence policy, getting results at one time or another involves journalists, with whom politicians have good reason for trying to get along.

Conflict Between Politicians and Journalists

If this were the whole story, we would find little to interest us for long. Journalists' main function would be to serve as conveyor belts. Politicians would hand journalists news releases, and the latter would roll off to print them, in much the same way as news seems to be made in totalitarian nations.

Experienced American politicians are not so naive about journalists. Yet, some, and perhaps all politicians at one time or other, are shocked by the news reports that result from events in which they have participated. When that happens, politicians claim that journalists distort and twist the facts, just to get the public to look at what they report.

Washington's Criticism of "Irresponsible Journalists." The experience is not new. An early draft of George Washington's "Farewell

Washington + the press

Address to the Nation" included a savage attack on journalists. Alexander Hamilton persuaded him to scratch it, but Washington remained unconvinced. What made our first president so touchy?

As the Revolutionary War began, Commander-in-Chief Washington urged colonial housewives to save old rags to be turned into newsprint. But the ungrateful editors began to criticize his battle strategies. Perhaps dealing the unkindest jab of all, some printed stories about drunken soldiers at Valley Forge. Washington contented himself with stating, perhaps through clenched teeth, the wish that "our printers be more discreet in their publications." Privately, though, he seethed.

Later he enthusiastically supported barring journalists from the Constitutional Convention of 1787 over which he presided. He arranged for tightly closed windows through that hot summer and an armed guard at each door to keep out snooping reporters. (James Madison's convention records reveal that no delegate — including Benjamin Franklin, patron saint of American journalists— raised the issue of an "open meetings" policy.)

During the deliberations someone gave Washington notes on convention proposals that a delegate had carelessly dropped in a Philadelphia tavern. Washington waited until the end of the day's session, then spoke bluntly of his distrust for journalists.

"I must entreat, gentlemen," he said, "to be more careful lest our transactions get into the newspapers and disturb public response by premature speculations." He then is reported to have bowed, slammed the paper on his desk, picked up his three-cornered hat, and strode from the room. Whoever owned the notes could claim them if he were brave enough to do so.

As president, Washington's attitude about the public's "right to know" remained unchanged. When Indians massacred six hundred soldiers on the frontier, most blamed the event on the ineptness of General Arthur St. Clair, whom Washington had appointed. Congress wanted to know how it happened, and critical newspaper editors did, too. The situation was similar to the suicide truck bombs that caused major tragedies among United States soldiers and embassy personnel in Lebanon during 1983.

President Washington announced that *he* would release the documents that *he* decided should be released "in the public interest." The rest would remain "confidential." We now call that presidential policy "executive privilege," a policy every president since has followed despite freedom-of-information laws or even public outcry.

Thomas Jefferson and Journalists. Washington was not the only American political hero upset with journalists. Newspaper editors and publishers are fond of quoting Thomas Jefferson on "freedom of the press." Jefferson said he would "not hesitate a moment" to choose a nation with newspapers and no government over one with a government but no newspapers.

But seldom do editors and publishers recall that Jefferson also said, "Even the least informed of the people have learned that nothing in a newspaper is to be believed . . . and I therefore have long thought that a few prosecutions of the most prominent offenders would leave a wholesome effect." Jefferson may have had an "enemies list" of journalists, just as Richard Nixon did.

Recent Leaders and Journalists. United States Supreme Court Justice William O. Douglas vigorously defended freedom of the press in his opinions. Yet, in his autobiography, he described journalists as "craven," "abusive," "self-seeking," and "depraved." During all his years as justice — from 1937 to 1975, longer than any other in history — the Supreme Court, he said, "got very poor news coverage." The reporters, Douglas wrote, usually wrote "news stories which the author of the court opinion would hardly recognize as descriptive of what he had written." Justice Douglas said he favored press freedom not because he respected journalists but because he thought government control of the news would be so much worse.

President Jimmy Carter, writing about his term as president in *Keeping Faith*, comments that he had "two unpleasant surprises. . . the inertia of Congress. . . and the irresponsibility of the press."

The point is easy to grasp — politicians have not always wholly admired American journalists or the way in which they perform their professional journalistic responsibilities.

What Politicians Complain About

Journalists tend to dismiss politicians' attacks as sour grapes. Even as able a reporter as Jack Germond could write in a moment of frustration, "One of the ways you can tell that a politician is in trouble is that he begins to whine about the press. Candidates slipping in the polls get testy about their failure to get their message across. Every political reporter has had the experience of being upbraided by a loser on election night."[5]

Conflicting Career Goals. Germond's criticism is justified, at least occasionally. But the basis of the conflict lies much deeper. Officeholders or politicians running for office cannot be expected to see the significance in political events precisely as journalists do. Politicians and journalists, with their different career goals, live by different rules. The two groups thus sometimes define "political news" in very different ways. Garrison Keillor, star of the PBS radio program, *Prairie Home Companion,* addressed a convention of journalists. He summed up his reasons for being wary: "We see things differently. If I were to suffer a violent death, you would regard it as a professional opportunity."

Superficial Political Reporting. Politicians tend to see reporters as a perpetual nuisance — forever reporting on sideshows rather than the center ring. The only remedy is to guide or control them. The politicians complain most about the kind of event journalists find newsworthy. Politicians say journalists too often are interested only in political events that attract readers and viewers. Politicians think journalists emphasize the superficial — political items that will shock or amuse readers — rather than reporting accurately the significant political facts.

They seek out "human-interest" stories. We once were following a broadcast of a presidential nominating convention when the television anchor booth switched from covering the political notables on the platform to an interview with a bearded "candidate for president" who said he campaigned in favor of free silver while riding on Greyhound buses between Utah and Oregon. We also have observed news stories concentrating on a mayor's peculiar habit of breaking crackers into his coffee, while generally ignoring the policies he was proposing.

Politicians see journalists as seeking to advance their own careers at the formers' expense by reporting events in ways that encourage controversy and build circulation or swell electronic media audiences. When the president makes a statement, politicians say, journalists try to start a controversy by picking the statement apart until they can encourage a negative reaction or division of opinion, preferably among members of the president's own party. Their attention to the real content of the statement seems incidental.

Strategy and Secrecy. President Reagan's deputy press secretary charged in 1982, as many other press secretaries had before him, that journalists go out of their way to make governing difficult or nearly impossible. Consider the matter of political strategies. Whether the president is preparing to deal with the new leader of the Soviet Union or with a recalcitrant member of Congress from Idaho, he will attempt to conceal his strategy. But that is precisely the kind of detail journalists want to rush into print. They encourage anyone involved in a strategy session, including secretaries who type the minutes, to leak information or documents.

© San Diego Union, 1986 by permission of Copley News Service

Politicians argue that labor negotiators, military commanders, and even journalists themselves keep their strategies secret.

Consider the problem that developed at the Pentagon in 1981. Jack Taylor of the *Oklahoma City Daily Oklahoman,* citing the Freedom of Information Act, asked to see "after-action reports" — memos that public information officers at the Department of Defense write after a journalist interviews a military officer. *Newsweek* reported that "these documents generally summarize what the reporter was after and what he learned." *Newsweek* quotes the reaction by reporter John Fialka of *The Washington Star* when he learned that Taylor had requested *his* after-action reports. "If I have to run the risk that some other reporter might see the questions I've been asking, then we no longer have competitive journalism."[6]

Here we find a journalist saying that if the news he is trying to nose out and the strategy he is following in interviewing officers were to become common knowledge, "exclusives" would be impossible. No doubt we could readily find a politician to paraphrase the claim — "If I have to let my political enemies know what I am trying to do and the strategy I plan to follow, then we can no longer have genuine political bargaining." Not unexpectedly, politicians feel wholly justified in hiding their strategies from snooping journalists.

Compromise and Secrecy. Another point of conflict is the need for secrecy during the bargaining itself. This need was the issue at the Constitutional Convention in 1787. No delegate wanted the citizens back home to read about the horse trading that went on or the threats and promises made in reaching any of the four great compromises that grew from the deliberations. Madison's notes were not published until long after every delegate had died.

President Woodrow Wilson, early in World War I, spoke glowingly and somewhat biblically about "open covenants openly arrived at." He meant that he opposed making treaties in secret. But by war's end he had enough of journalistic prying into the nation's international affairs. He then concluded that conditions of privacy were essential to treaty making; that is, if any of the participant nations were to be persuaded to give ground. Politicians notice that journalists want the same kind of secrecy for themselves.

Walter Bennis, former president of the University of Cincinnati, maintains that no organization (including a journalistic one) can function effectively without confidentiality in the proposals, steps, and discussions leading to its decisions. He describes how *The New York Times* scooped the profession in publishing the officially secret, but leaked, "Pentagon Papers" — a study of our participation in the Vietnam War.

The *Times* editors decided to condense this mammoth collection of documents for publication. In some places they had to add clarifying material — crucial decisions that they made in private. Bennis writes, "The editors surrounded their preparation of these stories with a secrecy and security the Pentagon might envy — renting a secret suite of hotel rooms, swearing each member of a small staff to total secrecy, confining them for weeks. . . restricting their communications to. . . those with the need to know, setting the stories themselves on sequestered, closely guarded typesetting machines. Thus the ultimate challenge to 'official' secrecy was performed in ultimate 'private' secrecy."[7]

Oversimplifying the Art of Politics. Politicians also complain that much of the reporting borders on giving citizens an oversimplified and overly moralistic picture of the complex political process. Some politicians conclude, after seeing the journalists' writeup of their actions, that journalists dislike and do not understand the art of politics. Politicians see journalists, especially television reporters, as seeking to condense and simplify everything to a good guys versus bad guys horse opera, or as reporting the political story as a soap opera, building in extraneous dramatics. Politicians suggest that television journalists have difficulty deciding whether they are in the information or entertainment business.

Bill Moyers, President Lyndon Johnson's press secretary — later a newspaper publisher and PBS and CBS news commentator — summed up the criticisms: "The rules of politics are negotiation, weaving, subtlety, nuance, trading, advancing, retreating, and so on. These are the things with which you sustain the political process. But television doesn't like nuance. And television doesn't like subtlety. . . . television deals in a world of simplicity and insists politicians play by the rules of television and not the rules of politics."[8]

The Politician's Dilemma

Politicians face a dilemma in their relationships with journalists. On the one hand, as we have seen, politicians often think that journalists cannot be trusted to report political events fairly. When reporters and editors talk about the public's right to know, politicians think they really mean the media's right to boost circulation and audience by printing or broadcasting sensational stories. Merely to attract attention, journalists sometimes make politicians look sinister or inept. For the same reason they might reveal political strategies or state secrets, and interfere with governing processes. Finally, what the journalists do report, politicians argue, is likely to be simplistic, distorting the meaning of the event.

Still, the politicians observe, journalists and their reports can be extremely useful. They can help build a politician's public image, improve reelection possibilities, and help pet political projects succeed.

How do the politicians handle the dilemma? Journalists, they conclude, must be handled properly. They need to be guided for their own good as well as the public's good. Politicians cannot depend on their self-restraint, must take care in giving them information, and must be sure they get the right slant. At the same time, it is essential to remain friendly and accommodating when possible. Politicians say to themselves, the time may come when I will need some journalist's help.

From the politician's perspective, then we sometimes see a love–hate relationship with journalists. More often, though, it is an attraction–rejection relationship, like that of a couple who cannot live apart but whose relations are strained when they are together. From the politician's side, the relationship is one of guarded cooperation.

JOURNALISTS ALSO NEED POLITICIANS

In the Hubert Humphrey story that opens this chapter, we notice that a *Minneapolis Star* reporter tagged along to this contrived media event. Was this just a crusty, cynical, but sympathetic reporter who wanted to help a young, struggling politician? Probably not. The episode benefited him as well.

Journalistic Payoffs of Political Coverage

Journalists, like politicians and the rest of us, have career ambitions. They want to advance in their profession or at least to maintain their status once they have reached a position that is likely to satisfy them during the rest of their working lives.

Starting out in a journalism career, as in politics, can be difficult. For many it means beginning with a job on a rural weekly paper or being a weekend reporter at a television station in a small market. If one gets a chance on a larger newspaper or television station, it may mean filing stories on the county commission or worse, the councils of outlying villages, or on zoning-board decisions. The reports draw little attention and the pay is low. But such reporters do not become anchor persons, city-hall reporters, or state-capital correspondents with higher pay by hard work or brilliant writing alone.

Importance of the Story. How do journalists achieve their professional ambitions? Ask yourself how that reporter's journalistic career might have benefited from the Humphrey story. First, he got a lead article on page one of the paper, something every reporter seeks. Second, he probably got a byline (his name attached to the story). Third, as his price for coming along, he got an exclusive — an important story no other reporter had. Fourth, he made a friendly contact with a young politician, one who might turn out to be successful and able to pass along other good stories and news tips in the future. Fifth, his editor and possibly his colleagues complimented him for the professional nose for news he displayed.

Reporters move up by "getting a good story." Getting an exclusive, which journalists once called a scoop, is even better. A scoop is an unambiguous example of the journalist's professional skill. It is an important story that no one else reports. A reporter may struggle along for years writing items for page 14 of Section D just before the want ads. Only a few colleagues notice. But getting a few exclusives that the wire

services pick up can make a big difference. A friendly and helpful politician may help a reporter become a bona fide local celebrity, at least among colleagues.

The opposite of this achievement — the ultimate journalistic disaster — is not to get a story other journalists did get, or to be given the story much later. A politician can sometimes arrange for that to happen as well.

Dan Rather wrote candidly about such journalistic career motivations. He was assigned to the White House, his first important break, by CBS. Just before his first presidential news conference a White House aide asked Rather to ask the president a "planted question."

What went through his mind as he considered the ethics of taking a "plant"? Rather wrote, "It wouldn't hurt for my bureau chief, Bill Small, to see me on my feet, getting recognized, and asking a question that produces a substantial answer from the President, one that may even be the lead news item that next day. Small doesn't know me all that well. I'm still trying to cut it. Then there was peer group acceptance. Yes, it might be nice to have a Tom Wicker or Bill Lawrence (both of *The New York Times*) notice that I had asked a useful question."

Rather's moral dilemma did not last. The president's aides prudently had also asked several other reporters to ask the "plant." Rather wrote, "My jaw fell open like a pelican waiting for a fish when the other fellow asked *my* question." And right then Rather resolved never again to accept a "plant."[9] But he did not give up the career ambitions that drove him to gain the respect of journalistic colleagues and become one of America's leading newscasters.

Politicians as a Source of News. As Rather and every other reporter knows, politicians are a major source of "big stories," even exclusives. They can make a journalist's career. David Claypool of the *American Daily Advertiser* got his big break when George Washington chose him for an exclusive, publishing the text of Washington's Farewell Address, an item reprinted with a credit line to Claypool in every other newspaper then published in America.

Several studies confirm the significance of political news. Leon Sigel sampled several years of *Washington Post* and *New York Times* front pages and counted the sources for the stories. He found that 46.5 percent were based on information that national officials supplied, 31.6 percent from officials of state and local governments. Only 21.9 percent came from nongovernment sources.[10]

Every ambitious reporter can readily see what kind of story gets on the front page or where the sources for such stories may be located. Journalists may not fully appreciate English editor Malcolm Muggeridge's analogy: "Journalists follow authority as sharks do an ocean liner, hoping to feed off the waste it discharges, with perhaps someone occasionally falling overboard to make a meal, and once in a while the whole ship going down and providing a positive feast."

The Rewards of Professional Reporting. James Deakin, veteran reporter on the St. Louis *Post-Dispatch*, wrote that it is difficult for hardboiled, worldly reporters to admit to idealism. They would rather say, "I became a journalist because I was too nervous to steal." But he argues that "public service is in the mixture of motives whose end product is the journalist."[11]

Like politicians, journalists are not wholly self-serving. The challenge to perform professionally, to do something clearly in the public interest, motivates journalists, at least in part. Even the most cynical see themselves as performing a useful public service, doing what *New York Times* columnist Tom Wicker describes as "monitoring those in positions of power."[12]

Journalists believe they "represent the public," serve as watchdogs who will reveal political corruption, misconduct, or ineptness in public officials. Reporting on unsafe, unhealthy, or unfair conditions and raising public awareness enough that politicians have to do something can be a source of quiet satisfaction.

Syndicated columnist Joseph Alsop received many honors and un-covered a number of big stories during his forty-two-year career. His "most pleasing moment," he remembers, occurred early in the Korean War. He and his brother Stewart helped force the Secretary of Defense to resign because, Alsop wrote, "we had shown up his endless lies." These are moments journalists savor.

Journalists Need Politicians. Once again we need realize only that the source for many such stories is an obliging politician who "leaks" the needed data. Watergate reporters Robert Woodward and Carl Bernstein were indebted to "Deep Throat," the pseudonym given an insider who guided the investigative reporting that eventually led to President Richard Nixon's resignation.

Whether journalists are interested only in advancing as journalists or they also are motivated by idealism, the path to success usually leads to the same doors — those inside which politicians live or work. On the journalists' side, then, we discover reasons for their maintaining friendly relationships with at least some politicians.

JOURNALIST CONFLICT WITH POLITICIANS

If politicians at times have a low opinion of journalists, the favor is returned, often intensely, as the following illustrations show.

Some Historical Criticism

We have no statements by journalists on their thoughts about President Washington's treatment of the press or his policy of "executive privilege." But we do know that poet and editor Phil Freneau described our first president as "the man who is the source of all the misfortune of our country." And the editor of the Philadelphia *Aurora* wrote in December 1796, "If ever a nation was debauched by a man, the American nation was debauched by Washington."

Nearly every statesman memorialized by a monument in Washington, D.C., or the fifty state capitols has received such journalistic criticism — some of it, perhaps, deserved.

Contemporary Criticisms

Jack Anderson, the national capital's most prominent investigative reporter, says about politicians, "One of the seemingly irreversible currents I have observed during 32 years of covering Washington politics is the hankering of our leaders to transform themselves from servants to sovereigns, to replace Abraham Lincoln's 'government of the people' with a government of privilege, majesty and omnipotence. . . the common practice has been to pursue aggrandizement and usurpation, often with mock humility."[13]

Or consider a column by Jack Germond and Jules Witcover on President Jimmy Carter. Their contempt for the president as politician jumps out of the page. Carter, they wrote, had been using the ominous technique of "newspeak" that George Orwell invented for his totalitarian novel, *1984*. They pointed with disdain to Carter's labeling the disastrous 1982 helicopter mission to rescue Americans held hostage in Iran as "an incomplete success." Orwell, they suggested, would have recognized the truth as opposite to what Carter said it was. They also commented on Carter's campaign statement to North Carolina tobacco farmers who were outraged at his antismoking campaign. Carter, they reported, said that the administration's goal was to make cigarette smoking "even safer than it is today."[14]

Journalists, it seems, operate on the principle that only their continual criticism, nagging, probing, digging, and exposing, or the threat of it, keeps politicians from indulging themselves with any dishonest strategy that comes to mind. Politicians, journalists tend to think, cannot be fully trusted.

The Journalists' Complaints

Journalists criticize politicians because they say most would like to have journalists report only what the politician wants reported.

Unnecessary Secrecy. Politicians, journalists say, try to suppress all news that may cast them in an unfavorable light. They act as if citizens do not have the right to know how the public officials behave and how they conduct public business.

Why, reporters ask, should strategy be kept secret? When an official such as the president is considering alternatives, reporters argue that the public has the right to know about them. James Deakin gives the journalist's view: "The people will pay, in lives, money, economic well-being or hardship, or in some other way. They will have to carry the can. So the final decision cannot be presented to them as a *fait accompli*, with no public debate over other possible courses of action."[15]

Some critics argue that President Johnson asked for the Gulf of Tonkin resolution, which involved us in the Vietnam War, without disclosing all the details. Not until much later did an admiral's message to the Pentagon that reports about the supposed torpedo attacks were erroneous become public. Ironically, Deakin commented, when Johnson was the Democratic majority leader in the Senate under Republican President Eisenhower, he argued that Congress should "be in on the takeoffs as well as the crash landings."

News Management. A related complaint by journalists is that politicians seek to control them and manage the news.

Every reporter, in time, seems to conclude that most politicians try to mislead reporters at least some of the time. Journalists are convinced that some, such as Presidents Nixon and Johnson, told outright lies. Former Secretary of State Henry Kissinger's explanation — "The press must understand that the official is there not to please them but to achieve his or her purposes" — is not wholly convincing. Reporters remember that presidents have harassed reporters who filed unfavorable stories by subjecting them to annual tax audits, wiretaps, and FBI checks.

It is clear, then, why journalists conclude that no politician can be wholly trusted to define political news properly.

The Utility of Open Warfare

Some journalists conclude that they cannot accommodate themselves to a relationship of guarded cooperation with incumbent politicians. Rather they decide that the only possible journalistic position must be one of barely concealed warfare. And some politicians, such as Presidents Nixon and Johnson, in effect declared war on journalists.

Cold-warrior journalists view any courtesy or deference to politicians as compromising their integrity. At times the Nixon and Johnson presidencies certainly encouraged such a posture. An example is the CBS claim to have on tape President Nixon's saying he thought reporters looked at him "with hatred in their eyes."[16] And Nixon persuaded himself that few journalists would treat him fairly, that most only wanted to "kick him around." Holding the view that people hate you, psychologists suggest, is likely to be a self-fulfilling prophecy.

Paranoia in the politician is countered with paranoia in journalists — a stalemate. Politicians begin to "stonewall" about even minor items. And journalists begin speculating about the politician's motives and wander further and further from factual reporting. One "news report" during the Nixon era used phrases common in describing the symptoms of schizophrenia to characterize the president's actions. The journalist did not *directly* suggest, though, that the president suffered from this mental illness.

The Necessity for Skepticism

When either side leaves common civility behind and resorts to declarations of open war, neither politician nor journalist profits. Nor do such declarations add to the public's store of knowledge. Thus journalists and politicians usually conclude that in one way or another they must generate an accord that both sides can live with; a peace treaty that allows both to observe at least the outward forms of politeness.

Such an accord, however, does not entirely eliminate journalistic skepticism about politicians' motives. Nor is the politician fully trusting of journalists.

David Stockman, budget director under Reagan, failed to appreciate this when, during Reagan's first term, he permitted William Greider of *The Washington Post* to tape a discussion in which Stockman expressed his doubts about "Reaganomics." Stockman perhaps imagined that at some later date Greider would, after getting his permission, unearth the tapes to show how prescient Stockman had been about the president's economic policies. If the policies proved successful, the tapes could be forgotten. But a short time later he found his recorded comments printed in an article Greider wrote for *The Atlantic*. Some thought Stockman might be fired. Instead, though, Stockman reported that the President had a session with him in the "woodshed."

Reasonable skepticism recognizes that the other party has different goals. It harmonizes well with the symbiotic relationship that usually provides benefits to both parties. The relationship between journalists and politicians is a game of mixed motives — the actors are partly supportive of each other and partly antagonistic.

To be war-minded or overly threatening is self-defeating. So also is trusting naivete. When journalists and politicians similarly define what is political news, as often occurs, they can work together harmoniously. And when their vantage points and definitions of news diverge, they find they must work at cross-purposes.

Again we arrive at the relationship described as guarded cooperation — a companionship of convenience in which both sides accept moments of friction and frustration along with moments of accomplishment.

DEMOCRATIC BY-PRODUCTS

In this closing section we examine the mostly unplanned effects of this relationship between journalists and politicians on the democratic system of governing.

Beneficial By-Products

Paradoxically, we find that guarded cooperation, with journalists and politicians each pursuing their own goals, helps democratic government function.

Legitimizing Political Opposition. Political information translates into political power. Citizens may learn that their governor has a detailed plan for raising taxes. Such information provides a basis on which citizens can agree and support, or disagree and oppose, that policy. News of the governor's plans may cause the governor to deny the report, clarify earlier statements, or scrap the plan.

If providing political information is legal, it follows that so too is criticism based on such information. Independent reporting of political events legitimizes those who criticize and even oppose the government and its policies, even when a majority of citizens do not agree with the critics. Independent news coverage proclaims that criticism of the government is not an act of disloyalty to the nation or subversive to its government — it criticizes only those presently administering the nation's affairs.

Such information also gives opponents of current policy an opportunity to seize the policy initiative from government leaders. Vietnam war opponents took the policy leadership from the Johnson administration. Many observers believe that viewers reacted to the horrors shown in televised reports from Vietnam — a Vietnamese officer executing a captured spy or Morley Safer's video clip of American soldiers using cigarette lighters to set afire the huts of villagers suspected of aiding the Viet Cong. Such news reports helped citizen critics to modify and finally reverse official policies and actions.

Thus, independent journalistic coverage is a vital component in the array of democratic institutions that undergird a "loyal opposition" — a group who offer to provide alternatives to current policies and actions. Without such information, the power of opposition parties or political leaders would diminish to impotence. Unofficial critics would have to go underground. And, as is common with many underground movements, its leaders and followers would increasingly lose touch with political reality.[17]

Building the Basis for Consent. Because politicians are the source of many political news stories, much of what is reported is, of course, favorable to them. But even when the stories are unfavorable they can help the politician.

Independent news coverage also legitimizes those who govern. Officials can argue that because journalists provide citizens with the information they need to select and evaluate officeholders, those selected to run the government have the right to govern: they have the informed consent of the governed.

Journalists help officeholders in another way. They may bring out political stories that distress opponents of the government. Not all anti-nuclear activists welcomed the attention given the person who threatened to blow up the Washington Monument in 1982 if the United States did not immediately declare a nuclear freeze. Nor were all right-to-life groups pleased with journalists' stories about radicals who dynamited abortion clinics in 1984. Leaders of both groups took pains to distance themselves from acts that they called bizarre behavior by a few extremists.

These Democratic Benefits Are Unplanned. We think these by-products are serendipitous outcomes of the interplay between politicians and journalists. This set of relationships is based primarily not on altruism, idealism, or planning in the public interest but on conflicting personal ambitions. Politicians often may have no higher goals than getting reelected, and journalists no more direct objective than to get a good story for the next edition or newscast. Neither group defines its daily task as enhancing or nurturing the democratic process. Nonetheless, that often is the outcome.

Nonbeneficial By-Products

But not all outcomes are beneficial to democratic societies. The situation is similar to the capitalistic system, which also depends on individual economic motivations to provide benefits. But unrestrained capitalistic individualism can result in victimizing the innocent, as by causing ecological disasters.

So too can unrestrained political or journalistic career ambitions. In their zeal to hold office at any cost, or their passion to get the "big political story" no matter what the price, both politician and journalist may go to excess and infringe upon constitutional freedoms and privileges.

The politician's goals occasionally lead to distorted, inaccurate, and self-serving information. Politicians' excesses in eliminating criticism are well documented; "Watergate" symbolizes these.

But journalists may be driven to excess for personal and crass reasons as well. Janet Cooke of *The Washington Post* had to return her Pulitzer prize in 1981. The paper's own editors, after checking her prizewinning news story, found that it was fiction. And Michael Daly of the *New York Daily News* in the same year was also found to have fabricated a story.

One cannot assume that all journalists or all politicians will always resist temptation when career rewards are high.

Who Decides What's Fit to Print? Reporters regularly face the more difficult choices — should they report all the stories they uncover? Should a reporter or editor withhold publication of a story because it is injurious to individuals or society or perhaps threatening to the survival of democracy itself?

The New York Times's famed slogan, "All the News That's Fit to Print," implies that because of poor taste or incivility or perhaps other reasons, some news is not appropriate for their publication.

When the *Times* editors devised that slogan, many journalists believed that they should not report or publish stories about personal scandal. Only long after the fact did the public learn about the extramarital affairs of Presidents Franklin Roosevelt or John Kennedy. Correspondent John Pierpoint of CBS writes that he and AP reporter Douglas Cornell accidentally became aware of such a Kennedy liaison. But in those days it was not the kind of story that would be reported.[18]

Nor did the nation learn until much later about our full losses in the Japanese attack on Pearl Harbor. Even today, television news will generally not show the bloody results of an auto crash but at most paramedics wheeling a covered body into the ambulance. And journalists still do not generally report on the private lives of politicians unless the story involves breaking a law or public scandal. The report on Senator Gary Hart resulted in a great deal of journalistic soul searching. Periodically, a journalist will hint that Congress or a state legislature has homosexuals, alcoholics, or hard drug users in its midst. But names are seldom mentioned.

And scholars have found 35,000 photos of President Roosevelt, only two of which show him in a wheelchair. Aides carrying the president into a meeting room, but out of the view of spectators, once lost their hand holds and dropped him, but no one snapped a picture.

Not all journalists agree, however. Some believe that all the news they can gather should be published. And some would add that any way in which they can gather news is justified. They figuratively wrap themselves in the phrases of the First Amendment and argue that they should not be subject to outside restraint, or be expected to show self-restraint. Like the swashbuckling reporters in the 1920s play about yellow journalism, *The Front Page,* they feel free to go after stories in any way that succeeds and to print everything they get.

Yet only a few television stations broadcast footage of Pennsylvania state treasurer R. Budd Dwyer, who, in a news conference, held a .357 Magnum revolver to his mouth and fired. He had been convicted for his role in a conspiracy and bribery case involving other state officials and a computer firm.

The handling that story got generally suggests that many editors and reporters are troubled by a sense of social responsibility. Such journalists face hard choices. Should editors publish information about new and sophisticated spy satellites carried by the space shuttles? Or should a magazine be free to publish instructions on making hydrogen bombs because of the government's declassification mistake, or print the names of American undercover agents abroad, which once was not against the law? One such CIA agent, Richard S. Welch, was murdered in Athens on December 23, 1975 after a small publication identified him as a CIA operative.

The Libertarian View. Some argue that journalists should not worry about the consequences of reporting a story — that is not their job. It is dangerous, they say, to limit freedom of the press. They argue that once journalists begin self-censorship of the news they collect, they will not know where to draw the line. Stories must be printed even when it means possibly doing harm.

Charles Eisendrath, a former *Time* correspondent, "vehemently disagreed" with those who would withhold footage of the treasurer committing suicide. He argued that "To deny the public an image of what happens in such a disaster is to deny them the basis for accurate judgement of their officeholders and the strain and tragedy they may encounter."[19]

Threats to National Security. Some politicians and a very few journalists favor a restrictive policy when some possible harm could occur from publication. They believe that the United States government, at least in some instances and especially during wartime, should closely monitor any information that is released for national security reasons. That was the justification the military gave in keeping reporters away from the invasion of Grenada in 1983. Public opinion pollsters found that Americans overwhelmingly approved of this decision, lest full reporting aid the enemy and expose American military personnel to greater risk.

Authoritarian and totalitarian nations embrace an absolutist national security position — whatever the government itself decides might endanger national security may not be published. The Soviet Union justified its decision not to report immediately on the Chernobyl nuclear disaster as preventing disorder and panic.

Conflicting Constitutional Freedoms. Not all citizens, and even all journalists, agree that it is right to publish all that can be collected — bomb recipes or lists of CIA or narcotics undercover agents. Some would regard such publishing as examples of "excess," especially if reporters obtained the information illegally. Others would argue that citizens and even politicians should be protected from hasty publication. Americans troubled by such problems generally hope for reasonable journalistic self-restraint rather than governmental regulation. In doing so they reject the libertarians' basic premise that journalists should be under no restraints.

More Americans would also reject the national security position. Some would argue that the Soviet Union's original suppression of the Chernobyl disaster news prevented victims from taking proper precautions and created more panic in the long run. Most of us reject any policy that approaches the totalitarian position — but we have come close to adopting it in national emergencies.

Freedom of the press, many believe, may conflict with other equally important constitutional freedoms. The Supreme Court has argued that this freedom, like others, should at times give way. But most Americans also favor taking some chances — generally favoring publication unless the probability of harm is high. We have to accept as the price of freedom the knowledge that some stories that are printed or televised may in the long or short run do some harm to our society or unfairly injure some citizens.

Charles Seib of *The Washington Post* agrees that the journalist should lean toward publishing rather than not when questionable items arise. But he points to three areas in which he believes journalists should consider self-restraint: national security, personal security of those whose lives may be endangered by publication, and most difficult area of all, an individual's right to privacy. Should the names of rape victims, especially if they are minors, be published?

Most Americans decide such questions pragmatically. Deciding whether press freedoms should give way in specific cases leads to questions such as: Whom will publishing the political item help? Whom will it hurt? Do the potential injuries tip the scales in favor of not publishing?

Consider the example mentioned earlier — publishing of instructions on how to make a hydrogen bomb, after the government had inadvertently declassified the information. The United States government tried to prevent a journalist from publishing this information, arguing that it would reveal secrets essential to the nation's security.

From either the libertarian or the absolutist national security position, deciding what to do is easy. One would publish without a second thought, the other would suppress without hesitation. But balancing the constitutional freedoms is more difficult. Who would benefit? The Soviet Union? No, they already have the formulas. China? No. Countries that might benefit are those with industrial capacity to make a bomb but without all the expertise — Israel? Argentina? Chile? Iraq? South Africa? Indonesia? Iran? Brazil? India? Pakistan? If published, would the information really help any of these nations to enter the hydrogen-bomb club?

On the other hand, is it desirable for the government to exercise prior restraint, preventing publication, when the potential harm may be only hypothetical and the danger cannot be demonstrated clearly? Would it be so bad if all nations had such weapons rather than just a few large nations? Or, isn't it likely that if one reporter was able to dig out the information that others now also have it? Haven't scientists from other nations already discovered the documents?

Each of us may weigh these questions differently. In the hydrogen bomb case the United States Supreme Court ruled in favor of publishing. The *Progressive Magazine* featured the story: "The H-Bomb Secret: How We Got It — Why We're Telling It." Few other publications, however, repeated the specific information.

A Closing Note

We are left with the conclusion that interaction between journalists and politicians in a free society will not always produce results that are seen as beneficial to all sides — both politicians and journalists sometimes violate democratic ideals. Politicians at times withhold or distort information and journalists may also distort stories for effect, or report stories that harm the innocent or the nation itself.

Society's goals — balancing the power of governing with the need to be accountable to the governed, the nation's security with the right to criticize, and the right to information with fairness to individuals — are not wholly consistent with each other and will always remain subject to tension.

But this mixture of benefits, spiced with some disadvantages, is perhaps all we have a right to expect of politicians and journalists in this less than perfect world.

NOTES

1. A number of students have listed the journalist's functions. Most lists include transmitting and interpreting information, and the watchdog function. Harold Lasswell adds "socialization of individuals in their social settings." As men-

tioned, we have used the classification in Delmar D. Dunn, *Public Officials and the Press,* (Reading, Mass.: Addison-Wesley, 1969) Ch. 2, "Reporters' Views of Their Work," pp. 7–22. Doris Graber discusses the Lasswell categories in *Mass Media and American Politics* (Washington, D.C.: Congressional Quarterly Press, 1980), pp. 4–9. See also the listing of the democratic functions of the press that Roger Fisher proposed for the 1972 Workshop on Government and the Media at the 1972 Aspen Program on Communications and Society, discussed in Bernard Rubin, *Media Politics and Democracy* (New York: Oxford University Press, 1977), pp. 83–84; and a listing Clayton Knowles and Richard P. Hunt devised in "Public Policy in a Newspaper Strike," *Columbia Journalism Review* 2 (Spring 1963): 28–33, and Carolyn Stewart-Dyer and Oguz B. Nayman, "Under the Capitol Dome: Relations Between Legislators and Reporters," *Journalism Quarterly* 54 (Autumn 1977): 443–453.

2. Joseph Schlesinger, *Ambition and Politics: Political Careers in the United States* (Chicago: Rand McNally, 1966). See also Norton E. Long, "The Local Community as an Ecology of Games," *American Journal of Sociology* 44 (November 1958): 251–261.

3. Douglass Cater, *The Fourth Branch of Government* (New York: Knopf, 1959).

4. Social psychologist Lloyd Sloan, immediately after the 1976 debate, compared a Notre Dame student sample who saw only the debate with a group who also saw the CBS analysis and another group who also saw the ABC analysis. Of those who saw only the debate, 47 percent thought Ford had won; 27 percent Carter. For those who saw debate and CBS analysis, it was 54 percent for Carter and 20 percent for Ford. For those who saw the debate and the ABC analysis it was 49 percent for Carter and 25 percent for Ford. Detroit *Free Press,* Nov. 27, 1976, p. 14A.

5. Jack Germond, "Losing Politicians Rap Press," *Lansing State Journal,* July 28, 1979.

6. *Newsweek,* Feb. 26, 1981, p. 81.

7. Warren Bennis, *The Unconscious Conspiracy: Why Leaders Can't Lead* (New York: AMACOM, 1976).

8. Quoted by Tom Shales in "Petty for Teddy," *The Washington Post,* Jan. 30, 1980, p. B11.

9. Dan Rather with Mickey Herskowitz, *The Camera Never Blinks* (New York: Ballantine, 1977), p. 286.

10. Leon Sigel, *Reporters and Officials* (Lexington, Mass.: D. C. Heath, 1973), p. 124.

11. James Deakin, *Straight Stuff: The Reporters, the White House, the Truth* (New York: William Morrow, 1984), p. 328.

12. Tom Wicker, *On Press* (New York: Viking Press, 1978), p. 186.

13. Jack Anderson, "Why I Tell Secrets," *Parade,* Nov. 30, 1980, p. 12.

14. Jack W. Germond and Jules Witcover, "The Era of Newspeak," Detroit *Free Press* (May 5, 1980).

15. James Deakin, *Straight Stuff,* p. 51.

16. Dan Rather and Mickey Herskowitz, *The Camera Never Blinks* (New York: Ballantine Books, 1977), p. 247.

17. Journalists were also initially regarded as subversive. For a discussion on how one type of media critic came above ground with the growth of democratic institutions in eighteenth-century England, see Charles Press, "The Georgian Political Print and Democratic Institutions," *Comparative Studies in Society and History* 19 (April 1977): 216–238.

18. Robert Pierpoint, *At the White House: Assignment to Six Presidents* (New York: G. P. Putnam's Sons, 1981), pp. 193–194.

19. Susan Fleming and Marc Gunther, "Suicide Photos Pose Dilemma for Papers, TV," *The Detroit News*, Jan. 23, 1987.

2

Journalists Declare Their Independence

A New England editor sent a young reporter to the nation's capital to collect political news. A few months later the reporter gave up and went home. He couldn't uncover enough stories to make his stay worthwhile.

Not because he didn't try. But he worked for a Federalist party newspaper when President Thomas Jefferson was leading the party then called "Republican." Jefferson funneled all his news to his own party's newspaper — *The National Intelligencer* — and froze out opposition-party reporters.

Frank Luther Mott, in his history of journalism, called this period "the dark ages of partisan journalism." During those days politicians dominated most of the journalists.

America's journalists — publishers, editors, and reporters — were then mainly errand runners for politicians. Newspapers not tied to a political party served as little more than bulletin boards of commerce and trade. Only a few independent journalists operated in the Benjamin Franklin mold in those early days. But no more! Journalists of today, perhaps more than at any time in our nation's history, flaunt their political independence.

President Theodore Roosevelt (1901–1909) did not have the advantage of playing to a national television audience. But he was well ahead of his time in recognizing the importance of remaining visible to the public, and the journalist's role in reporting his doings. To advance relationships with Washington reporters, "Teddy" Roosevelt opened up a special room to them in the new West Wing of the White House. Virtually every day he provided reporters with something newsworthy so that they would have a good story to file with their editors back at the newspaper office.

TR

friend to journalist –
realized importance of
relationships

CHAPTER OVERVIEW

In this chapter we examine first how American journalists evolved from captives of political leaders to the independent media agents they are today. We will focus first on how our form of government encourages independence. We next review how several interacting factors — capitalistic ownership of American media, developing technology, gradual democratization of American society, and legal rules directly affecting journalists — explains the journalist's evolving independence. Finally, we discuss whether journalists now dominate our political activities.

AMERICAN GOVERNMENTAL STRUCTURE AIDS JOURNALISTS

Governments are usually organized on the principle that those in power should be able to act quickly, decisively, and effectively. Officials of totalitarian governments, and most democratic ones as well, give these reasons for concentrating power in the executive. In contrast, the American system is decentralized.

American Government Is Anti-Teamwork

The American Founders designed a government on the principle of "separation of powers"; it is also known as the presidential or Madisonian system. Rather than concentrate political power, the Founders chose to splinter it. They were more interested in avoiding the danger of tyranny than in giving officials the power to act decisively.

The Separation of Powers. The Founders created a government in which president, legislators, judges, and administrators would reach office in different ways and therefore would be accountable to different constituencies. They set the terms of office at different lengths. They divided the legislature into two bodies, partly so that they might compete and check each other. They distributed legal powers so that officials in one branch could check and balance the powers of officials in other branches.

To only one office did the Founders give major coordinating power — the presidency. The chief executive is the only official who can lead and give some direction to the government. But even the president must lead as much through persuasion as by command. The power to persuade other officials does not rest solely on the president's legal powers or political skills — presidents are most effective when they can demonstrate popular support for their proposals.

The result is a government organized with an anti-organization bias. It is one of competing politicians with different career ambitions and interests, different power bases, and distinctive constituencies. Conflict and constant negotiation among its officials are common and expected. The system is anti-organizational because it encourages officials to compete with each other rather than work together as a team.

Structural Access for Journalists. How governments organize themselves determines the access reporters have to political information. As power in the American system is splintered, so too is information about policy making. The president is a major source of stories, but only one of many.

Some of those with whom the president deals are not completely loyal to him. Even those within his administration may be of doubtful loyalty. Nixon had his "Deep Throat," who leaked inside information to investigative reporters during the Watergate era. All recent presidents have experienced intentionally damaging "leaks" from within the administration — sometimes even from the cabinet officials they have appointed. And beyond the administration, in Congress and the bureaucracy, may be more persons whose loyalty is questionable.

Inevitably, information seeps from officials whose goals and careers conflict with the president's. No member of Congress feels obliged to keep a president's confidences on all matters. Moreover, the president may have difficulty identifying those who reveal his secrets to journalists and may not be able to punish them easily if they are found.

Nor are political secrets of the president's opponents wholly protected from journalistic revelation. The only branch of government with tight control over its information is the judiciary. But today's journalists have penetrated even the Supreme Court through the indiscretions of law clerks and leaks from the justices themselves. Those who hold public office find the American system both frustrating and useful in advancing their political careers.

Journalists, however, see the arrangement as close to ideal. The design guarantees reporters a great deal of political news. Officials are all somewhat independent of presidential or party control. Competing politicians leak information to journalists for the leaker's own political advantage. The outcome is that journalists have many access points from which to gather news items.

Few governments in the world offer journalists the same opportunities. Consider, as a contrast, the systems in such democracies as Great Britain and Canada.

Parliamentary Democracies. Many Americans may not realize how much parliamentary governments concentrate power in the controlling party's management team — the prime minister and cabinet. Cabinet meetings are confidential, as are discussions with other party members in the party caucus. Tidbits may leak but not information related in any way to national security, foreign policy, or financial matters.

The cabinet controls the release of most governmental information. During his period as prime minister, Winston Churchill held only one press conference. News on official policy becomes available to journalists only when the prime minister or other cabinet members announce it in Parliament. Before then journalists get only occasional hints or "official leaks" that the cabinet itself provides as trial balloons to get public attention.

In Britain, news leaks can be disastrous for the political careers of those who reveal information prematurely. Just a generation ago in Great Britain, Hugh Dalton, Chancellor of the Exchequer (second highest office in the government) resigned because he inadvertently leaked a story to the press. On his way to Parliament to present the annual budget, he stopped to chat with a journalist friend, John Carvel. Dalton briefly told of details in the budget message. Carvel immediately phoned a short item to the "stop-the-press" section of his paper, which delivered copies to Parliament while Dalton was speaking. The episode was known as "the budget scandal."[1]

And Sarah Tisdale, a low level civil servant, spent six months in jail in 1983–84 for giving *The Guardian* a memo from the Ministry of Defense. The memo discussed public relations plans in connection with the cruise missile.

The British government as well as that of Canada prosecutes those who leak information under their comprehensive Official Secrets Acts. The law in Britain covers such matters as data on outbreaks of infectious disease or food poisonings, minutes of municipal meetings, school records, medical or social work records, as well as civil defense plans and matters dealing with national security.

The act also contains the thirty-year rule — official papers are not released for public inspection for thirty years. Thus, only in 1984 did Britishers learn that Winston Churchill had a stroke in 1954 while he was still prime minister.

In 1986, the British government stopped English publication of *Spy-*

catcher, an intelligence agent's claims that thirty years before it had bugged the suites and meeting rooms of diplomats, including those of visiting Russian leader Nikita Khrushchev. He also charged that intelligence agents plotted against their own prime minister — Labour's Harold Wilson.

Still, news leaks on less important matters occur more frequently than in the past. In 1987 *The Independent* published details of *Spycatcher* and faced a government contempt citation. Two other London dailies then also published more details. Censorship imposed by confiscating printed magazines, as happened when *Time* magazine printed a story about the romance of King Edward VIII and the American divorcee, Wallis Simpson, would be loudly protested today. And royalty has become so popular a topic in political gossip that recently Queen Elizabeth sued a journalist for invasion of privacy. Yet the Queen still refuses to grant press interviews. But despite all this change, by American standards of journalism, news gathering in Britain and Canada is still tightly controlled.

THE STEPS TOWARD MEDIA INDEPENDENCE

Factors other than government organization also have had major influence in shaping the journalist's way of reporting political news. We consider four of them: (1) for the most part, media organizations have been profitable, capitalistic enterprises, (2) for competitive reasons they have sought out technological advances in printing and electronic communication, (3) as the social climate has changed and our society has become increasingly democratic, journalistic coverage has expanded to new audiences, and (4) the pattern of government regulation has varied.

Interacting Influences

The pattern of journalistic development tends to repeat itself as these factors interact with one another. At one time the media field is one of established enterprises. Then changes in technology and political climate generate opportunities for new entrepreneurs. The resulting competition, instability, and uncertainty encourage owners, editors, and reporters to be more aggressive in seeking readers' and viewers' attention. They push at the barriers of legal restrictions and accepted practices to gain the attention that translates into higher advertising revenues.

This ebb and flow of organizational change has produced periods of monopolistic control over the political news, and at other times, a diverse, fiercely competitive array of media outlets. Each condition generates differing opportunities for politicians and journalists as they attempt to manipulate each other to achieve their own goals and career ambitions.

Efforts to increase profits lead to new stability after periods of fierce competition. Generally, as in other capitalist enterprises, oligopolies or monopolies are created, leaving a few established enterprises in muted competition to drive out or absorb weaker firms. Survivors then redivide the pie. Government policy may prevent or slow journalistic consolidation, but to the extent it does not, we have periods of relative stability and less aggressive reporting.

The various phases in media development overlap. We review them here as manifested by innovations that upset established patterns beginning with the party press and continuing through the penny press, the yellow press, and the modern era.

The Party Press

In colonial times, establishing and operating a newspaper was a risky business venture.[2] Those who tried it usually turned to politicians to underwrite the risk. The price journalists paid was a degrading partisan loyalty.

Alexander Hamilton and friends helped establish the *Gazette of the United States*, edited by John Fenno. Besides paying the major expenses, they made sure that as the Federalist party newspaper, the *Gazette* received all government printing contracts during Washington's administration.[3]

Thomas Jefferson wanted a newspaper that would present an opposing viewpoint. As secretary of state, he brought poet Philip Freneau to Philadelphia and gave him a job as departmental translator. In his spare time, Freneau established and edited the *National Gazette*, mouthpiece for the Jefferson faction.[4]

The news in these papers was sparse and slanted to benefit their political sponsors. Editorials and political news stories berated the opposition mercilessly. Occasionally the editorial bitterness would spill over into duels and fistfights between rival editors. As we would anticipate, an editor could attract circulation and advertising mainly from hardcore party supporters.

Most editors of partisan newspapers meekly followed the political party's lead. But even in those dark days, we find instances of editorial independence, causing friction between journalists and their political sponsors. Charles Holt, a Connecticut Federalist, edited *The New London Bee*, but he saw fit to criticize President John Adams, also a Federalist.

The price Holt paid was prosecution under the Alien and Sedition Act, a $200 fine, and a three-month jail sentence.[5] For the most part, though, editors behaved themselves and attacked only political opponents.

The party newspaper reached its peak under President Andrew Jackson (1828–1836). Amos Kendall, editor of *The Globe*, was a close friend and intimate adviser to the president. He held no public office but was a member of Jackson's informal "kitchen cabinet," the policy-making arm of the administration. Kendall's publishing firm, of course, got all the government's printing contracts. In a new wrinkle, the Jacksonians insisted that all federal officeholders earning more than $1,000 a year buy a subscription to *The Globe*.

The Party Press in Decline. After Jackson, partisan papers began their long-drawn-out decline. Two actions by the Lincoln administration in the 1860s signaled the beginning of the end for the partisan press nationally. Shortly after taking office, President Lincoln declared that he would have no administration newspaper. He preferred, he said, "to skirmish" with all reporters. Later, he opened the U.S. Government Printing Office, ending the lucrative national government printing contracts for loyal editors.

Some editors until World War II maintained partisan affiliations in one-party enclaves such as the Democratic "solid South" or the Republican Midwest. But others recognized that too strong a tie might antagonize some readers or advertisers. Editors began using words such as "Independent" or "Independent Republican" on their mastheads.

The wire services organized nationally from 1900 on, also loosening party ties. They emphasized nonpartisan "objectivity" in reporting, because their reports went out to all papers, Democratic as well as Republican.

The decline continues to our day. After the 1950s most states became party competitive, at least at the presidential level. Yet, in one-party areas, we may still find county weeklies allied to the dominant party, in part to benefit from publication of local legal notices.

The Penny Press

Ironically, just as the party press was at its height, we find the philosophical roots and technological base of its successor, the penny press, already forming. Three important forces in the media began to evolve: a change in social climate that stimulated mass readership of newspapers, the formation of newspapers as profitable business enterprises, and technological breakthroughs.

By the 1830s the Jacksonians had expanded suffrage and were

trumpeting the virtues of "the common man." This democratic revolution in politics inspired a new kind of newspaper, one written to attract just such citizens. At about the same time, new technology made possible longer and cheaper press runs on inexpensive paper.[6]

Benjamin Day in 1833 established the first successful paper of this new breed, *The New York Sun*. Day charged a penny at the newsstand when established papers were sold only by subscription for six cents a copy.

The penny press also led to a new economic basis for papers, which newspapers, television, and radio still follow today: attract mass circulation, which will in turn justify high advertising charges. Publishers no longer had to depend on politicians for survival.

The penny press also changed the content of newspapers. To attract readers, editors specialized in lively coverage, exploiting the eye-catching news story. Lithography and new woodcut surfaces, developed around 1830, made it possible to produce drawings and cartoons for long press runs. Editors paid reporters to go out and dig up news rather than wait around for handouts from politicians or newly arrived ship captains. They presented political news as entertainment for the masses. But the stories were not only about the big issues in politics; they stressed human interest and emotion — crimes, political corruption, scandals in high society, and, of course, anything unusual, colorful, or exotic, from a two-headed calf to life in a Turkish harem.

Editors of the penny press — such as James Gordon Bennett and Horace Greeley — became celebrities. They freely expressed in their papers their own often unpredictable quirks and political prejudices. Almost all declared themselves political independents — they might

LUANN By Greg Evans

© News America Syndicate, 1986 by permission of North America Syndicate, Inc.

favor one party or candidate in this election, another in the next, and curse the whole lot in a third.

The Penny Press Becomes Respectable. As the nineteenth century wound down, the penny press gradually began to change. Newspaper publishing became a business proposition rather than a hobby for colorful editor-publishers. Successors to the original editors began to build stable, profitable businesses. They raised their prices, bought out local competitors, and became staid and respectable.

Yellow Journalism

The relative stability in the late 1800s, however, did not last, at least not in the nation's large urban centers. In the 1880s and 1890s a reincarnation of the "Great-Editor" papers appeared in big cities where new immigrant groups upset the old social patterns.

Some immigrants had difficulty learning English and papers in the native tongue sprang up to meet that demand. But Joseph Pulitzer and William Randolph Hearst found ways to design papers that would appeal to many other immigrants with the style that critics called "yellow journalism."

Hearst and Pulitzer challenged the more traditional papers by exploiting to the fullest the latest advances in technology. They made their papers easy to read and understand. They featured pictures and comics. The name yellow journalism itself derives from one of their innovations — printing the comic strip, "the yellow kid," in color. They introduced photoengravings and used every device of eye-catching sensationalism. They splashed red eight-column headlines across their front pages. Political cartoons appeared on page one. They offered heartwarming stories about children and dogs. They sponsored picnics and contests.

They also developed the "editorial crusade" as a circulation booster. Hearst said he wanted his news stories written so that readers would jump up from their chairs shouting "Oh my God!" And they offered the feature story and column, women's and sports pages, advice to the lovelorn, household hints, and lessons in etiquette.

The Tabloids. After World War I, tabloid-size papers designed to be read on street cars and buses entered the urban media scene. The tabloids added new competition in the nation's largest cities. Critics sometimes called *The New York Graphic*, "The Porno-Graphic," a clue to its editor's approach to news.

The Modern Period

Technological advances continued to create new media opportunities and intensify competition.

Radio and News Magazines. Both radio and the news magazines aimed at a more general national audience who wished to be better informed as well as entertained. From the crystal sets of the twenties, radio moved to the networks of the thirties with their influential newscasters and commentators, from Lowell Thomas to Edward R. Murrow. Presidents from Coolidge on used radio to address the nation. Radio newscasters reported political events such as the national conventions.

National news magazines, beginning with *Time,* added to the competition, aiming their publications at the professional class. Henry Luce, publisher of *Time,* emphasized a lively, personal writing style expressing editorial opinion in news copy.

TV Comes of Age. After World War II, the ownership of television sets grew rapidly, followed by the birth of a genuine televised news broadcast, out to capture viewers and advertising dollars.

The first television news broadcasts were low-budget, fifteen-minute, unopinionated reports — "talking heads" reading wire-service bulletins. Then, coverage of the assassination of President Kennedy in Dallas in 1963 revolutionized television news broadcasting. Everyone in the nation spent that weekend near the set. The experience revealed to network news directors new potential in techniques of presentation and the huge potential audience for action news. And this event fell just when television producers were looking for programs to fill the gaps left by the popular game shows. These had fallen into disgrace because the public discovered that many, such as *Twenty-One* and *$64,000 Question,* were rigged.

Then CBS went to a half-hour news program, quickly followed by the other networks. They substituted visual clips from the field and news anchors to tie the reports together for the announcer statically reading wire-service reports. Televised news reporting grew from an unprofitable public-service broadcast to a competitive profit-making venture with an ever more dramatic and aggressive style in reporting political events.

Television is thought to have killed off the old, established magazines such as *Life, Colliers,* and the *Saturday Evening Post,* or forced drastic changes. Many long-established newspapers also folded — the *Chicago Daily News,* the *New York Herald Tribune,* and the *Washington Times-Herald.* Afternoon papers seemed especially vulnerable, for it appeared that after work, people preferred to tune in the set for news.

New Media Enterprises. The Vietnam War and the 1960s radicalism spawned "underground" newspapers and magazines, a few of which survive, most notably *Rolling Stone*. "New freedoms" gave rise to *Playboy* and its imitators. Public radio and television seek out a specialized audience. And new market-identification techniques made profitable a host of other specialty, but short-run, magazines catering to a rainbow of interests. And in the supermarkets, weekly papers reminiscent of the yellow press appeared. Radio survived threats of imminent death inflicted by television in the 1950s by changing its format and specializing in music — soft rock, middle-of-the-road, and so on — and in a few cases in twenty-four-hour news broadcasts.

The Gannett chain launched a national newspaper, *USA Today*, full of brief stories, a format that one critic called "frozen television." Through microwave and satellite signal transfer the same newspapers are now printed at the same instant in several locations throughout a state or the nation. Now *USA Today*, *The Wall Street Journal*, or the newspaper published in a state's major city can thus find their way to the newsstand or front porch as quickly as the local newspaper. And national magazines such as *Newsweek* can produce special issues with advertising targeted to a region or local area. Meanwhile, in almost every large and small community, newspaper stands make available the major national prestige press — generally at a loss to the newspaper.

Commercial television in turn is threatened by new technologies. The 1970s brought cable television, with CNN round-the-clock news and other specialty networks. In the 1980s the network television news bureaus sharply cut back on staff. Pay-TV and growing use of videocassette recorders (VCRs) threaten some electronic media as well as the movie industry. Many VCR owners may prefer buying or renting movie tapes to watching regular television fare. Or they may record television programs and skip the commercials. In either event, the size of the television audience may drop and the value of commercial ads lessen. And now the cable industry is threatened by backyard downlink receiving dishes that take signals directly from satellites, without paying for the privilege.

THE MEDIA AS BUSINESS PROPOSITION

Today's media profits are 76 percent higher than those of all other American industries. Television gives a 90 to 100 percent return on investments.

Yet each of today's media ventures searches for a market large enough to give it viability and room for growth. Without a financially rewarding outlet, each faces possible extinction. And the stakes are high. Each television rating point represents 1.4 million viewers and is worth $30 million in annual advertising revenues.

The media scene as a business venture has gone through several stages. The era between World Wars I and II was one of general stability for newspapers outside the large urban centers. Using the technological advances in printing techniques, newspaper publishers in the large markets began following the methods of other capitalist entrepreneurs. They eliminated competitors by buying them out or merging with competing publications. The cost of establishing competing newspapers became prohibitive.

The peak number of dailies was 2,600 in 1909, when a steady decline began. The number of American cities with competing dailies dropped steadily from 61 percent in 1880 to 21 percent in 1930.

When radio became popular, many newspaper publishers established or purchased local stations. They followed a similar pattern in the early days of television. But not all competition for readers and viewers and advertisers could be thus contained.

Networks and Chains

New technologies made newspaper syndicates and chains possible, replacing local ownership. By 1923, the chains published 31 percent of the daily circulation.

The trend toward consolidating newspaper ownership into chains and eliminating two-newspaper cities continues — by 1984 chains controlled 79 percent of the daily and 88 percent of the Sunday circulation.

But the government limited the number of local radio or television stations that the networks could own. Thus independent stations became network affiliates rather than be owned outright.

Media Conglomerates

A number of media moguls began establishing holding companies taking in several types of media: newspapers, magazines, television channels, radio stations, movie-production companies. A change in the Federal Communications Commission rules, expanding from five to twelve the number of television stations a corporation could own, set off a spate of acquisitions in 1985.

The largest newspaper chain in 1985 — Gannett Company — owned 87 daily newspapers, including *USA Today* and *The Des Moines Register*, as well as sixteen radio stations, six television channels and the Louis

Harris opinion-polling organization. After buying the ABC Network in 1985, Capital Cities Communications, Inc., among other enterprises, owned twelve television channels, twenty-four radio stations, fifty-five cable television systems, and ten newspapers. (But CCCI had to sell off part of its combined holdings to get FCC approval for the ABC deal.)

Time for a while owned the *Washington Star*, and still owns the firm that publishes this text, *Life*, *Fortune*, and *People*, as well as Home Box Office, Denver Cable TV, the Book of the Month Club, a television production company, plus radio and television stations and other book publishers. Rupert Murdoch's News Corporation owned the *Chicago Sun*, the *Village Voice*, and the *New York Post* along with more than eighty publication and television operations in Australia, Great Britain, and the United States. He also owned 50 percent of Twentieth Century-Fox. His acquisition of television stations from Multimedia, Inc. formed the basis of a fourth network, called the Fox network.

Diversified Conglomerates. Government policy permits creation of conglomerates that combine media firms with nonmedia enterprises. Primarily an electronics company, RCA owns the NBC network and formerly owned Random House (book publishing). Xerox acquired that staple of the schoolroom, *The Weekly Reader*. *The Los Angeles Times* conglomerate includes the New American Library, a forest-products corporation (a source of newsprint), Denoyer-Geppert maps, *Newsday*, a Long Island newspaper, and other newspapers.

Storer Communications was associated with Northeast Airlines, and CBS owned the New York Yankees. *The Chicago Tribune*, which already owned WGN (the call letters stand for "World's Greatest Newspaper") radio and television stations, purchased the then hapless Chicago Cubs baseball team. And Boston Properties, whose main interest had been real estate development, owns *Atlantic Monthly Press* and *U.S. News and World Report*.

And because many media companies are stock companies whose shares are traded on stock exchanges, some media firms also have come under the partial but nonetheless influential ownership of general holding companies. The Berkshire Hathaway company of Omaha, Nebraska links ABC with the Washington Post Co., Time Inc., Affiliated Publications, Geico Insurance, and General Foods.

Implications For Political Reporting

Perhaps the major implication of contemporary media ownership is that media firm managers are pressed, more than in the past, to attend to profit-and-loss statements. Stockholders of the general holding companies or managers of conglomerates are likely to grow intolerant of media firms that do not contribute adequately to overall corporate profits.

We can anticipate that newspaper and television journalists will in turn be pressured to become more aggressive in their reporting — to report stories that sell newspapers or expand television audiences or to substitute entertainment materials for news. And pressure to produce profits may subject journalists to greater pressure from advertisers who object to some news reports. Group boycotts may also more easily intimidate media managers overly intent upon profits.

Major media firms may become casualties as owners put them to the profit test. The UPI wire service in 1985 filed for protection from creditors under bankruptcy laws. Primarily a tax-loss write-off for the Scripps-Howard chain until 1982, UPI was taken over by Mexican investors hoping to convert it into a profitable independent news agency.

The early radical criticisms of media ownership patterns, as this World War I vintage cartoon suggests, was fear of advertiser domination. The complex pattern of media ownership today may affect reporting in another way. How fairly will journalists be able to report stories on a strike at a subsidiary of the company that also owns the newspaper or

THE NEWSPAPER—HOUSE OF PROSTITUTION

television station? Some critics charge that they will think twice about printing "bare-fisted" editorials or reports about a "sister" company and especially its managers.

The media are still involved in a highly competitive environment despite growing centralization and the partial relaxation of government rules on electronic media ownership. Apprehension about monopolistic control over political reporting presently does not appear justified, for most communities still have competing news sources. Nor does it appear that pursuit of profits will starve the media. Individual outlets continue to have adequate resources for gathering and reporting political news.

A possible threat, however, is that the less successful firms will mimic techniques applied by the media that generate high profits. Individual media moguls such as Rupert Murdoch and Ted Turner of CNN are inclined to revive the "great-editor" approach. Other editors may decry Murdoch's "screaming politicized headlines and bare bosom photos" while also secretly admiring his ability to turn dying papers into profitable ventures.

GOVERNMENTAL INFLUENCES ON MEDIA OPERATION

Ordinary citizens, politicians, judges, and journalists continue to debate what the First Amendment to the Constitution means. It states, "Congress shall make no law . . . abridging the freedom . . . of the press." The outcomes of this debate are seen in acts of Congress and decisions by the U.S. Supreme Court. And they have shaped the media industry's organization and styles of political reporting. That influence has been especially important since the 1960s in freeing journalists from legal restraints.

In times of intense media competition, journalists crowd the limits of what may be published and that has been happening today. They seek to expand their freedom to publish information that may give them wider audiences. At the same time, media owners attempt to reduce competition by consolidations, and they pressure the government to relax laws against monopolies.

Let us briefly review these legal influences on today's reporting and media organization: (1) the rules of prior restraint on what can be published or broadcast, (2) policies on what must be published or broadcast, (3) restraints that apply following publication — the laws of libel; and (4) regulation of media firms as business enterprises.

Prior Restraint

Prior restraint is the legal term for preventing someone from publishing information. National security is the main reason given for such restrictions. Journalists argue that politicians unnecessarily classify as top secret many pieces of information that journalists suspect are marginally related to national security.

The United States information classification system operates somewhat differently from those of other democracies. Under our separation-of-powers system, American judges ultimately decide what information the government can legally keep secret.

The Pentagon Papers Case. A National Security Council staff member, Daniel Ellsberg, in 1971 began circulating to newspapers copies of a top-secret government study of how the United States became involved in the Vietnam War. The reports were prepared initially for the Department of Defense. When President Nixon learned of this dissemination, he sought to prevent publication. The Solicitor General argued unsuccessfully in the Supreme Court that publishing these reports would endanger national security.[7]

Students of the case conclude that had President Nixon limited his objections to specific sections of the study, he might have convinced a majority of the justices. But by trying to suppress the whole document, he lost; the Court allowed the whole study to be published. A number of newspapers published the "papers," also gathered later in a paperback. The charges against Ellsberg himself were dismissed.

The court's decision said to government officials that stamping "top secret" on a document does not necessarily mean that a newspaper that publishes it will be prosecuted.

Journalists are thus encouraged to dig out stories that may give them a competitive advantage. Nevertheless, officials in the executive branch have one major trump card — journalists cannot publish a top secret document unless they know of its existence and get a copy. Even with the openness of America's government, that is not always easy. In an effort to ease their problems in getting information, journalists encouraged two types of laws: freedom-of-information acts and laws permitting unrestricted coverage of public activities.

The Freedom of Information Act. In 1966 Congress passed the Freedom of Information Act, and in 1974 added strengthening amendments over President Ford's veto. The law permits reporters to demand and receive documents from the executive branch. Congress and the courts are exempt from the law, explaining why former Secretary of State Henry Kissinger gave his papers to the Library of Congress. Personal rather than official documents generally may be kept secret for thirty years. But congressional control of the Kissinger records probably provided greater assurance that his papers would not be released prematurely.

Officials in the executive branch need not produce every document asked for, or any document in its entirety. The act permits officials to withhold information including: (1) secrets involving national security or foreign policy; (2) internal personnel practices; (3) any matter exempted by law (the CIA succeeded in making it a crime to publish any CIA agent's name); (4) trade secrets or other confidential commercial information; (5) inter- or intra-agency memos; (6) personnel or medical files; (7) reports of law enforcement investigations; (8) reports on financial institutions; and (9) geological or geophysical data. Most states have passed similar laws; many of them more favorable to journalists than the federal law.

Administrators can impede release of information by giving themselves the benefit of the doubt. They can enforce exceptions rigidly as specific requests are made, a policy that journalists claim the Reagan administration followed. The Reagan administration also required journalists to pay for the document search unless the reporter could show that the items requested were clearly relevant to a news story and not excessively harmful to the persons involved. Congress subsequently eliminated this provision. Such practices, not wholly in keeping with the spirit of the law, hinder journalists. But overturning an administrative decision denying a request is time consuming and expensive. Many reporters instead seek other sources for the news.

Why are officials so skittish about releasing government documents even when national security is not at stake? For one thing, they say they have a right to prevent fishing expeditions, a practice frowned upon in congressional investigations. It refers to a probe conducted without a specific goal in mind in the hope that something unexpected and useful may turn up in the investigatory net. Thus, it seems likely that future administrations will follow some of the restrictive policies set by the Reagan administration.

Nevertheless, American journalists are still the envy of most other reporters in access to the news. British journalists broke an English spy case only because they could secure American documents through our Freedom of Information Act. Confronted with the papers, the Conservative party government admitted that the Queen's art consultant had been part of a Soviet spy ring during World War II.

Coverage of Public Activities. Open-meeting laws now cover all levels of American government. Again, the national law applies only to the executive branch but not to all its meetings; cabinet sessions and other high-level meetings are generally closed to reporters.

The judicial branch has been involved especially with news coverage of trials. At stake is the public's right to know versus the defendant's right to a fair trial. Some judges have concluded that journalists are more interested in entertaining readers and viewers than informing them. A 1954 conviction in the murder trial of Dr. Samuel Shepard, a physician in Cleveland, Ohio, was reversed because a higher court felt that a "carnival atmosphere" had been created by competing journalists. The decision suggested that in some circumstances journalists might be excluded from trial proceedings. In later cases the courts have attempted to spell out when the proscription might be applied. They have included eliminating journalists from some pretrial conferences at which a compromise settlement may be reached. Most courts have also limited admission of photographers and television cameras. A familiar journalistic response is to hire artists to sketch courtroom scenes.

Pornographic Materials. The issue of prior restraint has also arisen over defining pornographic materials. The courts have been reluctant to limit First Amendment rights in any substantial way. The only limitation thus far has been the "Miller test," which is applied to material after publication. Community standards should apply, the test holds, providing that they specifically define what is obscene in ways that meet court approval. A matter now intensely debated is prior restraint of obscene materials that involve children.[8]

But the FCC regulation that the electronic media may not broadcast the "seven obscene words" made famous by George Carlin has been upheld.

Government Required Broadcasts

The government began regulating the electronic media because only a limited number of over-the-air television and radio stations can reasonably operate in a community before interfering with one another's signals. The law presumes that the public owns the airwaves the broadcasters use and permits them to operate as semimonopolies.

Electronic media therefore must obtain a government license to broadcast which has led to rules governing what stations may broadcast. Radio and television broadcasters regard such regulation as an unfair restriction on their ability to compete with the print media.

In general, these rules have covered equal access for politicians, fairness in what is broadcast, and a required minimum of public-service broadcasting.

The print media, however, are all but free from government controls over what they may publish. No government agency requires newspapers to insert public-interest copy, or to set aside equal space for opposing views in their news columns, letters to the editor, or editorials. A Florida law once required newspapers to give politicians space in which to rebut criticisms, but the U.S. Supreme Court ruled that the law infringed on press freedom. Freedom of the press means something quite different for print media than it does for electronic outlets.

Equal Time. Congress devised the equal-time rule to broaden access to varying political views. If one political candidate or party receives free or paid broadcast time, stations must provide equal time at equally desirable hours and rates to all other candidates for an office. "All others," of course, includes candidates of minor parties as well as independent candidates for the specific office.

In practice, the equal-time rule restricts the access it is meant to encourage. Radio and television station managers are reluctant to risk having to give or sell prime time to the Vegetarians and Greenbackers just because major-party candidates received or bought broadcast time. Faced with having to supply politicians with prime-time programming during each campaign season, some station managers choose to allow none or to price time beyond the financial reach of minor groups.

Congress has made some exceptions to the rule. It excludes bona fide news events, news interviews, news documentaries, and press conferences. In 1960 Congress specifically excluded the Kennedy–Nixon presidential debates as a one-time exception. Networks televised later presidential debates by ingeniously bending the rules, carrying them as news events because the debates were privately sponsored events before live audiences. Minor-party candidates went to court seeking equal time but were rebuffed.

The Fairness Doctrine. Every now and then the president asks the networks for time to address the American public on a topic he says is important to the nation. Generally the president uses the opportunity to drum up public support for an issue that has opponents in Congress.

The networks and individual stations are not required to grant the president's request. But until 1987 if they did, the fairness doctrine required that the president's political opponents have time to respond. But in 1987 the Federal Communications Commission voted to abolish the fairness doctrine. Anticipating this action, Congress had made the doctrine law. But President Reagan successfully vetoed the act.

The FCC policy has been inconsistent. In 1941, WAAB, a Boston radio station, was threatened with nonrenewal of license because it broadcast editorials. Then in 1949 the FCC decided that the electronic media could broadcast editorials but only if they allowed equal time for anyone wishing to reply. The result was that near the end of local news broadcasts, a solemn-faced older gentlemen intoned the virtues of events such as the city's annual "clean-up day." He then dutifully offered equal time for listeners to reply "on the other side of the question." Few station managers want to start an endless free-for-all on controversial topics.

The fairness doctrine too did not always have the desired effect because the electronic media were reluctant to expose themselves, each time they dealt with a controversial topic, to demands by those who wanted to present "the other side." By presenting opposed views in their regular news programs they could legally reject claims for response time. The rule also affected how television handled controversial topics made in a presidential press conference — they arranged for or presented opposing views in "analysis" segments immediately following the news conference.

Critics say the fairness doctrine stifles debate. They also say the assumption that electronic media are semimonopolies is no longer true. They observe that one-newspaper towns are much more numerous than one-television or one-radio station towns. But influential members of Congress say they will continue efforts to reinstate the rule — fearing some views will otherwise never be presented.

Public-Interest Content. Until recently the FCC required television and radio stations to broadcast public interest programming — including news broadcasts — to benefit viewers. Some listeners or station managers may think public-interest programming is as exciting as watching traffic lights at work on Main Street. We were once invited to discuss a controversial state political issue on a local rock music station, only to find that our carefully chosen, recorded comments would be broadcast at 5 A.M. on New Year's day, right after the bars had swept out the last celebrants. The station manager no doubt logged the interview as part of its public-interest programming to satisfy the current FCC rules.

The FCC monitored stations by requiring them to turn in program logs, but set no minimum standards for quantity of public-interest programming. Licenses, though, are renewable every three years, and a station owner could expect the logs to be reviewed if someone challenged the relicensing. The FCC dropped the requirement in 1984 as part of the Reagan-supported deregulation policy.

Controlling content on cable television raises a more difficult question about regulation. Until 1984 local government boards granted franchise permits to cable television operators. Many used this power to make demands, such as providing public access channels for city-council meetings and other "public-interest" programming. In 1984, though, Congress changed the law, forcing cable franchise permits to follow national standards. Still, many franchise agreements continue to provide for public access channels. It is not clear what the station's responsibility is should a public access participant slander a racial, religious, or political group.

At the same time, the FCC eliminated regulations requiring that every local station be carried in areas where three or more television stations compete. This rule affects 75 percent of the cable companies and 90 percent of present subscribers. The cable industry is pressing for further deregulation so that they will not be required to carry a station having less than a 2 percent audience share. That proposal to the FCC is aimed at local-access channels. It might also reduce the number of PBS stations having cable outlets.

Public-interest programming thus is becoming a matter of market demand rather than government regulation. Competition for viewers rather than public policy determines content. For television network affiliates, news broadcasts will remain a key part of the daily program lineup. But independent television stations that feature movies or other special fare can present abbreviated news briefs and reduce "public-interest" programming. And because news is costly to gather, only a few major-market radio stations will continue to have news staffs. The remainder will rely on wire service reports and a brief rehash of the local newspaper. Still, station managers are aware that a new administration in Washington, appointing new FCC commissioners, might in time reinstate some public interest requirements.

The Law of Libel

Libel actions occur only after information has been published, but fear of a libel action can be a potent restraint. Until 1964, the media had to use extreme care in anything they published about politicians. In one case, a newspaper was successfully sued even though the item in question appeared in a syndicated column. Another case involved a textbook on state government. Its author described the trials that U.S. Senator William Langer of North Dakota faced for allegedly forcing state employees who handled federal funds to buy his partisan newspaper. His last appeal resulted in a hung jury, and the author neglected to say the senator had not been convicted. The publisher financed a free trip around the world for the senator as part of the out-of-court settlement.

The Sullivan Doctrine. Then in 1964 came the Sullivan case, involving *The New York Times* and a public official in Alabama. The U.S. Supreme Court ruled showing that the newspaper had published a false statement was no longer enough to prove that it had committed libel — if the falsehood were about a politician. Errors made in good faith, as in Senator Langer's case, would not be considered libelous. To win a libel suit a plaintiff must prove "malice" or a "reckless disregard for the truth" — that a journalist had to know he or she was publishing a lie or that the reporter had not taken reasonable steps to confirm the facts in the story.[9]

In 1967 the Supreme Court extended the Sullivan doctrine to "public figures." A public figure is a celebrity in the news such as a baseball player, movie star, astronaut, or any person widely known to the public. Celebrities generally are identified in the news story by name and not by title or occupation — Johnny Carson, Frank Sinatra, Eddie Murphy.

The Sullivan doctrine seemed to make it almost impossible for a politician to win a libel lawsuit; proving motivation is not easy. And some argued that journalists took advantage of this limitation. If Hollywood movie stars are to be believed, the editors of grocery-checkout magazines make up titillating stories about them. Politicians also claimed to be victims of journalists fictionalizing events to attract readers and viewers.

Recent "Sullivan" Cases. The Supreme Court under Chief Justice Warren Burger was more restrictive in applying the doctrine than was the Earl Warren Court that first fashioned it. In *Herbert v. Lando,* a producer of *60 Minutes* was quizzed at length and asked to describe what went through his mind as he prepared an allegedly defamatory statement. The justices were applying the same principle used in a murder trial, determining whether the person who pulled the trigger was motivated by "malice in his heart." Later Dan Rather testified at length about his motives in another libel action involving *60 Minutes.*[10]

But the first major break in publishers seeming immunity occurred in a case involving actress and "public figure" Carol Burnett. She sued *The National Enquirer* for libel and won a judgment of $1.6 million (later cut in half). An *Enquirer* story claimed she was intoxicated at a New York City nightclub. The story was false and a federal court accepted the argument that it was published without a careful check of its authenticity — "reckless disregard for the truth."

Other cases involving political figures followed. In 1985, General William Westmoreland, former Vietnam War commander, sued CBS for $120 million. He claimed a CBS documentary had maliciously reported that he had ordered subordinates to understate Viet Cong manpower and inflate their battle casualties. After weeks of courtroom hearings and millions in attorney's fees, Westmoreland, presumably following legal advice, withdrew the case. It was settled without CBS paying damages, although they paid their own legal fees and issued a statement that Westmoreland interpreted as a vindication. But CBS, and most who read it, thought it was nothing of the sort.[11]

Ariel Sharon, the Israeli minister of defense, sued *Time* for claiming that he had encouraged a Lebanese Christian massacre of Palestinians. The trial disclosed that the magazine had based a story on a nonexistent clause in a secret document. The Israeli government released the document. The jury ruled that *Time* had acted negligently and carelessly in reporting and verifying the story. But the jury refused to award financial damages because it found no actual malice.[12] Sharon and others treated it as a vindication.

In a third case, the president of Mobil Oil Company sued *The Washington Post* for a story that was derogatory about business deals involving his son. A federal appeals court panel overruled the trial judge, who had previously overturned a jury finding against the *Post.* The case was reinstated and is pending as we write.

Finally, after President Jimmy Carter left office, "The Ear," a gossip column in *The Washington Post,* reported that Carter had "bugged" the Reagans' living quarters during the transition period. He threatened to sue unless the paper admitted error. It did so.

In general, standards for "reckless disregard" vary according to the medium and the deadline under which each operates. Thus, magazine reports, analytical pieces for newspapers, and television weekly news reviews must meet a more rigorous standard of accuracy than do newspaper stories. Judges have ruled that the pressure of daily deadlines and lack of time to check every detail may excuse all but clearly intentional defamatory statements. Thus, the court's ruling that *The National Enquirer* was a magazine rather than a newspaper figured heavily in that case.

The Effects of Libel Actions. Whether judges will be more inclined in the future to decide that an inaccurate story about a politician or public figure was printed with "malice" or "reckless disregard for the truth" remains to be seen. At present writing, politicians are still fair game. A 1986 ruling held that the person suing must prove falsity of the report rather than the media outlet's having to prove the statement true. Still, public officials, especially after they leave office, can now be expected to bring cases more frequently when they think a printed or broadcast story is clearly untrue.

A fairly frequent outcome of libel cases has been a jury's finding against the media, only to have trial judges reduce the amount of the award or appeals courts overrule the verdict. A review of 120 cases in 1980–1983 found juries ruling for the plaintiff 83 percent of the time, but 70 percent of the cases were reversed on appeal. Journalist Jeff Greenfield suggests these jury actions show that the general public resents the claim by journalists that, unlike auto mechanics, physicians, or stock brokers, they need not be accountable to consumers.[13]

But is the threat of a libel suit an effective restraint? Publishers and broadcasters, especially those without the financial resources of *The New York Times*, *The Washington Post*, *Time*, or CBS, are likely to be hesitant in publishing material that may invite a lawsuit. Journalists say the financial and psychological costs of defending have a "chilling effect."

The Alton (Illinois) *Telegraph* lost a $9.2 million libel judgment in a case involving a local contractor. He claimed that a *Telegraph* reporter's notes implying the contractor had ties to organized crime reached a government agency and thus damaged his reputation. The newspaper had to file for bankruptcy to enable it to appeal. Even if the media company wins a case or a jury decision is overturned or the award reduced, publishers see that the costs are considerable, measured not only in dollars, but in damaged reputation, temporary paralysis of the news-gathering staff, and worry.

Regulation of Media as a Business

Does government regulation of the media as business enterprises threaten their freedom to report the news? In some cases the courts have suggested it might.

Taxation Issues. In the 1930s, the Huey Long administration in Louisiana imposed a special tax on New Orleans newspapers. The tax was ruled unconstitutional in part because the justices concluded that it was designed to drive three newspapers out of business rather than to raise revenue.[14]

In a 1984 case involving *The Minneapolis Star* a court ruled that a newly imposed sales tax on newsprint discriminated against the newspaper and jeopardized freedom of the press. Some argued that the case raised the issue of whether the media were not really immune from any but a general tax.

Concentration of Ownership. Special rules apply directly to ownership of the electronic media. The rules, however, indirectly affect newspapers, though not magazines. The Justice Department and the Federal Communications Commission attempt to ensure competition by limiting the number of outlets one company may own in a market area. In the future a company may not own both a newspaper and a television station in the same city. But present patterns are not affected.

Nationally, a corporation may own up to twelve VHF stations. Networks are limited to five stations. And a firm may not own television stations that reach more than 25 percent of the national audience. The FCC rules also limit a television network's cable television hookups to 90,000.

Government rules also encourage sales to minority-controlled corporations. Since 1978, Congress has allowed a tax break and avoidance of hearings if a license is lost, providing that the outlet is sold to a minority firm.

Losing a television or radio license does not happen often. But the conglomerate RKO-General lost its licenses for television stations in New York, Los Angeles, and Boston after the Securities and Exchange Commission had disciplined the parent firm for stock transactions. The licenses were lifted because the media firms had the same chief executive.

Members of Congress regularly introduce bills to limit the size of newspaper chains or change the estate tax law encouraging the sale of newspapers to chains. Thus far none of these bills has come close to passage. Federal law, however, does regulate joint operating agreements (JOA) between newspapers. The law permits two newspapers in the same community to collaborate on publishing, advertising, and other non-editorial matters if the papers are financially threatened and the U.S. Department of Justice concurs.

The Future of Regulation. As a nation, we have come to depend on electronic media for much of the news. Under the Reagan administration, the trend has been toward deregulation. But important regulations remain, such as the equal time provision.

If, as some suggest, we are close to the electronic wonder of having newspapers or the news they contain delivered through a television screen, the distinctions between what we now think of as print and electronic media may diminish. For government regulators, the issue could be whether to treat such enterprises the same way as they presently do radio and television. Or should these emissions be considered, as the FCC has in dealing with cable subscriptions, as not subject to major regulation because consumers can decide to buy or not buy the service?

INCREASED MEDIA FREEDOM AND POLITICAL REPORTING

All the changed patterns we have described have helped alter the relationship between politicians and journalists. This change itself has been rooted in the means by which citizens get political news. Before examining major characteristics in the new pattern, let us review how students of the World War II period found that citizens got their news then and how they formed their political opinions.

The Old Political Order and the New

Before television, students found that few citizens followed politics closely. Many voters cast a traditional ballot, supporting the same political party their parents and grandparents had. But a few did follow news events carefully, and a study of the 1940s called this small attentive public opinion leaders. These politically interested persons followed political stories in the newspapers or got political information from organizations: political parties: labor unions: or business, religious, fraternal, or even veterans' organizations.

A two-step or multistep flow brought this information to the less interested citizens. Opinion leaders at all levels of society acted as political guides for other citizens. The average citizen, busy with his or her own affairs, took political cues from these more knowledgeable citizens. Labor-union shop stewards or religious leaders or local business leaders advised others as to whom they should support to protect their interests. Where the old-style political-party organization held power, the precinct captain visited voters in their homes and suggested which candidates to vote for.[15]

The Changes in News Presentation

The modern age changed the traditional patterns. Fewer citizens vote with the consistency their parents and grandparents did. Partly attentive citizens no longer rely on cues from local opinion leaders — television reports now give them their political cues. TV journalists become today's opinion leaders.

Nearly all the trends we have reviewed also encourage modern journalists to become more politically independent. All have led to competition for mass audiences, a factor that has contributed greatly to this spirit of independence. And television has created a new style for reporting the news, one aimed to attract a mass audience.

Penetration. Political news now penetrates to all levels of society. Journalists beam much more information to ordinary citizens as it happens. Indeed even the functionally illiterate cannot escape its reach. In many homes the day opens with *Good Morning America* or the *Today* show. The mechanic, receptionist, barber, mother at home with children, dentist, and others are likely to be tuned throughout the day to music and "news on the hour." And an evening's television viewing begins with the evening news. Citizens become superficially familiar with political events as no one could conceive possible in the past.

More Confrontational Reporting. Because of competition, media entrepreneurs generously reward journalists who attract large audiences. A television advertisement for *The National Enquirer* that ended with a woman insipidly intoning, "And *I* want to know," characterizes a self-serving view of what some of the media hope the American public wants in news coverage.

For their own career advancement, journalists strive to satisfy the demands. Political news as entertainment that shocks, reveals secrets, has human interest, and is dramatic has high value in the industry. Reporting that is confrontational, antiestablishment, and adversarial wins higher salaries and perhaps a Pulitzer prize.

Personalized News. Political reporting concentrates on personalities and media celebrities. Of necessity it presents issues and events as displayed by individuals. When industrial waste discharged into a stream kills rafts of fish, environmental groups know that if the governor speaks out the alarm will gain more attention than if only the event is reported. A major beneficiary of personalized news is the president, who is never offstage for long.

But we are also learning more about a different cast of political figures. A few U.S. senators and representatives, who used to live in a dull gray world, suddenly are recognizable to millions. Moreover, those who participate in phone-in programs are also directly accessible — people from around the nation may call in and ask questions.

Created Media Events. The demand for more and more news is unending. Media news events are created political events, designed for visual appeal. Inevitably, the demand for filling hourly and round-the-clock newscasts expands the politicians' outlets for such news — incidents that earlier we called media events. Whether as innocent as a mayor's ribbon cutting to open a new brewery or a senator commenting on the latest hijacking or other act of terrorism, they are staged for the benefit of reporters, but also for the politician. For the latter media event, the stage is often international.

Nationalized News. In America, we are only beginning to have national newspapers. Washington and New York together have 6 percent of the country's population but only 9.6 percent of our national newspaper circulation. Nationally distributed papers such as *USA Today* or *The Wall Street Journal* still reach only a small percentage of the population. We still have 1,674 dailies and 9,000 weeklies. And, experts tell us, we could cover the whole country with just 100 clear-channel radio stations. Instead we have 7,100 AM and FM outlets. And we have 930 television stations in 285 markets.

The news these varied media outlets carry, though, is increasingly about national events. Radio and television depend on networks with their nationally advertised products. They feature national news to hold their audience. Any local story the networks carry has to be given a national twist. But look also at what is featured on page one of even the smallest local dailies. With the help of the Associated Press or United Press International news wires, they give us national and international news. Except for an occasional big story, the local and state political news goes on page three and beyond in the metropolitan or state sections.

The Dominance of Political News. Nationalizing the news means that more of the news that gets reported is political news. To interest a national audience, reporters are led to government, national and international. Even events such as natural disasters, gasoline shortages, or closing of a major plant draw in a political news angle: How will government respond? Few other topics matter to everyone in the nation.

Stephen Hess studied 153 stories in 22 newspapers outside of Washington and found heavy emphasis on the federal government even on Sunday, when Washington events are relatively scarce. He concluded,

"All the top stories from the community, the state capital, and other cities in the home state combined, do not equal the percentage from Washington."[16]

The Importance of Media Elites. Nine national media leaders — the two wire services (AP and UPI), CBS, NBC, and ABC, *The New York Times, The Washington Post, Time,* and *Newsweek* — are generally seen as the outlets that decide which political events of the day deserve emphasis, and how much play each story gets. As we will see in Chapter 3, critics of the media elite say that they also determine news slant or theme.

Michael Robinson and Margaret Sheehan conclude that the television networks follow the lead of the two major newspapers among the elite: *The New York Times* and *The Washington Post.* Stories that the editors of these papers decide to put on their front pages are also likely to be the lead stories on the evening television network news.[17]

But most newspaper readers get most of their news from the wire services, AP and UPI. Whatever they consider important gets front-page coverage locally.

The New Status of Journalists

At the turn of the century, the dashing and flamboyant Richard Harding Davis filed reports from foreign wars. Readers became familiar with his bylines and then with his dramatic personality. Ernie Pyle became a national celebrity reporting World War II and how the average GI experienced it. Radio listeners came to recognize the distinctive voices and styles of such newscasters as Raymond Gram Swing, Drew Pearson, Lowell Thomas, H. V. Kaltenborn, and Gabriel Heatter. Still, James Deakin observes, the most famous news columnist of the day, Walter Lippmann, and many of the well-known radio commentators, could walk down the street without being recognized.

Today's local and network television journalists find it increasingly difficult to keep from becoming part of the stories they report. Some television newscasters, and even syndicated columnists who make frequent television appearances, are as recognizable as Hollywood stars. We can hardly help but form personal identifications with the familiar "talking heads" on our television screens. At national party conventions, they, more than the politicians, get "the stare" and requests for autographs. As with other celebrities, what they do is news.

Consider this exchange from one of President Nixon's press conferences:

Dan Rather: "Mr. President, I want to state this question with due respect to your office, but also as directly as possible . . ."

President Nixon: "That would be unusual." (laughter)

Dan Rather: "I would like to think not. It concerns . . ."

President Nixon: (ironically) "You are always respectful, Mr. Rather, you know that."

That confrontation, of course, was on the next day's front pages. When Barbara Walters interviews the president's wife, we find newspaper accounts even before the interview is broadcast. Media people have even gotten involved in the nation's diplomacy. Walter Cronkite, in a live broadcast interview with President Anwar Sadat of Egypt and Prime Minister Menachem Begin of Israel, suggested that perhaps the two should meet. They did and that meeting led to the Camp David Accords.

Effects of New Status on News. What results when reporters become stars on their own televised news reports?

Such journalists become more than objective observers of a news event. They may in fact dominate the story they are reporting: How will Jennings treat the president at tonight's news conference? Will Mike Wallace trap the governor in a lie? Will Sam Donaldson's shouted question be heard over the roar of the helicopter engine and will President Reagan make an unscripted response? Viewers begin watching more for the interpersonal dynamics in the interview than for the substance of the news. The popular tendency to view issues and events in terms of personalities is reinforced.

As reporters' name recognition and reputation grow, they attract viewers. For the journalists themselves this appeal may mean rapidly rising salaries as networks compete for their services. Dan Rather earns $2.5 million a year. Others who also want to advance their journalistic careers are tempted to press for the dramatic. The job that should be news gathering and reporting assignments turns into a drive for personal publicity.

Moreover, star journalists also tend to influence the news itself. When they handle the story, Tom Brokaw, Roger Mudd, and other well-known reporters may give a political candidate or a demonstration more credibility and legitimacy than any of them deserves. And opinions expressed by journalists with large and loyal followings such as Walter Cronkite had may affect the outcome of a senatorial campaign or world events, as we have seen. Lyndon Johnson was said to have concluded the Vietnam War was lost after Walter Cronkite announced on the evening news that we would not win it.

As a result, some students have asked if we now have a media-dominated political system.

HOW INFLUENTIAL IS MEDIA REPORTING?

Eric Sevareid, television commentator for CBS, said:

> I have never quite grasped the worry about the power of the press. After all, it speaks with a thousand voices, in constant dissonance. It has no power to arrest you, draft you, tax you, or even make you fill out a form, except a subscription form if you're agreeable. It is the power of government that has increased. Politicians have come to power in many countries and put press people in jail. I can't think of any place where the reverse has occurred.

Politicians in the Watergate era and others might not so lightheartedly dismiss media power and influence. More than one will recall fellow politicians who indeed have spent time behind bars because of journalistic persistence.

But social-science researchers do not agree on just how much the media influence public opinion and, therefore, politicians. The important question is not whether media coverage can immediately affect individual political careers or influence the outcome of specific issues. That they do so occasionally, most politicians and journalists will concede.

The larger question is whether we have a media-dominated society and government, and if so, who controls what is reported.

The Early Studies

After World War I, when social scientists first became aware of the term "propaganda," some concluded that the media were almost unbeatable in brainwashing and mindbending.

The Allies' use of propaganda was claimed to have "gotten us into the war." Then a Russian scientist Ivan Pavlov rang a bell every time he fed his dogs red meat. Eventually, he found that the dogs would salivate when he rang the bell — even if he did not give them hamburger. He called this reaction a "conditioned reflex." Some scientists expressed an uncomplimentary comparison between America's newspaper readers and radio listeners and Pavlov's salivating dogs — they too could be conditioned to act on cue.

Reports followed about initial successes in advertising campaigns orchestrated by Madison Avenue. Some suggested that a concentrated media campaign could condition the public to buy anything, including political ideas.

Selective Effects. Turn-of-the-century political bosses were aware that media influence was selective. Middle- and upper-class neighborhoods with high percentages of newspaper subscribers, they noticed, tended to follow the anti-boss editorial endorsements by the metropolitan dailies. Newspaper influence was nil in machine wards.

Political scientists observed another instance of selective influence in the 1930s. Most newspapers endorsed the various opponents running against President Franklin D. Roosevelt. Some, including *The Chicago Tribune* outrageously slanted their news columns against him. Editors were accused of replacing the word "new" with "raw" when referring to Roosevelt's New Deal. Yet FDR won election after election, even carrying "Tribuneland."

At about this time laboratory experiments on media effects began. The researchers so refined their ideas about the importance of media messages that they made the press and radio appear nearly ineffectual, emphasizing the media's selective influence.

A distinguished social scientist summarized these results: "Some kinds of *communications* of some kinds of *issues* brought to the attention of some kinds of *people* under some kinds of *conditions* have some *effects.*" He then outlined several constraints under each heading. Under "communications" he reported that personal communication was more influential than impersonal, emotional more than rational, and so on.[18]

From the beginning, studies of editorial endorsements have come up with selective influence. Students find that such endorsements are most effective when (1) the newspaper's position already fits readers' predispositions, (2) voters' ties to both major political parties are weak, or (3) voters have few other cues or guidelines — in nonpartisan elections, for example, on ballot questions, or when they face proportional representation choices or very long ("bedsheet") ballots.[19]

A different kind of study dating from 1934 illustrated how the media influence those with few predispositions. Two social psychologists planted fake news stories about Australia in the college paper. They assigned some students to read the favorable and some the unfavorable stories. They found that 98 percent assigned favorable stories had a positive view of Australia and 86 percent assigned to read unfavorable stories had negative opinions.[20] And so the students' opinions, perhaps because they lacked previous knowledge, they were not directly involved, or a classroom authority figure assigned the article to them, were influenced by what they read. In these experiments students were not asked to act on their opinions, which, of course, would be another gauge of media influence.

And so the early media studies reached this unsatisfactory conclusion — sometimes "yes" and sometimes "no" — on how the media move public opinion.

More Recent Studies

Some social scientists argued that the results of media influence found in laboratory studies are highly questionable because the conditions are artificial and unlike those in the real world. Since World War II, researchers have emphasized field studies more than laboratory investigation.

Socialization: Creating a Political Climate. As early as 1959, Kurt and Gladys Lang argued that the media may account for the long-term shifts in voters' attitudes and perceptions that students of politics uncover.[21] Even though short-run effects may be negligible, cumulatively media messages may create a climate of opinion and thereby socialize readers and viewers.

Unconsciously the public adopts assumptions never subject to challenge, following a procedure that E. E. Schattschneider described as a "mobilization of bias."[22] In a major study of media influence, Colin Seymour-Ure argued that *The Times* of London, in favoring appeasement toward Hitler in the 1930s, made this policy seem an acceptable alternative for British citizens and politicians.[23]

Tom Wicker argues, as many others have, that television reporting and news commentary from Vietnam changed American attitudes toward the war and ultimately created a climate of opinion that changed American foreign policy.[24]

Arthur Miller and several political science colleagues studied trust in government immediately after Watergate in 1974. They reported that "readers of papers containing a high degree of negative criticism directed at politicians were more distrustful of government and somewhat more likely to believe that the government was unresponsive, than were readers of newspapers containing less criticism." This limited conclusion nevertheless confirms that repeated messages are significant in forming attitudes toward the government.[25]

These climate-of-opinion studies, however, have a problem: it is not always clear whether the media are influencing the public or vice versa. Newspaper, radio, television, and other journalists, along with their readers, are part of a larger community and themselves, of course, are not always in complete agreement on important issues. Were the editors of *The Times* merely reflecting the British public's views or were they creating them? Did journalists become critical of the Vietnam War after antiwar activists had demonstrated and thus already begun a shift in public opinion? And how long did the special effect of Watergate coverage take to wear off once President Nixon resigned?

We also have the troubling evidence of Nazi Germany. During the 1930s, journalists treated Americans to horror stories about the "bad seeds" being planted — the children educated in Nazi schools. Yet following the war, West Germany, at least, succeeded in creating and maintaining a functioning democracy, not an easy feat in today's world. The socialization of Nazi ideals apparently did not fully take.

But these criticisms aside, it is clear that many politicians are convinced that newspapers, radio, and especially television can and do create climates of political opinion about important and unimportant issues. That belief in itself, of course, significantly influences the way in which politicians will treat media representatives and how they will react to what they report.

"Uses and Gratification" Studies.   Selective-perception studies build on a different criticism of socialization studies: that viewers and readers do not passively accept media reports but screen out upsetting messages and skip over opinion columns or news stories that make them feel uncomfortable. They seek out media reports that reinforce beliefs they already hold.

Paul Lazarsfeld and his associates, in one of the earliest public-opinion studies, discovered that media converted few voters in Erie County, Ohio. They found that newspapers stimulated people to vote and solidified preferences they already held. Frequent newspaper readers during the campaign were found to be voters whose minds had been made up long before the campaign even began. They read papers that reinforced their views.[26]

Politicians, though, much prefer studies that provide recipes on how to change attitudes. Do media messages ever break through our guard? Or do we change our views only because of traumatic emotional experiences, such as being laid off in a recession, or the turmoil of being caught in the draft for a war like that in Vietnam?

Most of us have read a book that changed our ideas about a significant topic. Perhaps the same applies to news articles, columnists' opinions, or television commentaries. Under what conditions does this change happen? What prevents our screening out these challenging views? We do not know for sure, at least not much more than we learned from the earlier laboratory studies.

Agenda Setting. Political scientist Bernard Cohen observes that the media may not be very successful in telling us what to think. But, he writes, they are often "stunningly successful" in telling us what to think about — screening events for us, not changing our attitudes.[27] They are influential, Cohen suggests, because they tell the rest of us what the important issues are.

Politicians have long recognized the political weight of news coverage in agenda setting. A news story such as the shooting of John Lennon, for example, may capture national, state, or local attention and fuel demands for gun control. Or a series of factual articles exploring a condition in depth may make the topic a public matter — what a fire trap the local auditorium is, why a basketball star such as Len Bias dies from drug overdose, how state legislators are taking trips to sunny climes at public expense, or how the president's policies favor the Southwest over New England and the Midwest. Such stories may force politicians to take political action in response.

A series of studies examined how newspaper readers ranked issues of the day, and later, the issues in an election campaign. The researchers chose newspapers that gave page-one prominence to different issues. They found that readers ranked issues just as the newspaper that they read did. These readers did not necessarily accept their newspapers' editorial stands, but they did accept the idea that the issues newspapers played up were those they should think about.[28]

In 1982 Shanto Iyengar and his colleagues conducted an experiment on how television influenced viewers' opinions about which issues were important. They took broadcast news stories but repositioned some of them and to various test groups showed "newscasts" with heavy concentrations of different types of stories such as defense problems, pollution, and energy. After a week of such experimental "newscasts," viewers usually ranked issues according to the topic concentration of the "newscast" for their group. The researchers conclude that "Network news programs seem to possess a powerful capacity to shape the public's agenda."[29]

Political commentators almost always try to be agenda setters. Political cartoonist Bill Mauldin writes of using his editorial cartoons to get his audience's attention on a subject. And then, he adds, "what the readers do about it is their own business. Our particular society was founded on the idea that if enough people get interested in an issue, the majority will come up with the right answer most of the time. I like to think that's true."[30] NBC News anchorman Tom Brokaw, in a commercial promoting his program, echoes this theme.

Politicians also sometimes set media agendas by getting reporters to focus on issues they want emphasized. President Reagan was also "stunningly successful" in getting the nation to look at politics according to his priorities. Even journalists, who remained unconvinced about the value of cutting taxes, spending more on defense, or downgrading social expenditures, found the president putting these issues on their front page and making them the top story on their news broadcasts. He had placed them on the political agenda for action.

But whoever starts the ball rolling, journalists or the politicians themselves, both know that the political events that get media attention in time also land on the political agenda for action, if they are not there already — to that extent we have a media-dominated society.

A Closing Note

We have seen how restraints were removed from the media as they changed from party-dominated organs to profitable businesses and were more fully able to take advantage of the openness of American government. This independence has been abetted by loosening legal controls and a more democratic climate of opinion. Politicians today face journalists who operate in a highly competitive market. Their professional careers depend on their ability to dig out attention-getting stories about politicians — stories that may help a career, threaten it, and even destroy it.

But has the profession come so far that journalists now in fact dominate the political scene? Can they dictate what politicians must do? We believe they cannot. But asking whether journalists dominate politicians is different from asking if media coverage dominates the political process. Politicians and social scientists have come to recognize that media coverage today is a paramount influence on politics.

Politicians have a major advantage in controlling the content of journalistic coverage. For every news story about government and politics some politician almost always has a monopolistic hold over the commodity the journalist needs most — the political story itself. At the same time, politicians deal not with a media monopoly but with individual, competing journalists. They can still pick and choose whom to favor, playing one journalist off against others. Some reporters will provide favorable treatment for an exclusive story or a leak.

Few reporters can afford to antagonize important politicians. It is significant, we think, that the Watergate coverup was uncovered by two unknown reporters, not by the men and women who daily covered the

White House and looked to its occupants as major sources of news. If a major politician or groups of politicians subtly or directly refuse to deal with a reporter, that reporter has difficulty surviving in the trade. A once rising career in journalism may suddenly plummet.

In the background lies also the possibility that a retaliatory Congress may toughen regulatory policies, particularly for the electronic media. Speeches by Vice President Spiro Agnew during the Nixon years echoed this threat. Or officials may make gathering of news more difficult by cracking down on leakers or by ordering employees to channel all media inquiries to the departmental press officer. None of these orders is ever completely successful, but they can harass journalists, at least for a time.

Part of the politician's skill in setting agendas can be used to deflect criticism. In 1985, President Reagan visited a cemetery in Bitberg, Germany that held remains of forty-seven Nazi storm troopers. A number of news commentators concluded that he had finally committed an error from which he would not recover. But Reagan came right back, changing the topic of journalistic and public discussion. He proposed that the national income tax be overhauled and reporters dutifully reported the growing discussion. Bitberg dropped from the news.

Do not conclude, though, that politicians do not sometimes have good reason to fear journalists. The uncertainties of American politics dictate otherwise. The journalists may score points and sometimes dominate the relationship and even influence political outcomes, yet politicians, for the most part, can hold their own in the relationship and then some.

Watergate, Jimmy Carter's experience, and the Iran-Contra scandal suggest one definite conclusion: it takes combined bad luck, inattention, blunders, political treachery, and perhaps even an inclination to commit political hara-kiri for the relationship to turn against the politician.

NOTES

1. George Brown, *In My Way* (Harmondsworth: Penguin Books, 1971), pp. 46–47.
2. Michael Schudson, *Discovering the News: A Social History of American Newspapers* (New York: Basic Books, 1978), pp. 14–17. The historical review presented here is based mostly on Schudson's excellent study. Omitted are the early commercial papers reporting on ship cargoes and sailings.
3. James E. Pollard, *The Presidents and the Press* (New York: Macmillan, 1947), p. 8.
4. M. L. Stein, *When Presidents Meet the Press* (New York: Julian Messner, 1969), p. 19.

5. James E. Pollard, *The Presidents and the Press* (New York: Macmillan, 1947), p. 48.

6. Schudson, *Discovering the News*, pp. 12–16.

7. 403 U.S. 713 (1971).

8. 413 U.S. 15 (1973).

9. 376 U.S. 254 (1964).

10. 441 U.S. 153 (1979).

11. "Westmoreland Takes on CBS," *Newsweek* 104 (Oct. 22, 1984): 60–72 and "The General's Retreat," *Newsweek* 105 (March 4, 1985): 59–60.

12. "Absence of Malice," *Newsweek* 105 (Feb. 4, 1985): 52–58, and "A General Loses His Case," *Time* 125 (Feb. 4, 1985): 64–66.

13. Jeff Greenfield, "Press Challenge," syndicated column in *Lansing State Journal*, May 10, 1984.

14. Grosjean v. American Press Co., 297 U.S. 233 (1936).

15. Elihu Katz and Paul F. Lazarsfeld, *Personal Influence: The Part Played by People in the Flow of Mass Communications* (Glencoe, Ill.: Free Press, 1955).

16. Stephen Hess, *The Washington Reporters* (Washington, D.C.: Brookings Institution, 1981), pp. 94–95.

17. Michael J. Robinson and Margaret A. Sheehan, *Over the Wire and on TV: CBS and UPI in Campaign '80* (New York: Russell Sage Foundation, 1983), pp. 286–289.

18. The standard sources are Joseph Klapper, *The Effects of Mass Communication* (Glencoe, Ill.: Free Press, 1960), and Sidney Kraus and Dennis Davis, *The Effects of Mass Communication on Political Behavior* (University Park: Pennsylvania State University Press, 1976).

19. Frank Luther Mott studied the newspapers' position in presidential elections between 1792 and 1944. He concluded that "there seems to be no correlation, positive or negative, between the support of a majority of newspapers during a campaign and success at the polls." "Newspapers in Presidential Campaigns," *Public Opinion Quarterly* 8 (1944): 348–367; Harold Gosnell studied eight elections between 1930 and 1936. He correlated the editorial position of the five Chicago daily papers with census tract circulation and voting results. Where *The Chicago Tribune* and *The Chicago Daily News* were widely read, Roosevelt's gains were small, but Roosevelt sharply increased his support in homes receiving foreign-language newspapers. More recent studies include: James E. Gregg, "Newspaper Editorial Endorsements and California Elections, 1948–1962," *Journalism Quarterly* 42 (1965): 532–538; Michael Hooper, "Party and Newspaper Endorsement as Predictors of Voter Choice," *Journalism Quarterly* 42 (1965): 281–284; Maxwell McCombs, "Editorial Endorsements: A Study of Influence," *Journalism Quarterly* 44 (1967): 545–548; John E. Mueller, "Voting on the Propositions: Ballot Patterns and Historical Trends in California," *American Political Science Review* 63 (December 1969): 1197–1212; William M. Mason, "The Impact of Endorsements on Voting," *Sociological Methods and Research* 1 (1973): 463–495; Robert Erikson, "The Influence of Newspaper Endorsements on Presidential Elections:

The Case of 1964" *American Journal of Political Science* 20 (1976): 207–233; John P. Robinson, "The Press as Kingmaker," *Journalism Quarterly* 51 (1974): 587–594 and 606; and Steven L. Combs, "The Electoral Impact of Newspaper Editorials," a paper delivered at the annual meeting of the Midwest Political Science Association, April 19–21, 1979, in Chicago.

20. A. D. Annis and N. C. Meier, "The Induction of Opinion Through Suggestion by Means of Planted Content," *Journal of Social Psychology* 5 (1934): 65–81.

21. Kurt and Gladys Lang, "The Mass Media and Voting," *American Voting Behavior*, Eugene Burdick and Arthur J. Brodbeck, eds. (Glencoe, Ill.: Free Press, 1959) pp. 217–235.

22. E. E. Schattschneider, *The Semi-Sovereign People* (New York: Holt, Rinehart and Winston, 1960), p. 61. But see also Peter Bachrach and Morton S. Baratz, *Power and Poverty: Theory and Practice* (New York: Oxford University Press, 1970), pp. 43–46.

23. Colin Seymour-Ure, *The Political Impact of Mass Media* (London: Constable, 1974).

24. Tom Wicker, *On Press* (New York: Viking Press, 1978), p. 11.

25. Arthur H. Miller, Edie N. Goldenberg, and Lutz Erbring, "Type-Set Politics: The Impact of Newspapers on Public Confidence," *American Political Science Review* 73 (1979): 67–84.

26. Paul Lazarsfeld, Bernard Berelson, and Helen Gaudet, *The People's Choice* (New York: Columbia University Press, 1948).

27. Bernard Cohen, *The Press and Foreign Policy* (Princeton: Princeton University Press, 1963), p. 13.

28. Maxwell McCombs and Donald Shaw, "The Agenda Setting Function of Mass Media," *Public Opinion Quarterly* 36 (Summer 1972): 176–187; Donald Shaw and Maxwell McCombs, *The Emergence of American Political Issues* (St. Paul, Minn.: West, 1977), and Ray Funkhouser, "The Issues of the Sixties: An Exploratory Study in the Dynamics of Public Opinion," *Political Science Quarterly* 37(1973): 62–75.

29. Shanto Iyengar, Mark D. Peters, and Donald Kinder, "Experimental Demonstrations of the 'Not So Minimal' Consequences of Television News Programs," *American Political Science Review* 76 (December 1982): 848–858; and Roy L. Behr and Shanto Iyengar, "Television News and Real-World Cues and Changes in the Public Agenda," *Public Opinion Quarterly* 49 (Spring 1985): 38–57.

30. Bill Mauldin, *What's Got Your Back Up?* (New York: Harper and Row, 1961), Foreword.

3

☆ ──────────────────────────── ☆

The Journalists
Whom
Politicians Face

Science writer Isaac Asimov has claimed that wars, great political leaders, plagues, and disasters — the events we often find leading the evening newscast or on page one of our newspaper — are of little overall importance for humanity. What matters, he says, are the advances in technology: the Wright Brothers' flight at Kitty Hawk, the computer, satellite communications, and other scientific discoveries.[1]

Perhaps Asimov is correct. But for a daily diet most of us find the big events that get the headlines of greater interest. What is it about these events that attracts our attention? Knowing the answers to this question is essential to journalistic success and our understanding of the journalists whom politicians face.

CHAPTER OVERVIEW

We begin by reviewing the qualities that journalists seek in their political stories. We examine how the demands of a medium itself shape the news that is reported. We see how journalists choose the style they believe appropriate in reporting the news. We consider accusations of journalistic bias and evaluate how well journalists cover the news under all these constraints.

JOURNALISTS DEFINE POLITICAL NEWS

We find three parts in the journalist's definition of what is politically newsworthy. They say political news is about (1) events which involve government officials, politicians, or a political issue; which (2) are current enough to be unfamiliar, and which (3) are interesting. We add a fourth consideration: the events that news organizations cover can be reported at a cost that editors consider reasonable.

Journalists are seldom far from the vicinity of the nation's top politician. Nor are many situations too mundane for network television if the visuals seem interesting. Here, President Gerald R. Ford (1974– 1977) permits networks to televise a swim in the White House pool. For Ford, it may have been an effort to counter a growing myth among journalists that he was clumsy and unathletic.

Political Events

At the heart of this definition is the "event." News is about activity, about someone doing something, described in journalistic jargon as a "news peg."

We think of political events as spontaneous, even unpredictable, like defection to the west by a Soviet diplomat. But politicians also plan pseudo-events — happenings designed to attract media coverage — what we call media events.

A good deal of what we read in our newspapers or see on television covers such manufactured events. Some are designed to draw attention to an issue or to a politician. President Calvin Coolidge, that dour New Englander, donned tribal headdress in South Dakota, a memorable scene that held no political significance unless it was to show he was not as aloof as had been thought.[2]

The News Event Must Be "Fresh"

Nonjournalists sometimes overlook how important timeliness is to journalists. Journalists are supposed to inform readers and viewers about events of which they know nothing about. Think how bored you become by hearing the same news again and again. Many radio stations with hourly newscasts have a rule that only the most important events may be reported more than three times. And even these must be updated with a new slant or new details.

Timeliness counts especially when media outlets compete. Journalists know that delay in getting the news out increases the likelihood that people will learn about it from other sources. When several newspapers in a city compete for readers, being first with a major story or even a story with as little eternal weight as last night's baseball results is essential. The reputation of the newspaper depends on it.

Television and radio call attention to their timeliness with news flashes: "We interrupt this program to bring you a special bulletin...." or "We switch you now to our correspondent in. . . ." Often such "bulletins" are little more than promotional teasers during the breaks in popular programs such as the Bill Cosby show to entice viewers to watch the next regular news program. Television also counters radio's "on the hour news" with "news updates" between scheduled programs. Electronic media often use recorded segments but try to make them seem "live."

Newspapers once put out "extras," special editions for street sale to report extraordinary events such as the death of a president. But the print media can no longer beat the immediacy of radio and television. Newspapers' "in-depth" reports, however, can provide fresh news by going into detail that electronic media do not have time to include.

Though most newspaper stories are from five to twenty hours old, print journalists try to make them appear current. Douglass Cater describes how he and other wire-service reporters prepared the "overnight" — a story composed the previous evening but giving the impression "when it appears the next day that it covers that day's events."[3] Occasionally, even weekly news magazines postpone publication at the last minute to cover a major "breaking story."

This induced hunger for timely news can create trouble for politicians. Political news often occurs in the form of a breaking story that creates a demand for new facts. The Watergate and Iran scandal stories that plagued Richard Nixon and Ronald Reagan were kept alive for months. Persistent digging by journalists turned up fresh details, which they nourished to evoke critical comments and the desire for more information. A statement you will often hear on television news is, "We still have unanswered questions, Dan." The president and members of the administration are likely to regard such journalists as busybodies engaged in malicious troublemaking.

Political Stories That Interest the Public

Reporters once talked about having a nose for news, a feel for stories that would attract attention. What separates an interesting political event from the ho-hum?

Events with Human Interest. Many people like to read and know about murders, treachery, mystery, scandal, and bizarre happenings in real life. Scandals entangling politicians in high places, such as Senator Edward Kennedy's accident at Chappaquiddick, are political events with some of the same emotional attraction we find in novels, movies, and television soap operas — drama with a touch of tragedy and sometimes of comedy. They involve the mysterious and unpredictable element we call personality. People watched how Senator Dole, when he was chairman of the Senate Finance Committee, would handle budget requests from the secretary of the Department of Transportation because DOT Secretary Elizabeth Dole was his wife.

Conflict and Competition. In 1985, journalists focused at length on a relatively small request for funds. President Reagan proposed that

Contra's

$14 million be given a rebel band fighting the Nicaraguan government. Recalling Vietnam, many opposed this request. The battle between the White House and Capitol Hill became intense. It was a great human-interest story.

In 1984, Senator Howard Baker retired as Republican majority leader. Journalists immediately began questioning possible contenders for that spot, attempting to find out whom individual senators and even the president would support. They heightened the sense of competition by suggesting that Senator Robert Dole was the front-runner but that he did not have quite enough votes to win. We may not sit on the edge of our sofas waiting to see who wins the contest, but nonetheless, the race captures our attention.

By this time the common element in these political events shows clearly: each carries a heavy dose of controversy and competition and an outcome that is in question. Eliminate the political conflict and these, not to mention many political stories in today's paper, would get no more than passing journalistic attention and barely tweak our interest. Conflict provides drama. We wonder how the president will respond and what he will do next; we are curious about who will win.

The more uncertain the outcome in such conflicts, the more our interest climbs. Journalists thus seek to play up the horse-race aspects of politics, what will happen next, and how the president will handle future issues if he loses. Political scientists criticize them for horse-race journalism but they know viewers and readers will be interested. We are also attracted by political controversy because it signals possible change — what is new is news.

But notice also the two-sides bias. Journalists habitually report any conflict as though it had only two sides. Lumping all the contestants on one side or the other simplifies the report and gives the appearance of balanced reporting. But the approach may not convey the diversity of opinion that really surrounds the issue.

Political Celebrities.   Because we are so attracted to human-interest stories, journalists create a cast of media characters, the grist from which to manufacture further news stories, and those are the persons we know as celebrities.

Celebrities make news just because of who they are. Mostly they are sports and entertainment personalities, but a few are politicians. Whatever they do is news, political news if a celebrity speaks out on a public issue or becomes associated with a politician.

Media celebrities are identified by name only. We don't need to be told that Ann-Margret is an actress or that Cher sings, nor do we need their full names. Some we recognize by a nickname or catch phrase, such as, "He-e-e-re's John-n-n-ny!" or, in the political arena, "the Peanut Farmer" or "the Great Communicator."[4]

Questionable real-estate practices in New York City ordinarily do not qualify as national political news. But when John Zaccaro, husband of the 1984 Democratic vice-presidential candidate Geraldine Ferraro, pleaded guilty to a misdemeanor, reporters counted on readers becoming fascinated, and they dug and dug to give us more data. We were expected to scour the reports for new revelations.

The president outranks all others as a political celebrity. (Within states, the chief political celebrity is probably the governor or a U.S. senator.) If, as President Reagan did, the political celebrity eats white coconut jellybellies to keep his energy up, it's political news. If he has an illness, undergoes a medical procedure, says he enjoys reading westerns as President Eisenhower did, or starts wearing a hearing aid, the media dutifully report these as political events because the subject is a political celebrity.

Authorities. The next best story for a journalist is a political authority. Authorities get into news stories because of their expertise or their official position, as when the head of H&R Block publicly discusses a new tax law.

Henry Kissinger, when secretary of state for Presidents Nixon and Ford, was a political celebrity and he now, perhaps, ranks as a media "authority." Reporters called him for quotes when Mikhail Gorbachev became head of the USSR. On national economic stories, journalists called Alan Greenspan, former chair of the Council on Economic Advisers. During 1984 he was quoted twenty-two times in *The New York Times* and in the *Washington Post* twenty-four times. Today he heads the Federal Reserve Board.

Political scientist Richard Scammon often appears on election night broadcasts to explain voting trends. Reporters call on political scientist Norman Ornstein for comments about Congress. The list might include former Notre Dame President Rev. Theodore Hesburgh on liberal Catholic views, pollster Pat Caddell on the future of the Democratic party, or NAACP director Benjamin Hooks on civil rights. Community or state politics reporters also have their own lists of authorities for use on local or state stories.

Some authorities are called upon often because journalists can count on them to generate forceful, succinct, and sometimes humorous remarks — with no hedging!

Incumbent politicians usually fit into the authority classification.

They are quoted only when the event touches their own office or position. A proposed change in social-security benefits brings comments from aging Representative Claude Pepper. But his preferences for candy or reading materials are not political news except perhaps in his home state, Florida, where he is a celebrity.

Wide Influence. Journalists also seek out political stories that affect large segments of the population. If national television shows an unemployed worker, it does so to suggest that unemployment is at least a regional or perhaps a national problem. President Reagan showed his disgust with such reports when he asked, "but why is it news that some fellow out in South Succotash someplace has just been laid off that he should be interviewed nationwide?"

For the journalist, local or national, the more Americans affected, the stronger the appeal, and the greater the audience. A federal tax increase or cut has a higher appeal than a similar action in a state or community. And an increase in the personal income tax means more interest than does a similar increase for corporations.

We are interested because the events may affect our lives. A report that 2,000 people in India died from an industrial accident might be reported under "World Roundup" columns. But when we learn that a United States company is involved and that it has similar facilities in West Virginia, the news becomes a highly influential political story. Suddenly we are interested and begin wondering whether similar problems lurk in our town or whether trucks loaded with these dangerous chemicals are moving through our state.

Political Events Nearby. Fred G. Bonfils, legendary editor of the *Denver Post*, instructed his reporters, "Remember that a dogfight on Champa Street is a bigger story for us than three thousand Chinese drowned in a typhoon." We are especially interested in political and governmental events that happen in our own neighborhoods. Presumably, they may affect us or we may know some of the persons involved. We may be generally interested in prison security. We will have only passing interest if the prison break takes place 500 miles away unless it involves a local person or angle. Such reports may be lead stories elsewhere, but will be reported under "national roundup" in our local papers and be mentioned briefly, if at all, on national radio news or television. But if some escapees are thought to be seen hitchhiking on a nearby freeway, our interest rises sharply. We want more details.

Reporting at "Reasonable" Cost

Not all political events are reported in the media. Journalists may not know about some of them, or if they do, they may not recognize their importance. Newspaper space and air time are limited. Some stories get bumped for other "practical" reasons.

War correspondents sometimes risk their lives to bring us the latest news. And occasionally reporters are kidnapped and held hostage by terrorist groups in the Mideast and elsewhere. But these are exceptional cases. Editors and reporters avoid such risky situations except for the most important stories. Some stories may appear to be risky for other reasons — the potential for a libel suit, for one.

Media outlet owners remind editors that they have limited staff and money. Reporters may not be available for an extensive investigation of possible local political corruption or for many trips to the state capital.

Reporting also involves personal energy costs. Editors and reporters prefer to report political events that fit their routines. They like stories that require little extra effort to report.

Reliance on Official Sources. The preference for easy-to-gather news contributes to heavy reliance on official sources: the White House, Congress, governors' offices, criminal courts, the legislature, police stations. Such offices are on reporters' beats, places they visit regularly for news.

The procedure becomes institutionalized as reporters check in daily with official sources. In turn, officials know that reporters expect them to provide a peg on which the reporter can hang a story. A symbiotic relationship forms, with each helping the other.

Beats normally do not cover unofficial sources, partly because these sources may be in inconvenient places and because reporters may not know of them. These sources usually have to seek out the reporters, rather than the reverse. Thus, political events such as the Watts civil-rights riots of the 1960s, the rise of the women's movement, and the Moral Majority's wide influence caught reporters unprepared. These were not political events that occurred on their regular beats. The *Los Angeles Times* had no reporters or sources in Watts when violent civil-rights riots broke out there.

Cooperation with Incumbents. Ease of getting a story also explains why journalists so often cooperate with incumbent politicians in reporting media events — stories staged to get publicity for the politician or an issue. The event is likely to occur at a convenient time and place, scheduled by politicians to make sure journalists have it in time for their deadlines.

During a 1985 debate over seating a representative in a disputed congressional race in Indiana, Republican House members walked out after the Democratic majority voted to seat the Democrat. As Republicans left the chamber, Democrats heckled, "Get out there by 3 o'clock. We know you want to appear in the best light." The implication was that Republicans would miss the "photo opportunity" for the network news that evening if they delayed too long. We suspect Republicans smiled knowingly as they marched out of the House chamber.[5]

Seeking out media events that nonincumbents attempt to stage takes special effort and some risk. The journalist may come up empty after going to great trouble lugging television cameras or waiting around for hours for something to happen at some out-of-the-way location. Seeking the predictable story and jazzing up the treatment is easier.

Geographic Overreporting. The national networks overreport events in New York and Washington and the eight to ten other cities where they have camera crews. Similar local events occurring in Waterloo, Iowa or San Angelo, Texas are not carried unless the story line involves a well-known person or it fits in with a current nationally dominant theme or trend. Then the network may accept a feed from a local affiliate. Dispatching crews to remote locations is costly and is done only if the political story has unusual national importance.

Examine the list of authorities appearing on national television. You will notice that it is rather short; most are within easy reach of network headquarters in New York or Washington.

The medium one chooses shapes the content of one's message.

HOW THE MEDIUM AFFECTS REPORTING

Marshall McLuhan argued that the medium is the message — that the medium one chooses shapes the content of one's message. Here we look at the special requirements print and electronic media impose on journalists who use them and distinguish how the events reported in the two types of media differ.

The major difference between viewing print and electronic news presentation is that printed matter allows for discontinuous viewing. Electronic media do not. If you become bored with this printed page you can skip to another. You can return to it later or reread a section as often as you wish. And you can read it to fit your own schedule.

The electronic media of over-the-air radio and television, and cable television give you information in a continuous flow. Recorders aside, you can skip only by switching channels or turning the thing off. You have to listen or view the report as it is broadcast; viewing the news when it is convenient for you is not possible except perhaps on cable news or by VCR.

The difference in attention that the two forms of media require lead to their handling news events differently.

Attentiveness and Printed News

Every day the print media carry many political stories and other features that we may completely ignore; including editorials, recipes, financial news, or sports data. They also carry political stories that appeal to many minority tastes. They can provide regular reports on politics in outlying suburbs or political events in Bulgarian villages. A newspaper can provide a daily state-by-state political rundown as *USA Today* does. It can feature political news for specialized groups — Spanish speakers, women, blacks, business executives, or labor.

The print media will also cover political stories "in depth." If you are not interested in reading an analysis of the politics of Zimbabwe, your eyes can skip through it or pass it entirely. The reporter knows or hopes that some readers may even put the article aside to read carefully when they have time. Print journalists know they are catering to an audience with specialized tastes and expectations. And their papers and magazines provide space for extended political analysis. The only restrictions on such reporting are the financial costs of news gathering and limited space.

For all these reasons, specialists in every field including politics find that television and radio do not wholly replace reporting in print.

Attentiveness and Electronic News

The big worry in over-the-air electronic media is boring their mass audience, which loses them viewers or listeners. Television needs enticements that the trade calls eye candy — visual presentations that attract viewers. From these demands flow standards for television reporting of political news.

Brevity. Reports must be brief. One minute and fifteen seconds per item — about 100 to 120 words — is the usual outside limit on the evening news. One television broadcast would fill a little more than two columns on the front page in a standard newspaper.

General Interest. Network television and radio items must have general interest because the audiences are general. Even a local television station with a market area of two or three counties, as many have, cannot hope to report all that is happening in more than a few local governments within its viewing area. Television is therefore attracted to events of general interest — national over state news, state news over local, and larger local units over smaller ones.[6]

Emotional Influence. Material broadcast on television must have emotional content. Reuven Frank, executive producer of the NBC Evening News, says that "The highest power of television journalism is not in the transmission of information but in the transmission of experience. Joy, sorrow, shock, fear — these are the stuff of news."[7]

Thematic Influence. Frank also writes in his memorandum to his news staff, "Every news story should, without any sacrifice of probity or responsibility, display the attributes of fiction, of drama. It should have structure and conflict, problem and denouement, rising action and falling action, a beginning, a middle, and an end. These are not only the essentials of drama; they are the essentials of narrative."[8] Television news, he states, must do more than report the facts: the "four w's" — who, what, where, and when. It needs an interpretive theme that ties the facts into a story and makes a point.

Heavy Editing. Edward J. Epstein, in studying NBC network news found that only half the stories were presented live, the equivalent of viewing nature through a mirror. The rest, he concluded, were news manufactured in the television newsroom.

An editor or producer set a theme or slant for the story in advance. Field reporters were then told to get the film footage that would support the theme. Groups were often stereotyped to fit familiar themes. Editors and producers in the studio would then splice pieces of film and add sound and voice lead-in to construct a news story with that interpretive theme. They would end up using as little as 5 percent of the film shot. Segments that did not support the theme were cut.[9]

Local news programs, especially in small markets, usually have less editing and therefore less thematic coherence.

Other Media Differences

The print and electronic media differ in other ways affecting their journalists' ways of covering events.

Permanence. Printed matter is more lasting than material that is broadcast on radio or television frequencies. Readers and librarians clip stories and may preserve them for years filed by topic for quick and easy reference. Rarely does anyone record a news broadcast, except perhaps the stations themselves or a few students of the media, and only the most memorable footage is ever rebroadcast.

Print journalists pride themselves on being the medium of permanent record and maintain that print reporting has greater prestige. Print reporters say they feel more pressure to be accurate. They put down electronic reporters as little more than entertainers, whose best efforts soon disperse into thin air.

Viewer Involvement. Print media necessarily depend on reports of what happened hours or even days ago. Electronic media sometimes let us see or hear a political event as it happens. Television news can show us what the actors in the story looked or sounded like — you see the president addressing the European parliament, the soldiers in El Salvador under fire, hear the sound of an IRA bombing raid and see the smoke still rising. Some of these images are etched in our minds.

Cameras may also distort reality with false rosiness. With close-in focusing, a small crowd can be made to seem sizable. Demonstrators may knowingly march with relatively wide spaces between participants and violent acts may take place only when the crew has the camera lights turned on.

And one political argument is never put to rest: does the camera really reveal or can it gild reality with false color? Does it reveal a politician's true character, or can a skillful politician successfully fake sincerity and honesty? Politicians appear to believe that it doesn't hurt to try to improve appearances. When Democrats regained control of one U.S. Senate committee in 1987, they moved Republicans to the other side of the chamber to give Democrats a better camera angle.

Newspapers try to overcome these electronic advantages by livening up their pages with photographs, cartoons, graphs, and colored print. Boxed materials provide background information about how an issue developed, how an interest group got organized, or how a politician got started. They are able to avoid oversimplifying a story or falling into the trap of ascribing legitimacy to a small demonstration that makes it to television news.

Print journalists also can base their reports on what politicians tell them in private, rather than on only what the camera is able to film or the microphone record. Print reporters can inform readers about the subtler forms of politicking, those not easily shown visually. They may describe in detail how "Cap" Weinberger really managed to gain support for his defense proposals.

The Reporting Staff. The media also differ in news-gathering ability. Print media need details. Thus the typical newspaper is labor intensive. Television needs pictures. It depends on sophisticated equipment to give us capsule accounts.

Television journalists have to deal with the problems of getting equipment to the news scene. Even with hand-held cameras the job is cumbersome. Commonly the reporting team is a crew attempting to get a few minutes of footage. Most radio stations need even less for their audio. A small tape recorder and a few reporters suffice. Recordings can be received by phone — incumbent politicians often provide "news bites" that can spice up the local news program. Newspapers, even small ones, must have large staffs — regulars and stringers — to get the local detail and fill their "newshole."

Transmission Time. Getting stories into print and into readers' hands, even with modern technology, is a relatively slow procedure. The struggle to be first to report a political event is now fought among electronic media. Networks vie to be first with the news or to predict election outcomes. Newspaper journalists can do little but predict winners and watch as the networks announce the news.

Print journalists respond by using their staff advantage for exclusives and occasional investigative reports such as the continuing series Woodward and Bernstein wrote for the *Washington Post* on Watergate. Newspapers can no longer be first with the story of the State of the Union speech, but they can give thoughtful analysis in some depth. They are also better able to handle political stories of some complexity or subtlety.

Media Restraints and Politicians

Some politicians such as President Reagan profit by their personal appearance and effectiveness as television or radio performers. The more leisurely pace of print reporters favors other politicians, authorities who can "background" journalists over lunch or a sip of scotch.

The varied media needs provide opportunities for some politicians or officials to stay in the news even on weekends. Television interview programs such as NBC's *Face the Nation* provide news mentions through the weekend. President Reagan's Saturday radio broadcast, which in itself had a small audience, was nonetheless reported heavily in both print and electronic media each weekend.

THE JOURNALIST'S APPROACH TO REPORTING

Publishers and editors felt a surge of relief to get out from under the politicians' thumb, and be able to criticize politicians as they pleased. Political reporters were happier still. Independent of political patronage, they could report as they pleased, requiring only the blessing of their editors and publishers or network executives.

Editors as Gatekeepers

News editors determine which stories a reporter will be sent out to cover and how those reports will be handled. Some reports may never be published or broadcast; they may be sharply cut; some receive praise, others criticism.

From their editors' actions, reporters get subtle and sometimes not so subtle cues about the kinds of stories that are wanted. Other cues come from fellow journalists.

In a competitive market for news, still many of the decisions on how a story will be handled, and even which stories will be covered, are left to the individual reporter. They use this independence to approach their responsibilities in political reporting in different ways that greatly affect the content of news.[10]

Today's More Aggressive Journalists

Modern reporting produces facts from more sources than reporting of a generation ago. Most journalists feel they are doing a better job of reporting. Some journalists' ways of gathering news, though, and the way of presenting their stories, are not without critics.

Ann Landers describes what happened when she filed for divorce: "Reporters and camera crews camped out for days in my lobby and on the sidewalk outside. . . . It was terrible. . . . One reporter, who had been a friend of mine, got up to my apartment after conning the doorman into believing she was there on a personal visit. I wouldn't let her in. She just wanted to talk, she said. I was certain that she had a camera and wanted a picture of me looking depressed or anguished. I just couldn't believe this attempt to invade my privacy. Television is the worst. Television reporters present themselves as having the perfect right to be anywhere, to ask any question."[11]

A *Time* cover story in late 1983 gave this assessment of the modern journalist:

They are rude and accusatory, cynical and almost unpatriotic. They twist facts to suit their not-so-hidden agenda. They meddle in politics, harass business, invade people's privacy, and then walk off without regard to the pain and chaos they leave behind. They are arrogant and self-righteous, brushing aside most criticism as the uninformed carping of cranks and ideologues. To top it off, they claim that their behavior is sanctioned, indeed sanctified, by the U.S. Constitution.[12]

Senator Eugene McCarthy, 1968 independent candidate for president on an anti-Vietnam platform, says the media giants act as if they consider themselves sovereign states. "I have been waiting," he says, "for CBS to put out its own postage stamps."[13]

What has earned journalists this reputation? In part, they have earned it because journalistic approaches to reporting over the last twenty years have evolved from the objective to the interpretive, to the adversarial, and beyond.

"Objective" News Reporting

As newspapers evolved into businesses, the value of nonpartisan news stories grew. Fledgling news services early in this century such as Associated Press and later United Press International, produced nonpartisan reports because newspapers representing so many shades of political opinion used their product.

News-service reporters were instructed to report only the facts; opinions were to be reserved for the editorial page. Editors blue-penciled speculation and interpretation from cub reporters' stories. Journalists thus could be generalists who knew little about the subject they covered — only specialists had opinions, they were told; reporters just collected facts. The reporter remained out of the story, an anonymous figure who received no by-line. The target audience was as broad as possible. The kind of behavior such reporting encouraged was respectful attention to what politicians told them.

Objective reporting required journalists to present their facts in order of importance, beginning in the first paragraph with the who, what, when, and where of the story. Subsequent paragraphs gave less important facts. This style allowed the makeup person to lop off one or more ending paragraphs, knowing that these covered the least important facts. It also gave a very technical and impersonal flavor to news reports.

The strength in the objective approach was that reports are backed with many facts — editors stressed factual accuracy. Because the reporters could not voice their own opinions, incumbent officials were ready to cooperate with them. Objective reporting thus would give most emphasis to official news.

Criticisms of Objective Reporting. Journalists and others criticize this approach because they say it is not really objective. Choosing the stories to be reported and the facts to emphasize in themselves involved bias. The defense was that professional editors with a "nose for news" assigned and reviewed the stories to be covered and published.

Some reporters claimed too that objective reporting left them captives to the public officials who provided the facts to be published. Objectivity, critics said, makes reporters apologists for the system, reporting what is told them without comment.

Critics also argued that the "objective" stories did not interpret the significance of the facts. The whys or shoulds and even the so whats were left out. The antics of communist-hunter Senator Joseph McCarthy were reported deadpan, without comment. The senator was skilled at using reporters to portray him as a fearless fighter of subversion, and reporters could do little about it. Dutifully they reported each new charge he made. But the significant political news story was seldom reported: the senator produced no proof for his charges — he just issued new charges.

Reporting in the objective style by taking facts out of chronological order also made it more difficult to figure out the sequence in which events occurred. If a president fired a staff aide, reporters would report that fact. It might be difficult, though, to put together just how the event took place. That the aide had been suspected of leaking information a week before might appear far down in the story or be dismissed as speculation.

Doonesbury   **by Garry Trudeau**

A last criticism was one that defenders of objectivity proudly accepted: the writing was often dull and boring. Better to be dull, they said, than to hype up stories, as yellow journalists did or expect readers to accept reporters' opinions, as in the partisan press.

Interpretive Reporting

To meet the shortcomings in objective reporting, newspapers began adding to their news sections stories labeled "news analysis," usually identifying the news analyst with a byline. Television newscasts also frequently add a "commentary" to the evening report.

These reports are built around a theme; an interpretation that adds the whys, whats, and hows as well as background details. If a story were about a general who, in a coup, had taken over the government of a Central African nation, the news analysis would tell anything that was known about him and his policies and speculate on what might happen next rather than concentrate on who shot at whom and how often the air force bombed the imperial palace.

Some journalists also introduce interpretive material into unsigned news stories by presenting alternative and conflicting interpretations of political events, usually with quotations in alternate paragraphs from persons with different political views.

Interpretive reporting requires a different style of reporter. Getting explanatory material sometimes means asking incumbents embarrassing and even hostile questions. Reporters must seek out sources other than the official ones. For the incumbent official, this kind of reporting means less control and influence over what is reported. Reporters, must ask themselves what Senator Jones's statement means, whether they should ask someone of the opposite party, or maybe get a different angle from someone at the local university. They thus attempt to make sense of the facts in stories that are otherwise strung together in prescribed format.

The best interpretive reporters attract sophisticated readers because they build unpredictability into their reports, conveying a sense of fairness by allowing their analysis of facts to include politicians of varying persuasions. Predictable interpretive reporters, however, may attract audiences who agree with their likely conclusions.

Criticisms of Interpretive Reporting. The value of any interpretive analysis depends on perceptiveness in the person interpreting the events. Physicians might well object to reporters' interpreting how well a politician is recovering from a heart attack. Politicians may also feel offended by an unskilled reporter's clumsy interpretation of political events. Bylines thus are usually attached to "news-analysis" stories and increasingly to "news stories."

And any reader may rightly ask if the themes that journalists develop are reasonable given the facts. Or are journalists simply putting into the story their own political prejudices or those embedded in conventional wisdom?

Any day now, you will probably see a news story in which a politician claims that the media treated him or her unfairly. The complaint might be not that the facts were wrong but the "spin" or theme of the story was improper. Judy Belushi, widow of John Belushi, said of reporters who interviewed her after her entertainer husband died of a drug overdose: "Before they talk to you, they know what their story is going to say. When they interview you, they're just waiting for you to say the things that fit [the story they came to write]. [14]

Adversary Reporting

Even more than interpretive reporting, the adversarial style is a matter of journalistic manner and attitude. Such journalists maintain a hostile, critical, and cynical view of everyone in power. The public image put out by most politicians, they suspect, is false, their public statements disingenuous, their moral pronouncements hypocritical, their motives self-serving, and their promises ephemeral. The politician is guilty until he or she can prove innocence.

Sam Donaldson of ABC wrote: "If you send me to cover a pie-baking contest on Mother's Day, I'm going to ask dear old Mom why she used artificial sweetener in violation of the rules, and while she's at it, could I see the receipt for the apples to prove that she didn't steal them. I maintain that if Mom has nothing to hide, no harm will have been done. But the questions should be asked. Too often, Mom, and presidents — behind those sweet faces — turn out to have stuffed a few rotten apples into the public barrel." [15]

If they are to expose what politicians are really like and keep them from using the media to their own advantage, adversarial reporters think they must be completely independent of politicians. Refusing to report facts exactly as officials present them, these journalists may assume that the facts provided are self-serving, and at best, only part of the story. Reporters, they say, should do more than interpret events; they should be watchdogs, ferreting out information that the public "has a right to know." Their job, they say, is to do investigative reporting.

Adversarial journalists dig out facts in every way possible; often questioning legal restraints and the self-restraints that friendship, loyalty, or civility impose. Fred W. Friendly, an associate of Edward R. Murrow, wrote, "A good journalist has a lot of shoe leather, a conscience, and the ability to see the world from the wolf's point of view."[16] Robert Pious in his book on the presidency wrote that "the legacy of Watergate is wolfpack journalism."[17]

They aggressively seek out nonofficial sources, or by promising publicity or even threatening, encourage leaks, especially from administrators not in sympathy with elected officials. Some adversarial reporters' belief in independence is so deep that, even when a judge orders them to reveal their sources and release their notes, they refuse. Anything is better than having their sources dry up and to gain that information they probably had to guarantee confidentiality. They also object because they feel journalists should not in effect become aides to law enforcement officials.

Adversarial reporting often turns up information that would not otherwise be available, perhaps uncovering political wrongdoing that had long escaped notice. Many journalists value the adversarial approach because it is the style that wins Pulitzer prizes and brings prestige to the reporter. Jack Anderson won a Pulitzer for reporting a leak from the National Security Council, a leak later traced to a Navy enlisted man. That adversarial reporting can be a quick ticket to the top, Woodward and Bernstein found from their Watergate reports. It can also lead to top audience ratings, as Mike Wallace demonstrated on *60 Minutes*. Media outlets facing intense competition often seek out and reward adversarial reporters.

Criticisms of Adversarial Reporting. Politicians generally despise adversarial reporters. Among the more defensible reasons is that they make governing more difficult. Insiders and others who oppose an executive's policy may leak negative information or reveal details prematurely to stymie unpopular programs. Almost every president since John F. Kennedy, and many before, battled treacherous leaks by aides who claimed to be loyal. Such reporting may also make criminal justice, military tactics, and espionage more difficult to manage.

Unwittingly, adversarial reporters also make a significant trade: no longer prisoners of official sources, they become entrapped by those who leak information. To be sure, official sources often provide information that puts themselves in the best light. But unnamed sources frequently do likewise, and they also manipulate reporters. Their information, of course, may be equally suspect, especially because it is provided anonymously. Information accepted without careful verification can lead to publication of false charges and ruined careers, a point made in the movie *Absence of Malice.*

Reagan aides said about a reporter they regarded as overly aggressive: "when the questions are too strident, he makes the president look good." Donaldson agrees. "We play into our critics' hands if we push something when we don't have any news."

Adversarial reporters are perhaps more tempted than others to grow lazy and sloppy, avoiding truly investigative work. A reporter once told us half jokingly when we asked if a story about a politician was really true: "that's the kind of story that's too good to check out." A Dr. Carl Galloway sued *60 Minutes* and Dan Rather for slander, claiming that he was not involved in medical fraud as had been reported and that the signature on the incriminating document was forged. After the verdict in June 1983, jury foreman David Campbell, who had sided with CBS, told reporters, "I think the consensus [among jurors] was that Galloway had not signed that piece of paper." They argued, however, that Rather and his producers believed he had, and therefore the journalists had not acted in reckless disregard for the truth. The doctor lost his case on a 10 to 2 verdict, but the adversarial reporters of *60 Minutes* also lost something in this close examination of their procedures.

Adversarial reporting almost always leads to an antiestablishment bias that may blind reporters to relevant facts. It may also unwittingly give antiestablishment protestors legitimacy they do not deserve, just because reporters accept their criticisms or complaints as newsworthy. A reporter, too intent on prosecuting all politicians or just getting a good story, may slant the data or leave out important information.

Surprisingly, adversarial reporting may also result in less rather than more news, and news that is less reliable than under objective reporting. Reporters with chips on their shoulders often cut themselves off from official sources of information. One wonders why anyone agrees to be interviewed by the staff of *60 Minutes*. Politicians with less choice may find it necessary to talk to an adversarial reporter but may feel he or she has already been put on trial and found guilty! Officials may become very cautious about what they reveal, may stonewall reporters, or give choice stories only to those on whom they can depend to file reports with a favorable spin or theme.

Adversarial reporting fascinates many readers and viewers, as the popularity of Jack Anderson's columns and *60 Minutes* suggests. But it repels others. Critics argue that the steady decline in the public's regard for journalists evident in polls is impelled by such reporting. The quotation from *Time* earlier in this section appears to be directed mainly at adversarial reporters' practices.

Advocacy Journalism

Rather than merely question the motives of all public officials, or favor a political party, advocacy reporters seek to advance an ideological point of view. Such point-of-view journalism, of course, is similar to the old partisan reporting, and is most frequent in the alternative or underground press of the right or left. Their target audiences hope to get specialized information on issues that the mainstream journalists overlook.

Some conservatives argue that since the Vietnam War and Watergate, journalists for mainstream publications have employed advocacy reporting to encourage social change. They point to a survey of 104 top television executives, not all from news divisions, revealing that two-thirds believed television programs should help lead the way to social reform.[18] Journalists, though, vigorously dispute this charge. Stephen Hess, in his study of the Washington press corps, argued that journalists were rarely ideological — most, he concluded, were apolitical. Morton Kondracke, executive editor of *New Republic*, agrees. Most journalists, he says, are "trendy liberals, not hard-line ideologues."[19]

A major flaw in advocacy reporting is that ideology often colors the presentation of facts. The reporter also runs the risk of becoming a propagandist, seeking facts to support a point of view and ignoring any that do not. The temptation to distort is there, but perhaps stronger is the unconscious distortion that occurs when a journalist reports an event with a preconceived political view of what must have occurred.

The New or Now Journalism

During the 1960s, some journalists began experimenting with reports using fictional techniques. Most such reporting in the print media appears in specialty magazines. Sometimes authors of novels have fictional characters meet political leaders such as Theodore Roosevelt or Abraham Lincoln. Television "docudramas" employ this mixture of fact and fiction extensively.

The fictional techniques may include creating composite characters. One journalist, writing about New York prostitutes, combined the true experiences of many women into one, whom she called "Red Pants." The writer felt that in this way she captured the essence of life as a New York prostitute, more than if she had faithfully reported experiences of several women.

Other writers using these techniques telescope political events or report them in a new order to heighten the dramatic effect. Or they make up plausible quotations and put them into a politician's mouth.

Woodward and Bernstein, to add drama to their book on Watergate, *All the President's Men*, reported conversations roughly as they judged they would have happened.

Now journalists argue that the technique is often a better way of reporting the essence of the truth than a strictly factual report. A skilled writer can also make the story fascinating reading.

Journalists using this technique risk temptation to distort or suppress facts to fit their fictional framework and dramatic theme. Moreover, the writer can easily reason that because the account is partly fictional, liberties can be taken with other known facts. Walter Lippmann, listing factual errors in a biography of John F. Kennedy, wrote, "In the mistakes I know about there is the same pattern: always the mistake is a fiction which intensifies the drama of the story."[20]

Today's Reporting

Politicians may be tempted to conclude that almost all of today's journalists are adversarial, at least they are more numerous now than a generation ago. But that is an overstatement.

Career Differences. When we catalog journalistic ambitions, we see that the adversarial approach appeals most to journalists wanting a quick climb up the journalistic career ladder. Reporters with static ambitions, satisfied to work out the rest of their careers in their present position, are likely to report objectively but to interpret the data politicians give them. Some may be co-opted by the official who is their steady source of news.[21]

Media Differences. Approaches to reporting are likely to differ according to the reporter's competitive situation and job. Most print-medium editors still prefer objective reporting, placing interpretive pieces in separate, byline columns or giving opposing views in alternating paragraphs. The two highest prestige papers, *The Washington Post* and *The New York Times*, are major exceptions. As the *Post* challenges the *Times* for national newspaper leadership, each depends on investigative reporting and adversarial practices to demonstrate its preeminence.

In the fiercely competitive network business, a point or two in the ratings is worth millions in advertising revenues. National television journalists, Austin Ranney observes, are likely to couple open bias against all politicians with antiestablishment feelings characteristic of adversarial reporting.[22]

Reactions to Criticism. The networks are aware of findings like those in Michael Robinson's report, that people who follow national politics entirely on television are significantly more confused and cynical than those who use other media as well.[23] Calculated changes in Dan Rather's appearance — hair style, clothing, and even an effort to create a friendlier emotional tone — were the CBS News prescription when he took over as anchor from Walter Cronkite. These changes clearly made him seem less adversarial. Perhaps network anchor reporters need to appear friendly and reassuring and the correspondents can be more confrontational.

A more accurate appraisal of the general run of journalists, we think, is that most reporters are convinced they need to be more skeptical than reporters were in the past. They owe the reader or viewer an interpretation of political events to make their stories understandable, they feel, and within limits they will dig more than reporters once did to get viewpoints other than those gathered from official sources. This media environment isn't as comfortable, for many politicians, as it once was.

ARE THE MEDIA BIASED?

During the 1920s and through the New Deal period, charges of media bias came from the radical left. George Seldes, a former *Chicago Tribune* reporter, wrote several books attacking his former employer and other media giants. Socialist Upton Sinclair contributed *The Brass Check*.[24] The business office and large advertisers, they claimed, dominated America's newspapers and twisted the news to fit their prejudices.

The new left today continues asserting that media biases favor establishment views and interests. The news is written and broadcast, they say, to defend wealthy media owners and discredit the radical left and those who lead liberal social movements. The entertainment programs are designed to lull the masses into accepting the status quo.[25] Significantly, they say, the media today form the *third* largest industry in the United States.

Until recently, Democrats too complained that the news was slanted against them. During the 1952 presidential election campaign, Democratic candidate Adlai Stevenson observed, "It would seem that the overwhelming majority of the press is just against Democrats; not after a sober and considered view of the alternatives, but automatically, as dogs are against cats. As soon as a newspaper. . . sees a Democratic candidate it is filled with an unconquerable yen to chase him up an alley."

STAYSKAL
85 TAMPA
TRIBUNE

A PLOT TO TAKEOVER CBS WAS PUSHED TODAY BY SOME NARROW-MINDED, MANIPULATIVE, RIGHT-WING, FLAKY CONSERVATIVES WHO THINK THEIR WEIRDO VIEWS AREN'T HANDLED FAIRLY BY OUR MORE LIBERAL AND INTELLIGENT NEWS STAFF!

© Tampa Tribune, 1985 by permission of Wayne Stayskal

Bias for Liberals?

Today, conservatives and Republicans most frequently attack newspapers and television for bias. President Eisenhower lashed out at journalists in the 1964 Republican national convention, setting off an unexpected standing ovation from the delegates. Some even shook their fists at the television control booths. Vice President Spiro Agnew in 1969 revealed that the same sensitive nerve had been tweaked. In a Des Moines speech he warned against "a small and unelected elite" in the media whom he described alliteratively as "nattering nabobs of negativism." He claimed that the prestige press, in deciding what to emphasize in the national political news, favored liberal views and Democratic party positions and were negative about all Republicans.

What has changed? The media scene is no longer dominated by the monopolistic newspaper publishers, who openly influenced news content. They were Republican. We offer this tentative hypothesis: Media owners are more likely to guide news policy during periods of stable semimonopoly than they are during times of intense media competition. When competition is fierce, as it is today at the national level, journalists who attract large audiences do far more in shaping what is printed or broadcast. Sam Donaldson and Mike Wallace are prized properties.

The Political Affiliations of Journalists. Studies indicate that a majority of reporters vote Democratic. Leo C. Rosten in his study of Washington correspondents found most voted Democratic in 1937. A 1973 National Press Club–American University study stated that "most of the correspondents interviewed conceded that a majority of the press corps probably votes Democratic."[26] Stephen Hess reached similar conclusions in 1981.[27] S. Robert, Linda Lichter, and Stanley Rothman in the 1980s found that more than 80 percent of leading reporters and editors voted Democratic in each election from 1968 to 1980, and only 4 percent of the students studying journalism at Columbia University favored Ronald Reagan in the 1980 election; 85 percent described themselves as liberals.[28]

Conservatives have accused the three television networks, and especially CBS, of political bias. What evidence do we have suggesting that reporters' or executives' liberal sympathies introduce a partisan slant in news reporting? Edith Efron of *TV Guide* examined television coverage in the 1968 campaign. She counted the number of times the evening network news announcers mentioned candidates Nixon, Humphrey, and Wallace. Then she coded each mention as for or against the candidate. (See Table 3.1.)[29]

Efron concluded that the networks were consciously biasing the news in favor of the Democratic candidate. Network officials responded by attacking her procedures, pointing out that she omitted from her tabulations speeches by the candidates, poll results, and questions on holding debates. They also disputed some of her classifications.

Table 3.1
Network Evening News Coverage of Candidates, 1968 Presidential Election

	Words for and against each candidate								
	Hubert Humphrey			**George Wallace**			**Richard Nixon**		
Networks	**For**	**Against**	**Total**	**For**	**Against**	**Total**	**For**	**Against**	**Total**
ABC	4,218	3,569	7,787	1,353	3,373	4,726	869	7,493	8,362
CBS	2,388	2,083	4,471	1,079	1,282	2,361	320	5,300	5,620
NBC	1,852	2,655	4,507	1,041	1,821	2,862	431	4,234	4,665

Source: Edith Efron, *The News Twisters* (New York: Manor Books, 1971), pp. 32–34.

Structural Bias. Political scientist Paul Weaver rechecked Efron's data. He concluded that despite some errors in measuring, and some questionable classifications, these flaws did not significantly alter her results, especially those on candidate Richard Nixon. The ratio of unfavorable to favorable comments was between nine and seventeen to one, so large that even if every challenge were granted, the anti-Nixon result would not change.[30]   *structural bias*

Weaver argued, however, that Efron's study did not demonstrate political bias. Rather, the results demonstrated the political effects of structural bias, caused by the characteristics of the medium itself. He suggested that the anti-Nixon statements resulted from television's effort to get and hold viewers' attention by making the 1968 election "interesting."

Weaver explained that when the race began President Richard Nixon was far ahead. As election day approached, Hubert Humphrey, after a poor start, began to narrow that lead. Network coverage treated the campaign as a horse race, in effect cheering the underdog's effort to close the gap. Some pollsters argued that if the election had been held one week later and the trend had continued, Americans would have elected Hubert Humphrey rather than Richard Nixon.

Weaver argued, as did Walter Lippmann, that the bias could be attributed to television's dramatizing a political theme. In doing so, Weaver says, the networks gave challenger Humphrey more favorable comments than defender Nixon, intending not to change the outcome but to attract more viewers.[31]

Later Election Studies. Although the television networks objected to Efron's conclusions, the 1968 study was instructive for them: be alert to the possible political effects of structural bias.

Richard Hofstetter repeated the study of network coverage in the 1972 campaign. He observed a great similarity in the three networks' ways of treating the Republican and Democratic candidates. Whereas CBS was slightly less favorable toward President Nixon, ABC was slightly more favorable. One surmises that the networks were themselves keeping count.[32]

In 1980 and again in 1984, Michael Robinson analyzed all network evening news broadcasts from Labor Day through the election. His preliminary report in 1984, like that of 1980, expressed one major criticism — that the networks overused such adjectives as "right-wing" and "conservative" to describe Republicans but seldom used the terms "left-wing" or "liberal" to describe Democrats. He concluded, "But let's give the networks credit where it's deserved: real partisan bias is one thing the network news people are not committing in this campaign."[33]

In a later report with Maura Clancey, though, Robinson stated that "Reagan and Bush received much worse press on network news than the opponents they defeated so handily." The basis of their study was what newscasters said.[34] But other recent research suggests that the message viewers remember is less what is said and more what is shown in the visuals, an area the Robinson-Clancey study specifically omitted. In visuals, Reagan excelled over challenger Walter Mondale. We will discuss later how the Reagan team in office used this influence to their advantage.[35]

Political Fairness and Bias.   The Efron study should be questioned on other points as well. She assumed that all network staff would insert a liberal bias rather than recognizing that this addition was the question to be examined. Her critics also suggest that she failed to demonstrate a link between the broadcasters backgrounds and the news they produced. Epstein commented on how remarkable it was that reporters were not "restrained from expressing their unfavorable opinions about Nixon or even induced to express favorable opinions."[36]

In her study she also seems to assume that all candidates should receive equal coverage in word totals and an equal number of for and against comments, a version of the equal-time doctrine. But should minor-party candidates receive the same attention as candidates of major parties? Should networks remain uncritical if one candidate is racist? Politicians and journalists, of course, will differ in defining fair treatment.

Social or Style Bias.   David Broder of *The Washington Post* writes that "reporters are by no means any kind of cross-section. We have a higher socio-economic stratification than the people for whom we are writing." His colleague Lou Cannon added, "The gulf is growing between reporters and working-class Americans."[37]

The Rothman and Lichter studies support the observation. They also reveal that practicing and aspiring journalists' strong "liberal" views are related to social rather than economic issues, a condition that Kondracke called "trendy liberalism." When questioned on social issues, most favored affirmative action in employment, feminist positions such as abortion on demand, and vigorous government action to protect the environment. More upsetting to socially conservative groups were opinions on such matters as adultery, homosexuality, belief in God, pornography, and handling of criminals. The aspiring journalists' heros were Ralph Nader, Gloria Steinem, and Edward Kennedy.

If one were to devise an agenda of behavior that the social liberals in our society feel is appropriate, working journalists would subscribe to most of its tenets. But so too would the elites in most other institutional areas in our society: higher education, the arts and sciences, "mainline" religion, and even prominent Republicans and business leaders. These are opinions associated with an upper middle class.

Yet on economic issues the working journalists were far from "strongly liberal." Their position was closer to what the new left charges them with — uncritical supporters of the capitalist system. Eighty-eight percent did not favor government ownership of industry; 86 percent believed that abler people should earn more money; 73 percent thought the nation's political, economic, or social institutions were not in need of radical change; and 70 percent said the private-enterprise system was fair to workers. Many (63 percent) even stated that less government regulation of business would be good for the country.[38]

Stephen Hess calls this *style bias*, suggesting that "reporters are most attracted to a political style that might be characterized as elegant, urbane, and cosmopolitan." Ideology aside, they prefer a John Kennedy or a George Will to a Jimmy Carter or a Gerald Ford. And so, he says "it is possible for a 'liberal' press to be anti-George McGovern and pro-William Buckley."[39]

According to Peter Clark, former publisher of the *Detroit News*, such cosmopolitan social bias colors news content. He claims that "public opinion has been radically transformed in a decade" and that the themes of the prestige press emphasize intellectual values over traditional values such as family, nation, patriotism, law and order, and material success. He suggests that the assumptions implicit in this view are: "America can solve its problems with good intentions, education, university-trained expertise, rational analysis, earnest conversation, peaceful efforts, and sophisticated compromise."[40]

Hodding Carter, state department press representative under President Carter and later PBS chief correspondent and anchor of *Inside Story*, an analysis of media coverage, claims that journalists have unintended social myopia. "They mix on and off the job only with those of their own class. News organizations," he argues, "are run mainly by upper middle class, white males. Information which does not come from the designated messengers, including, of course, in-house 'radicals,' is rarely accepted or disseminated. . . . Only recently has a Jerry Falwell been portrayed as something more complex and significant than a redneck exploiter of redneck yahoos."[41]

Hodding Carter's prescription is to assign reporters to the "unexplored ghettoes — not simply of race and class, but of economics, science, academic research and religious revival."

Most critics accept the idea that structural bias is almost inescapable. Most also reject the idea of a media conspiracy, that reporters or editors consciously slant the news to fit their own political prejudices. But the criticism that unconscious social bias clouds news reporting seems to us highly relevant. It is a criticism that continues to surface, from blacks; from minority religious and ethnic groups including Jews and Arab-Americans, fundamentalists, and Catholics; from blue-collar ethnics, southerners, westerners, citizens in outlying areas; and from others not in the mainstream or the successful upper middle class.

Ethnocentric Bias. Herbert Gans, studying the enduring values as revealed in the media through the last two decades, heads his list with ethnocentrism. He reminds us that we want to believe the best about our nation and sometimes avoid facing up to its inadequacies. Seymour Hirsh found it hard to convince others, with his reports about GIs gunning down My Lai villagers in Vietnam, until the evidence became overwhelming.[42]

Americans have become somewhat more skeptical about our own nation in recent times. Certainly journalists have not found it difficult to report stories like the one about the manual prepared with help from the CIA for Nicaraguan guerrillas that suggested murdering fellow guerrillas to create martyrs.

But, as we will discuss in a later chapter, in a way we, like any other nation, are parochial in reporting and viewing news. Reports about other nations are sparse. Latin American reporting is generally limited to such topics as war, coups, and drugs. In our eyes and in the media reports we read and view, the world revolves around the United States and its interests.

HOW WELL DO THE MEDIA COVER POLITICS?

It sometimes appears that no one is satisfied with the way the news is reported, including many journalists themselves. Consider these criticisms.

Accuracy. Frank Mankiewicz, George McGovern's political director in his 1972 candidacy and former president of National Public Radio (NPR), says, "Sooner or later everybody will know the dirty little secret of American journalism, that the reports are wrong because sooner or later everybody will have been involved in something that is reported. Whenever you see a news story you were part of, it is always wrong. It may be a rather unimportant error, but it also can be an important one."[43]

Brevity. Walter Cronkite says the lack of news time causes spotty news coverage. After nineteen years as anchor of CBS News, he stated, "It is impossible to cover the news in a half-hour show. We have a responsibility we simply can not discharge."[44] And even with full-time news programs such as that of CNN, the news is packaged in half-hour time blocks and repeated each hour.

Coverage of Issues. Thomas Patterson and Robert McClure, studying television coverage of the 1972 campaign, concluded that television emphasized pictorial values even when the events had little lasting political significance, those shots that David Halberstam, a Pulitzer prize-winning reporter, called tele-gestures. These were endless footage of candidates, sitting on a hay mower, watching someone install Chevrolet windshield wipers, or strolling through Brooklyn eating blintzes. They concluded that viewers could learn more about candidates' stands by looking at their political ads.[45]

Hyping the News. Michael Kinsley observes how British royalty provides titillating stories for American journalists, bent on capturing the audience's attention. "This approach," he writes, "is actually in the great tradition of British journalism, which often strikes a posture of 'Shame on those who say Princess Margaret is having an affair (pictures on page 3).'"[46]

Ignorance. Charles Peters, editor of *Washington Monthly,* says that because political journalists are generalists rather than specialists, they are ignorant about government and politics. "The drama of an election can be reported without any knowledge of government. If the candidates want to avoid the issues, so does the reporter."[47]

Pack Journalism. One of the most observant of media critics, Timothy Crouse, followed reporters covering presidential candidates in 1972. He criticized reporters because everyone followed the wire-service lead and filed the same stories. If reporters filed slightly original reports, they were apt to get calls from the home office asking why they were seeing events differently than the wire services reported. He also says that because reporters herd together on the same assignment "they tend, after a while, to believe the same rumors, subscribe to the same theories, and write the same stories." Following this path, they are likely to neglect other facts or themes.[48]

Thoroughness. One relatively old study examined how all the media in an area handled a day's news. Researchers in the Rand Corporation and the Journalism Department of the University of Michigan recorded and analyzed all electronic broadcasts and collected all local print media published during twenty-four hours in the Grand Rapids–Kalamazoo area (June 2–3, 1969). They included the output of three television stations, eight FM and thirteen AM stations (two from Chicago), and two newspapers.

The quantity of coverage varied between 3 percent and 17 percent of a station's broadcast time. As we would expect, electronic news was far less complete than newspaper coverage. The newspapers devoted roughly 250 words per item, the electronic media 64 words.

To assess quality of coverage they studied how stations reported the main story of the day, a ship accident that occurred at 6 A.M. Eight of the radio stations got the story out only between 6:30 and 7:15 A.M. A number did not add new details as they came in over the wire, instead, repeating their first bulletin every time. The newspaper stories were from five to twenty-three hours old.

The researchers also found numerous errors in fact and interpretation, especially in smaller radio stations where disk jockeys read the news. Errors crept in when radio announcers rewrote items to make them sound fresh and different from those which might be heard on another station. In handling local news, both radio and television stations usually read handouts from politicians or public officials, checked a few sources regularly, such as the sheriff's office, and then added paraphrased items from last night's newspaper.[49]

Implications for Politics

There you have our litany of criticism. Are these instances of poor journalistic practices typical or unusual? Most critics would probably say such faults can be found in many news outlets, adding that readers are also offered some excellent reporting in newspapers and television.

Political philosophers have long argued that a democracy's effectiveness depends on a well-informed citizenry. The media are the principal sources of information about our elected and appointed officials. Is the quantity and quality of news coverage good enough for democratic government to function adequately?

Political scientists may be too demanding in what we think citizens require. Dan Rather observed that "many Americans really do not want to be told what their government is doing, any more than they would want to know what went into the grinder to make the hot dog they are eating." Many readers and viewers probably are getting as much news as they want or can absorb. We know of little evidence suggesting a general public yearning for more sophisticated and detailed presentation of the news.

Journalists probably will never be able to inform the public as well as the early and even latter-day theorists of democracy assumed they would. Yet we are probably closer to the democratic ideal of the informed citizen than at any time in the past. Citizens do turn from their private interests to decide on vital public questions, as they did in the Vietnam War period, in the Watergate era, and on our policies toward Iran and Central America. Public opinion has proven to be neither monolithic nor static.

Let us give credit to the media because reporters provided the information that has allowed for such reassessments of policy choices, which are after all what democratic theorists promised would occur where the media were free to report political events.

A Closing Note

We have looked at how journalists go about their trade and seen their career ambitions, their structural conditions, as well as their social prejudices shape their way of covering political news.

For the national public official and the elected politician the media world is not friendly, as it was just a generation ago. The pressures to get the news first and beat the competition with coverage and interest have moved more reporters to interpretive and some to adversarial reporting.

Journalists themselves believe this change has resulted in better news coverage — stories that are fairer and more thorough than in the past. It has also brought more criticism to the media; happily, some of it is healthy self-appraisal. Timothy Crouse's reaction to the coverage he and others gave to candidate McGovern in 1972 illustrates: "We spent tons of ink on that guy and I'd be willing to bet that on the night he got the nomination we hadn't told anybody in the United States who the hell we were talking about, what kind of man he was."[50]

NOTES

1. In James Hilton's novel *Goodbye Mr. Chips,* he creates a schoolroom in which a classics teacher tries to keep the students' attention while bombs are exploding outside. He says they think the bombs are important, but they are wrong. The only things of lasting importance are the Greek and Roman writings in the book before them. These will be remembered long after the bombs are forgotten.

2. Historian Daniel J. Boorstin called these "pseudo-events," and considered them a kind of poison, showing that more and more, the content of our news content was made up of these contrived political incidents, not spontaneous news events. See Daniel J. Boorstin, *The Image: A Guide to Pseudo-Events in America* (New York: Harper Colophon Books, 1961).

3. Douglass Cater, *The Fourth Branch of Government* (New York: Knopf, 1959).

4. Daniel Boorstin says the media consume most celebrities so quickly that in a few years they have died out of the news and been replaced by new ones, e.g., Geraldine Ferarro. He claims that you can tell a person's age by the celebrities he or she knows about — Clara Bow, Wrong Way Corrigan, Senator Everett McKinley Dirksen, Jack Paar, Senator Sam Ervin, Jr., Congressman Peter Rodino, Bing Crosby, Walter Cronkite, Jody Powell, James Watt, Jesse Jackson, Henry Kissinger, Gary Hart, and so on.

5. *Newsweek* (May 13, 1985).

6. Ben H. Bagdikian, *The Information Machines: Their Impact on Men and the Media* (New York: Harper Torchbooks, 1971).

7. Quoted by Austin Ranney, *Channels of Power: The Impact of Television on American Politics* (New York: Basic Books, 1983), p.130. Originally reported in *The Washington Post*, March 18, 1982, p. A1.

8. Quoted by Edward Jay Epstein, *News from Nowhere: Television and the News* (New York: Random House, Vintage Books, 1973), pp. 4–5.

9. Edward Jay Epstein, *News from Nowhere*, Chapter 1, pp. 3–43.

10. This section is based on Paul H. Weaver, "The New Journalism and the Old — Thoughts after Watergate," *The Public Interest* (Spring 1974): 67–88.

11. "Your Story, But My Life," *Time* (Dec. 12, 1983), pp. 84–85.

12. See the discussion of investigative reporting in William A. Henry III, Richard Bruns, and Christopher Ogden, "Journalism under Fire," *Time* (Dec. 12, 1983), pp. 76–93.

13. John R. Roche, "McCarthy Hits Media's 'Mythical Castle,' " syndicated column, (June 14, 1977).

14. *Detroit Free Press,* Sept. 22, 1984, p. 14D.

15. *Newsweek* (March 2, 1987), p. 59.

16. William A. Henry III, Richard Bruns, and Christopher Ogden, "Journalism under Fire," *Time* (Dec. 12, 1983), pp. 76–93.

17. Robert M. Pious, *The American Presidency* (New York: Basic Books, 1979), p. 417.

18. S. Robert Lichter and Stanley Rothman, "Media and Business Elites," *Public Opinion* (Oct./Nov. 1981): 42–46, 59–60.

19. Morton Kondracke, "Is the Press Responsible for Weak Foreign Policy?" *The Detroit News*, May 24, 1984.

20. Quoted in Edward Jay Epstein, *Between Fact and Fiction: The Problem of Journalism* (New York: Vintage Books, 1975), pp. 120–141.

21. The categories "progressive" and "static" are taken from Joseph A. Schlesinger, *Ambition and Politics: Political Careers in the United States* (Chicago:

Rand McNally, 1966), p. 10. He applies them to politicians rather than journalists.

22. Austin Ranney, *Channels of Power*. See Chapter 3, pp. 64–87.

23. Michael J. Robinson, "American Political Legitimacy in an Era of Electronic Journalism: Reflections on the Evening News," ed. Douglass Cater and Richard Adler, *Television as a Social Force: New Approaches to TV Criticism* (New York: Praeger, 1975), p. 101.

24. George Seldes, *Freedom of the Press* (New York: World, 1935); *Lords of the Press* (New York: Julian Messner, 1938); and *Tell the Truth and Run* (New York: Greenberg, 1953). See also Upton Sinclair, *The Brass Check* (Upton Sinclair, 1919). Seldes in his recent autobiography defends today's journalists: *Witness to a Century: Encounters with the Noted, the Notorious, and Three SOBs* (New York: Ballantine, 1987), p. 473.

25. Robert Cirino, *Don't Blame the People* (New York: Random House, Vintage Books, 1972).

26. Cited in Stephen Hess, *The Washington Reporters* (Washington D.C.: Brookings Institution, 1981), p. 87.

27. Leo C. Rosten, *The Washington Correspondents* (New York: Harcourt, Brace, 1937) and Stephen Hess, "Is the Press Fair?" *Brookings Bulletin* (Fall 1974), pp. 6–10.

28. S. Robert Lichter and Stanley Rothman, "Media and Business Elites," *Public Opinion* (Oct./Nov. 1981): 42–46, 59–60.

29. Edith Efron, *The News Twisters* (New York: Manor Books, 1972).

30. Paul Weaver, "Is Television News Biased?" *The Public Interest* (Winter 1972): 57–74.

31. Weaver, "Is Television News Biased?"

32. C. Richard Hofstetter, *Bias in the News: Network Television Coverage of the 1972 Election Campaign* (Columbus: Ohio State University Press, 1976).

33. *Detroit Free Press*, Sept. 25, 1984.

34. Maura Clancey and Michael Robinson, "General Election Coverage: Part I," ed. Michael Robinson and Austin Ranney, *The Mass Media in Campaign '84* (Washington, D.C.: American Enterprise Institute, 1984), p. 27.

35. Dean Alger, "Television, Perceptions of Reality and the Presidential Election of '84," *PS* 20 (Winter 1987): 49–57. Alger discusses unpublished work by Doris Graber.

36. Edward Jay Epstein, *Between Fact and Fiction: The Problem of Journalism* (New York: Vintage Books, 1975).

37. Quoted in James Deakin, *The Straight Stuff: The Reporters, the White House and the Truth* (New York: William Morrow, 1984). Deakin points out that the 1982 recession may have made reporters more sensitive to economic issues.

38. S. Robert Lichter and Stanley Rothman, "Media and Business Elites," *Public Opinion* (Oct./Nov. 1981): 42–46, 59–60.

39. Stephen Hess, "Is the Press Fair?" *Brookings Bulletin* (Fall 1974): 6–10.

40. Peter Clark, "The Opinion Machine: Intellectuals, The Mass Media, and

American Government," ed. Harry M. Clor, *The Mass Media and American Democracy* (Chicago: Rand McNally, 1974) pp. 37–84.

41. Hodding Carter, "The Myopic Press," *Newsweek* (Dec. 7, 1981), p. 25.
42. Herbert J. Gans, *Deciding What's News* (New York: Random House Vintage Books, 1980).
43. "Your Story, But My Life," *Time* (Dec. 12, 1983), pp. 84–85.
44. Quoted in David Halberstam, *The Powers That Be* (New York: Knopf, 1979).
45. Thomas E. Patterson and Robert D. McClure, *The Unseeing Eye: The Myth of Television Power in National Politics* (New York: G. P. Putnam's Sons, 1976).
46. Michael Kinsley, "You Yanks Have Gone a Bit Barmy Over the British," *United Features Syndicate,* Nov. 14, 1985.
47. Charles Peters, *How Washington Really Works* (Reading, Mass.: Addison-Wesley, 1980).
48. Timothy Crouse, *The Boys on the Bus* (New York: Ballantine Books, 1972), p. 7.
49. The findings are summarized in Ben H. Bagdikian, *The Information Machines: Their Impact on Men and the Media* (New York: Harper Torchbooks, 1971), pp. 144–156.
50. Timothy Crouse, *The Boys on the Bus,* pp. 6–7.

4

The Politicians
Whom Journalists
Face

Even in pretelevision America, politicians found being media conscious helpful in winning votes and public approval.

Theodore Roosevelt was perhaps the first prominent politician to exploit his own media potential. Knowing Monday was usually a slow news day, he released White House news every Sunday; his stories would get top billing. He also exploited his personality to the fullest, living "the strenuous life" while in the White House. He chopped wood, hunted bear, and with his children took point-to-point hikes that required walking across, under, or through whatever they came upon. The image he projected said that he was having a "bully" time as president.

These news reports of the president's varied activities also symbolized Roosevelt's approach to national policy making: shake up a stodgy government and a nation grown a bit dull under statesmen in the mold of William McKinley and Rutherford B. Hayes.

Today's aggressive politicians, from president to city councillor, no longer passively accept everything journalists serve up to citizens. Politicians, like journalists, have become calculating and careful about everything that may appear in print and on television. They aggressively seek favorable attention. They plot and plan to get favorable coverage.

CHAPTER OVERVIEW

Our focus in this chapter is the kind of political stories that politicians believe bring them public approval. We will look at how their preferences lead politicians to approach journalists and the reservations they sometimes have about how journalists report political events. We will then review how today's media-conscious politicians work to get favorable news coverage, and how they try to manage political news. We will review their attempts to guide reporters' interpretations of political events and their efforts to manage potentially damaging stories and counter actions to control reporters and political associates.

THE KINDS OF NEWS COVERAGE POLITICIANS WANT

Politicians regard as most important the media stories that reach the people they regard as their constituents. For some the constituency is the district they presently represent. But ambitious politicians also want favorable coverage in districts they may later seek to represent. Most also count as a significant constituency one or more interest groups that support them: senior citizens, labor unions, business groups, tobacco growers, environmentalists, and others.

Politicians who aspire to higher office — senators, governors, and vice presidents who hope to be president — are likely to encourage journalists to emphasize different aspects of their records in news stories than those stressed when they ran for the office they now hold.

Thus each politician makes individual judgments on the kinds of stories that may help or hurt his or her political career at a particular time. Even though individual constituencies may "require" specific types of stories, most politicians have some general qualities they desire to see in news coverage about themselves, qualities that go into the desired public image.

Creating a Favorable Image

The first goal of politicians is to be noticed in a flattering context. Journalists noted that most of the members of Congress on the Iran–Contra hearings panel wore red ties and blue shirts — advice given by television technicians. But politicians also want news stories, and a truism that doesn't carry us very far is that politicians want stories that bring public approval, stories that will advance their political careers. In creating this good image, public-relations specialists emphasize the personal intangibles that voters seem to respond to.

Revealing Biographical Anecdotes. Journalist Jeff Greenfield observed that reporters are "bewitched by the revelatory biographical anecdote," interesting details that illustrate aspects of a politician's character or personality. Reporters particularly thirst for biographical detail on a politician who climbs suddenly to the political stage, as did Gary Hart, Geraldine Ferraro, and Jimmy Carter. Politicians cooperate by digging up incidents revealing their sterling qualities.

Greenfield brings up a story that Jimmy Carter's staff passed along to the White House correspondents. The president recalled how back in Plains, Georgia, his family had gathered around the radio in 1938 to

This was a moment of great joy and pride for underdog Harry S. Truman (1945–1953) and one of substantial embarrassment for the early pollsters and some newspaper editors, whose early editions incorrectly reported a Truman defeat. Pollsters had confidently forecast that Thomas E. Dewey would easily defeat Truman in his bid to win the presidency. But because of the final results in 1948, pollsters acknowledged that their monitoring of voter opinions had stopped too soon. Truman's victory led to a reappraisal and revamping of polling techniques, the major change being the continuation of polling up until and through election day.

listen to the boxing rematch between Joe Louis and the only one who had beaten him, Max Schmeling. Blacks, who did not own radios, were invited to listen out on the lawn through the open windows. Louis knocked out the pride of Hitler's Germany in the first round. Filing quietly back to their own quarters, the blacks only then celebrated. President Carter suggested how greatly race relations had improved since 1938 because of southerners like his parents and others, including, in case you missed it, Jimmy Carter himself.

Ronald Reagan, reporters were told, worked as a lifeguard during summers in high school and cut eighteen notches in a stick for the people he saved. And Gerald Ford was an all-American center at the University of Michigan. One supposes that even President James Buchanan let it be known through his secretary that he had been expelled from college for boyish pranks, through he was soon readmitted.

Heroism and bravery are also solid grist for these mills. President John Kennedy and Vice President George Bush, through their publicists, reminded voters of their World War II heroics: about the sinking of PT Boat 109 and the subsequent lifesaving swim, or that Bush's plane was shot down at sea. Perhaps the most repeated and revealing biographical detail in President Reagan's political career was his statement, "I guess I forgot to duck," after being shot in an assassination attempt.

Politicians also fight off journalists' coverage of traits that might detract from their favorable image. During the 1984 campaign, on a live interview with candidate Gary Hart, Roger Mudd repeatedly asked Hart to do his imitation of Teddy Kennedy. With a frozen smile, Hart kept refusing; he was incensed. In his fundraisers later, he used this one-liner: "I hear Roger Mudd wants to be an anchor. When I get to be president, I'll talk to the Navy about that." (Mudd earlier had been demoted as co-anchor of NBC's Evening News.

B.C.   **BY JOHNNY HART**

© News America Syndicate, 1987 by permission of Johnny Hart and Creators Syndicate, Inc.

But some thought the 1987 revelation that former TV evangelist Pat Robertson and his wife had a child ten weeks after their marriage helped rather than hurt his presidential campaign — it humanized him, they said.

Such biographical anecdotes are so helpful that sometimes partisans invent them. William Henry Harrison, a Virginia aristocrat, was supposed to have liked nothing better than living in a frontier log cabin, drinking hard cider. The anecdote they told of his opponent, Martin Van Buren, a tavern owner's son, was that he perfumed his sideburns. And supporters, not satisfied by painting Abraham Lincoln as "the rail splitter," called him "Honest Abe," claiming he had walked ten miles to return two cents in change that a customer left on the counter of his store.

The Faithful Public Servant. Politicians try to show they are doing what they promised to do, faithfully serving the public. They require only that the story make it *appear* that they are on the job, for appearance is worth as much as or more than reality.

For executives such as a president or governor, this appearance means seeming to lead, being in control, and having that undefinable charisma that makes citizens trust them and accept their vision of the future. Pictures of the president in the Oval Office conferring with advisers or greeting foreign dignitaries on the portico of the White House remind voters that their president is on the job.

Many Democrats believed Reagan won in 1984 because of his public image — his projected on-the-job portrait was calculated to make citizens feel better about themselves and restore their pride in America and confidence in the future.

Personal Competence. A crucial part of a politician's image is appearing to be personally competent, physically, mentally, ethically, and politically.

In American society, creating an image of physical vitality is perhaps the keystone in constructing the appearance of personal competence. President Reagan conveyed this impression through news stories about his chopping wood and horseback riding, and by being seen on television returning from Camp David in blue jeans and western style shirts. Jimmy Carter did it by carrying his own bags onto helicopters or by being seen with his suit jacket slung over his shoulder as he walked around. But he also undid his image of good physical stamina when he appeared to collapse after a ten-kilometer race.

Others have taken physical risks to provide news stories showing their physical vitality. During his 1944 campaign, Franklin Roosevelt rode in an open car through New York City in a driving rain, a gesture that brought on a cold that persisted to his death. Sixty-eight-year-old William Henry Harrison, at his inaugural in 1841, rode to the capitol on a white horse through cold and stormy weather, symbolizing his fitness to lead. He then took off his hat and delivered a speech an hour and three quarters long. He caught cold and a month later died of pneumonia.

President Eisenhower had special health problems. Over a two-year period that included his reelection campaign, he suffered a heart attack, had a serious operation for ileitis, and perhaps raising questions about his mental competence, underwent a mild stroke. James Deakin describes how Eisenhower's press secretary, James Hagerty, guided news coverage through these troublesome periods. Hagerty's assignment was to convince voters that the president was physically competent to serve and be reelected, especially because many voters still had fresh memories of President Roosevelt's physical problems during his last term, and some remembered President Woodrow Wilson's struggle at the end of his term after World War I.

In each incident Hagerty delayed news of the real illness from twelve to twenty-four hours, until the crisis was over. To explain why Eisenhower canceled his appointments, Hagerty reported that the president was suffering a stomach upset, or a headache, or a chill. Hagerty ordered that no one talking to reporters use such anxiety-raising medical names as "stroke" (the doctors called it an occlusion of a small branch of the middle cerebral artery on the left side). The UPI in desperation called it a "heart attack of the brain," a description that gave Hagerty little consolation.

Within a few days after each incident, Hagerty had a parade of cabinet members visit the president, ostensibly to consult him on current problems. At the same time, he had President Eisenhower sign a string of minor bills. Two days after the ileitis operation, he had the president send a foreign policy message to the Senate. Each day of the convalescence, Hagerty had an Eisenhower recovery story for reporters — the president was reviewing his State of the Union address or he was issuing a statement to the Big Four foreign ministers meeting in Geneva.

The reporters suspected that these stories were a charade staged by the staff, but they were obliged to print them. And as soon as the first day of danger was past, Hagerty and the doctors gave reporters more news than they could possibly handle about the illness. For the seven weeks after the stroke, Hagerty scheduled four briefings a day, always emphasizing how remarkably the president was recovering and that he was on the job.[1]

Reporter Bob Woodward much later claimed that President Reagan's seemingly rapid recovery from an assassination bullet was also a media show. He was much closer to death than the public knew, according to Woodward.

Mental Ability. Few Americans seek scholarly intellectuals for public officials. And yet they want as president a person who is articulate and knowledgeable, in command of the facts and cool under pressure.

But in 1987 when Reagan switched his story about the arms deal and said he was unable to remember authorizing the shipment, these doubts returned. Forty-four percent of a Gallup poll sample thought him too old for the job.

Moral and Ethical Values. One hardly need comment on how politicians scatter through their speeches references to God, home, and family, representing their own high moral and ethical qualities. In the next presidential address televised from the Oval Office, take a look at the pictures resting on the credenza behind the president — for most presidents' spouse and family are all there subtly conveying dedication to family values. Or observe that Senator Joseph Biden concluded he must withdraw from the 1988 presidential race when reporters revealed he had misrepresented his law school record.

Political Competence. For the executive, political competence means being in control, on top of issues, setting the political agenda, gaining public approval. For a legislator it means association with important policies.

Press agents and image builders can most easily suggest political competence with stories of crowds warmly greeting the politician and how many leaders consult with him or her. President Nixon was thought to have taken foreign journeys, including his famous trip to China, to bolster his image as a competent politician.

President Carter, through stories of his cabinet dismissals, his flip-flops on issues, or his speech which was described as suggesting a "malaise" in America (the word was not in the speech, however), demonstrated political incompetence. During the Iranian hostage incident in 1980, Carter accepted the proposition that America had no more important task than to free the forty people held at the American embassy in Iran. In doing so, Carter permitted the Iranian government to dominate our public agenda.

In a similar situation in 1985, President Reagan was more careful when faced with the forty-three airline passengers held hostage in Beirut.

Without diminishing the incident, he let it be known that it was only one of the many problems with which a president must deal.

Politicians attempt to influence and manage the public agenda with publicity about their "vision for a better America." They give their programs appealing names to increase their visibility and recognition. Since Theodore Roosevelt's "Square Deal," we have had "The New Freedom," "The New Deal," "The Fair Deal," "The New Frontier," "The Great Society," and the "Second American Revolution."

Legislators jealously guard their identification with their chosen issues. They demand their right to be recognized as sponsors of bills that are popular and to be present when the president or governor signs the bill. Representative Claude Pepper of Florida has become the spokesman for America's senior citizens. Former Senator Warren of Wyoming, a state then interested in tariffs on wool, prided himself on being "the greatest sheepherder since Abraham."

POLITICIANS TRY TO MANAGE POLITICAL NEWS

Politicians agree with journalists that political news should consist of reports about current and interesting political events. But they disagree with some of the journalist's ways of deciding what is "interesting."

Politicians Define What's News

At the heart of this disagreement are differences in career objectives. Politicians think journalists too often equate "interesting" with "entertaining." To catch the public attention, politicians say that journalists dramatize political events in ways that distort their meaning. They may so report political events as to give the reading and viewing public a wrong impression, or more precisely, an impression that the politician feels is less favorable to her or his interests than is justified. This distortion can heavily damage a political career.

Politicians worry especially about the interpretations resulting from these reports, recognizing that public perceptions, rather than reality, are the basis for a good deal of political action. If the public becomes convinced by gruesome serial murders that the state has a major problem with its parole policy, politicians may feel forced to respond to that perception, whether it is true of not.

Realizing this interaction brings us very close to saying, as we saw in Chapter 1, that politicians believe journalists, unless discouraged from doing so, will report political events which may attract attention but which, for various reasons, politicians feel should not be reported at all. Or they will so define political events as to arouse public perceptions that hurt the politician or the issues he or she is associated with.

Most politicians conclude that part of their job in politics or government is guiding journalists in reporting political news. From their point of view this task is little more than self-defense.

Such guidance requires that the politician: (1) exercise as much influence as possible over story content and interpretation, (2) use damage-control techniques when breaking stories are potentially threatening, (3) exercise control over the journalists themselves, and (4) dry up leaks of confidential or potentially damaging information.

CONTROL OF STORY CONTENT AND INTERPRETATION

Influencing coverage begins with determining, as closely as possible, the facts that journalists will be given to report. Sometimes the politician is eager to supply facts and information. In other instances control may mean denying journalists information or concealing facts as thoroughly as practical.

Making Information Easy to Report

Knowing and understanding that journalists define political news as events covered at reasonable cost helps politicians guide what the journalists report. It may even influence the spin they put on the event.

Providing such news may give the politician an advantage. Journalists may be so busy reporting this news that they will have less time to dig around for political stories that might be more threatening. Supplying information is a subtle way of influencing the facts and information that journalists come across.

Advantages of Incumbents. Politicians in office, especially the president and governors but heads of major departments as well, have a big advantage in making events easy to cover. Their offices usually are on assigned "beats." Reporters either check in regularly or are permanently stationed close by. Executives know reporters want and expect a news story every day, and generally try to provide something favorable to themselves.

Incumbents also try to employ aides who are experts in getting favorable media attention. Within the past ten to fifteen years at the national level, new technocrats have taken over media relations. At the state level, governors and most major department heads now have at least a small public-relations staff. Locally, such media specialists perform more frequently as consultants in election campaigns, though mayors of major cities may have media staffs rivaling those of the governor.

The permanent political aides, who manage the politician's public appearances, also prepare news releases and arrange briefing sessions. During a speech, the specialized technocrats worry about details such as camera lighting and background, the flow and syntax of words, and they make sure that the journalists and the other "right" people have advance copies of the speech. They may also arrange for the politician to appear on television and radio programs, prepare commercials, or handle direct-mail appeals.

The prepared news release is an easy way for the reporter to prepare a political story favorable to the politician. Politicians know that some journalists will print their news releases with little change. But even when they do not accept the original without change, reporters are likely to incorporate some handout details in their stories because the releases at least carry accurate quotations. And the handouts spell out the details so that no journalist can claim to have misunderstood them or the way in which the politician would like to see them reported.

Skillful staff members are always looking for ways of helping the boss. A student asked a television reporter visiting one of our classes what difference the governor's new press secretary had made. The reporter considered momentarily and then described a recent event. The governor's new aide had told representatives of the statewide television network that the governor's televised speech would end at about 8:22 P.M. The television journalists prepared for an instant analysis that would follow the speech. But the governor's remarks ran till 8:27, just long enough for an announcer to summarize the high points, following which the stations returned to regular programming. The reporter did not think that sequence was accidental, but he also could not help admiring a media pro who knew his job.

Staging Media Events. Politicians and their aides expect to have to manufacture news stories, which we have been calling "media events."

To satisfy the media craving for news and to illustrate something they regard as politically important, they stage little dramas as political entertainment. Often the event is scheduled just to keep public attention on the politician; it may also keep eyes away from something else. The *U.S. News and World Report* carried this report: "Ronald Reagan won't get much rest after his busy ten-day tour of Europe. Aides already are setting up a series of summer trips in the United States. Aim: Keep the President in the public eye to prevent Democrats from seizing all the attention with their national convention."[2]

To get media attention, politicians must find a way to create an event dramatizing the issue or a point they wish to make. A speech, a public appearance, or a press conference are standard media events. So too are legislative hearings and investigations, or a blue-ribbon commission report. These may provide information that most knowledgeable people are already aware of, but the facts will now be given special media prominence. The hearing also reinforces the appearance that the politician really cares and is on the job.

Knowing that the business of journalism is competitive, politicians are aware that journalists will report even obviously contrived media events, especially if the visuals are good and other journalists are likely to file a story on the event. Creating or taking advantage of potential "photo opportunities" for the evening news is a daily chore for White House staff, and occasionally for staff serving other politicians as well. Timing counts, especially for "the other" politicians. Their media event, pushed aside by other breaking stories, may be forgotten.

The ritualistic and ceremonial duties that presidents and other executives must live with offer many opportunities for media events. Governors are shown signing bills and giving the pens to the chief legislative sponsors; the photos are sent to media outlets in the home district.

Visiting celebrities are an occasion for other photo opportunities. The winning sports team visits the White House or the governor's mansion to receive special recognition. Jimmy Carter visited the World Champion Pittsburgh Pirates' dressing room after the final game to congratulate them. Politicians ask entertainers and other celebrities to visit. Nancy Reagan invited comedienne Joan Rivers for a special event, and Jimmy Carter had the Rev. Billy Graham conduct worship services in the White House. Performances by classical artists may even be broadcast on PBS, as when Jimmy Carter was president.

A twist is to have national politicians or members of their families appear on television entertainment programs: Richard Nixon said the stock line "Sock it to me" on *Laugh In*, Gerald Ford was seen on

Saturday Night Live, and Nancy Reagan on *Different Strokes* publicized her campaign against drug abuse.

Mayor Federico Pena took part in a media event publicizing the Better Air Program for Denver. Each day residents selected by car registration-plate numbers were asked not to use cars to get to work. The program was to help combat Denver's "brown cloud," and the mayor was photographed taking a bus to work.

Political incumbents have the easiest time in planning elaborate make-believe events. Their staffs, knowing publication deadlines, can plan striking visuals, such as showing Ronald Reagan drinking beer with blue-collar workers in a Boston tavern. They are also available to handle complicated arrangements, know most reporters by name, can get them to the site, or will choose a location to which reporters have easy access, and can handle all other details that will result in the event's being reported.

The oldest clichés that incumbents still use are poses in their best clothes, carefully spooning out a shovel of dirt to start the new sports arena, cutting a ribbon at its entrance either when completed or, shortly before an election, suggesting that it will soon be open. Having an official toss out the first baseball to start the season amid cheers of supporters is another well-used media event. In the past, a favorite was a having politician's daughter smash a bottle over the prow of a ship to be launched. The photographers snap pictures, television cameras grind away, and reporters record pithy quotations in their notebooks. Everyone treats the occasion as a political news story.[3]

As we will see, out-of-office politicians and those demanding attention for little-known social movements find the going more difficult. They are likely to stage demonstrations in the form of sit-ins, strikes, marches — even illegal acts such as hijackings — to reach journalistic coverage.

Beware of Backlash! Politicians should be aware that they cannot be too careful. Generally reporters, insatiable for stories, cooperate with politicians in reporting these media events. They may even suggest improvements. But sometimes reporters turn on politicians, describing how a carefully engineered but phony media event was planned and executed. Careful editors may occasionally tell reporters after a while to revisit a media-event site to see if anything really happened.

When presidential candidate John Anderson visited New York City's depressed Bronx during the 1980 campaign, journalists reported how his staff rushed him in and out of the poverty area, pausing just long enough to snap pictures. Jimmy Carter made a similar stop in the Bronx during the 1976 campaign. In 1980, reporters recalled the event, showing the sordid buildings, where nothing had improved. Their stories suggested that these politicians were exploiting the misery of the poor by using them as a backdrop for a campaign stop.

Mayor Pena of Denver also came a cropper. On the first day of the Better Air Campaign the front page of the *Denver Post* described how at 7:23 A.M., with a *Post* photographer in tow, the mayor stepped on a bus to go to his office for a PBS radio interview. Reporters found out, however, that a police car then went back to the mayor's home with his press secretary, who then drove the mayor's car to City Hall to have its radio fixed. That detail too was in the story — in the first paragraph, in fact, along with a quotation from the press secretary, who "seemed annoyed when questioned about the event, explaining that under the Better Air Campaign a car must be left at home only 'if that's possible.' " The story mentioned too that, "At a kickoff event Wednesday on the 16th Street Mall, Pena told Denverites, 'media from all over the nation are watching us here.' "[4]

The media event may go wrong, as when the champagne bottle launching a ship will not break, however hard or often the senator's daughter swings it. Or, as at a Reagan rally during the 1984 campaign, an eleven-year-old girl whom politicians patted on the head proclaimed that her daddy and mommy were going to vote for Mondale. Republican officials announced that her decision meant she could not attend the 107th annual Easter Egg Roll on the White House lawn. Nancy Reagan opportunely interceded, creating another media event. She phoned the girl, and said, according to Sheila Tate, Mrs. Reagan's press secretary, "I want you to come to the Easter Egg Roll as my special guest. You tell your family I'm sorry. I'll see you here at the White House."

During the 1985 farmers' financial crisis, Michigan's Governor James Blanchard promoted a bill in the legislature giving low-cost loans to keep farmers from bankruptcy. He staged a media event on the farm whose owners were getting the first loan under the program. Next day a reporter called the farmer's wife to ask how the loan had been arranged so quickly. She reported that their bank had already approved their loan. "We didn't really need the governor's loan," she said, "but we'll take it. It cuts our interest rate from 12 to 7 percent."

Most commonly the spoilers are opposition hecklers or demonstrators. The television cameras and reporters can be expected to tell about the botched media event, because reporters will believe it holds more human interest than a perfectly staged one. And doing a followup story that may be unfavorable also lets the politicians know that journalists were not taken in by the affair. A politician cannot be too careful.

Making Information Seem Special

A leak is information someone secretly gives to a reporter. Leakers want reporters to keep their identities secret.

Politicians know that such leaks have an off-the-record, confidential quality that seems irresistible to many reporters. Something that is secret, they often believe, must be important. Reporters hope leaked information will give them an exclusive.

"Official Leaks." Politicians manufacture "official leaks" because the technique improves the chances that the information will be reported. Senator William Fulbright, piqued because reporters paid so little attention to Foreign Relations Committee hearings, suggested he should have held secret sessions and then "offically" leaked the information.

Ben Bradlee of *The Washington Post* argued that "A leak isn't a leak unless somebody gets wet. If a member of the National Security Council staff releases information, it's a leak. If Henry Kissinger tells James Reston of *The New York Times*, it's just policymaking."[5] Such officials, he says, are just trying to get added media attention.

A string of official leaks may be part of a dramatic buildup, often for a speech the politician is to make, as when a staffer leaks tantalizing hints about what the president may say in his speech to the United Nations. Such leaks have the added advantage of getting the story reported twice.

But an official leak may be part of a complicated political strategy. The politician may want to float a trial balloon to gauge public reaction: "The governor is reported to be considering asking the state legislature to pass a mandatory seat-belt law." Or it may be a way for the president to show displeasure with a colleague, without doing so officially. After President Carter fired him as Secretary of Health, Education, and Welfare, Joseph Califano claimed White House aides leaked attacks on cabinet members such as himself. President Carter, he claimed, could have stopped them, implying that the president did not wish to do so.

Or the president and his staff may leak advance news to a reporter who they hope will then treat them with special kindness. The motivations behind leaks are endless. Frank Cormier, in his biography of Lyndon Johnson, says the president used official leaks to get a network television correspondent he did not like taken off the White House beat. He had his staff aides leak phony "scoops" to the unsuspecting journalist.[6]

Some motives are harder to fathom. During the 1985 Shiite hijacking of TWA airliner, the president readied a commando squad to rescue the hostages in Beirut. This plan was leaked almost immediately, destroying the possibility of a surprise rescue. Why? Some said leakers wanted to impress journalists that they were important enough "to be in the know." Or perhaps they were uneasy about the mission and chose to scuttle it. And, of course, it is possible that the president never intended to use the squad at all, but alerted it only to let the public know America would be tough this time, or as a warning to the hijackers.

Whatever the purpose of an official leak, Bradlee is right. It is unusual for anyone to get wet, but if someone does, it is seldom the politician or the staff who leaked the information. Hodding Carter III, spokesman for the State Department during the Iranian hostage crisis, wrote, "official sources are like official anything — largely self-serving."[7]

Plants. A "plant" is a more devious way of getting information to journalists. The staff asks a third party to release the information, or, as we saw Dan Rather do in Chapter 1, to ask the president a set-up question at a press conference. Plants launder sources of information in ways that conceal or disguise where the information came from.

A successful plant should be carried out so smoothly that the journalist who reports the information is unaware of the original source. Jack Anderson reported that Senator Thomas Eagleton, George McGovern's first running mate in 1972, had been arrested for drunken driving in his home state, Missouri. When reporters checked the records, they found the report was false. Anderson claimed he received the story from a source in Missouri and printed it because he knew someone else would if he did not. Some suspected that the real source was the "dirty-tricks" department of the Nixon Committee to Re-elect the President.

The Reagan administration ran a "disinformation" campaign against Libya by planting stories so that foreign and American reporters would suggest that an attack against that country would soon occur. American journalists who published the story objected later that it undermined faith in the United States government as a source of news. The story was given to them in a string of plants.

Occasionally plants backfire. Republican Senator Charles Percy was critical of Hamilton Jordan, Carter's chief political strategist. A planted story claimed Percy had accepted free plane rides from a corporation doing business with the government. The company denied the rumor, stating it did not even own a plane. A reporter then revealed that Jody Powell, press secretary for President Carter, was the source. Powell admitted to the plant that turned out to be a clumsy attempt to smear an opponent, and apologized.

Controlling the Interpretation Given Events

In releasing information, the politician cares about the interpretation that will be given. How will the information affect public perceptions?

Controlling the journalist's way of interpreting political events requires forethought and some subtlety. Assume that a number of major industries have announced they are moving to states with a more favorable industrial climate. A legislator who wants to propose a bill regulating industrial disposal of waste in streams has a problem with perception. He or she wants the legislation defined as an environmental protection bill rather than as another regulation driving industries out of the state and causing unemployment. The legislator will be searching for some way to dramatize the waste problem as an environmental issue. Photos of fish floating belly up in a stream near an industrial plant would be helpful.

The problem such politicians face is getting publicity for an idea or a concept or a condition. The politician may want journalists to report that the nation's schools have a bad drug-abuse problem, that air pollution in Denver is reaching crisis levels, that our public health system is in jeopardy, or that Nicaragua is planning to invade its neighbors. But journalists stubbornly say they report only events — they need a news peg. Part of the job before the politician or his staff is to supply an event calling attention to the issue as the politician wants it perceived — a media event.

National politicians also agonize at length about how television journalists end their news reports on events that do occur. The reporters often add a brief interpretive comment, putting a "spin" on the story. The news report may be a story showing the president announcing a plan to help his party pick up congressional seats in the coming election. The spin might be an added comment such as, "And the polls indicate he will have an uphill battle in winning those seats." Journalists aptly called Reagan's White House staff the "spin doctors" because of their efforts in guiding such interpretations during the 1984 election campaign. All politicians and their staffs and the consultants they hire now attempt spin doctoring. But they have no magic formula for ensuring that the interpretation will always be favorable. The only guideline politicians follow is, "Give it some thought before you release the information."

DAMAGE CONTROL ON BREAKING STORIES

Almost daily politicians, especially those in major offices, face a political news event that they are expected to respond to. It may be a potentially damaging event for them. Such "breaking stories" can be among the most difficult media problems a politician faces.

Breaking Stories

Ronald Reagan gets the news that Shiite Moslems have blown up the U.S. Marine barracks in Lebanon with heavy loss of American lives. Presidential candidate Walter Mondale learns that reporters are asking about financial statements of his running mate, Geraldine Ferraro, just as an election campaign begins. Jimmy Carter has to deal with a story about his brother Billy's ties to Libyan leaders. Or Richard Nixon hears burglars have been caught in the Democratic party headquarters at the Watergate apartment complex.

As the story unfolds, the politician wants the public to believe that he or she has the problem under control. Politicians also want to put opponents on the defensive and state the case in such a way as to invite others to join and support their side.

The politician may know very little about what has happened, and worse, may not know how much reporters know. Should more information be released? Perhaps some facts should be held back for release when some sort of victory can be claimed.

No one has pat answers on how to handle such media problems. We review here some of the tactics politicians use, and how they have sometimes helped and sometimes proved damaging to their careers.

Controlling the Spin. A basic necessity is to guide reporters and the public to so interpret the event as to help, or at least will not harm the politician.

The Reagan administration emphasized after the event that no one could protect a marine base in Lebanon and be 100 percent effective against suicide attacks. They wanted the public to reject the view that the president had not prepared for this probable danger. Geraldine Ferraro wanted citizens to recognize that she and her husband had paid their fair share of taxes — if she had made any mistakes, they were honest ones. The Nixon administration worked hard to assure the public that the Watergate break-in was the work of a few marginal zealots not associated with the president's reelection campaign. And Carter tried to show that being president did not mean he could control his brother's actions.

Diversionary Stories. A politician caught up in a breaking story may release diversionary news. This tactic works best with such smaller embarrassments as those which relatives of a president sometimes cause. It may also work if the president acts quickly to deal with the problem.

Thus, Department of Interior Secretary James Watt resigned under pressure. President Reagan expressed regret and then turned the nation's attention to other matters. After the attack on the marines, some critics held the Reagan administration staged the invasion of Grenada.

Releasing the Bad News. Politicians may choose to release bad news that they know will become general knowledge sooner or later. Geraldine Ferraro admitted finding a $30,000 error in her income-tax report and immediately paid what was owed. Senator Edward Kennedy released the story of his impending divorce in February 1981, timing it to follow his unsuccessful campaign for the Democratic presidential nomination and long enough before the next national election that it would then be little more than a dim memory. Kennedy offered no explanations except to express regret and to say that details of a divorce should remain private.

"No Comment." A riskier tactic is to refuse to answer all questions, which may lead the public to equate silence with guilt. Silence may also leave the opponent's interpretation of the event the generally accepted one.

But the politician may also gain some advantages by refraining from explanations, to gain time to think and assess public reaction. Initial silence also makes time to get all the facts and make sure that political allies take the same line. And refusal to comment may be forgiven if the politician can later present an acceptable explanation, such as wanting to check the facts before making a full disclosure, to protect others, or to avoid a breach of national security. And the politician can sometimes hope that the story will drop out of the news and be forgotten as more important events obscure it.

Stories involving a legal action such as an indictment or trial, as in the Watergate investigation, do not just go away. Nor will political enemies who work to keep it alive, perhaps through a congressional investigation or a journalist's persistence. A group such as Common Cause, Right to Life, the ACLU, or the Moral Majority may also keep pressure on an issue by raising it whenever the politician gets into the news or appears in public.

Using Surrogates. Politicians frequently provide information through another person, a surrogate such as a press secretary or other aide. On minor matters the substitution gives the impression that the public official refuses to dignify a charge by answering it directly. But having someone else do the talking also prevents the politician from getting into more trouble by misstating the facts, being caught in a lie, showing ignorance of details, or saying something that may come back to haunt.

If reporters' questions become too pressing, the surrogate can plead ignorance on some points, or may suggest that the politician "really meant to say . . . ." Using a surrogate also allows the politician to "clarify" the surrogate's remarks later. Surrogates are acceptable for minor issues, but reporters expect politicians to speak out in person on anything major.

Meeting Criticism Head On. Politicians can also face any charges and defend their decisions or actions. To be successful with this tactic, though, the mood or tone in the response must be carefully managed. The typical Reagan response was lighthearted and not defensive, folksy but tough and determined, and usually appealed for unity and decency and avoidance of cheap politics. Geraldine Ferraro followed that formula in a lengthy televised revelation of income-tax data. She was less than successful, however, when she half-jokingly said she was not sure how her "Italian husband" would react if asked to reveal his own income-tax data.

Another defense is to say that everything is legal and proper; no crime has been committed. Anything that was done is customary, routinely done by many others in the past. The difficulty is that times and values change. Practices acceptable in the past may be objectionable today. John F. Kennedy and Lyndon Johnson and perhaps Franklin Roosevelt secretly recorded conversations with people in the Oval Office. But after Richard Nixon, no governor, senator, mayor, or president will lightly try it for a while, or at least be caught altering or erasing conversations.

Admitting a Mistake. Politicians sometimes confess they were wrong . . . but. The next breath usually outlines circumstances that make the error forgivable.

Geraldine Ferraro stated that an accountant the family had used for many years made the $30,000 error in her income tax, suggesting the image of an old family retainer who was now less efficient but who could not be cruelly cast aside. President Kennedy successfully defused criticism for the disastrous Bay of Pigs invasion of Cuba by admitting that military and intelligence sources had misled him.

President Reagan in a speech on the Iran–Contra scandal admitted that somehow what began as an opening to moderates in Iran became a trade for hostages. This he said was a mistake for which he took full responsibility. Mike Royko in a column titled "It Takes a Lot of Courage to Admit You're Right" pointed out that in this speech, Reagan had admitted to four "mistakes": that he had been too trusting, too compassionate, too statesmanlike, and that in the past his managerial style had been too perfect.[8]

The politician may confess to being partly to blame for not making a situation fully clear, or making a poor choice of words. Politicians, not sensitive enough to know how the suggestion infuriates reporters or that many of them now carry tape recorders, may also claim to have been misquoted.

Attack! Politicians can also react by questioning the motives of their severest critics, implying they are engaged in dirty politics. Or, as Lyndon Johnson and Richard Nixon frequently did, they may suggest that influential persons or groups — publishers, editors, or reporters, perhaps — are trying to trash them. Politicians may also suggest that disgruntled ex-employees are at the bottom of charges against them. The Reagan administration, with this intent, dismissed as groundless charges that the president was not committed to aiding female workers.

The attack response may include tricks reminiscent of Hitler's "big-lie" tactic — if the lie is big enough, people won't believe it's a lie. In 1986, the United States exchanged with the Soviet Union a Russian embassy staffer who had been caught spying. Meanwhile the Russians arrested a United States journalist, Nicholas Daniloff, on spying charges in Moscow. When the respective governments released the two, President Reagan asserted that the releases were unrelated. Later Reagan called Oliver North, a key person in selling arms to Iran in exchange for hostages and converting proceeds from that sale to illegal aid for the Nicaraguan Contras, "a national hero."

Sometimes politicians will stand by a statement or colleague and "tough it out." Zealous supporters will admire the politician for statements beginning with, "I make no apologies . . . ." President Reagan stood by Edwin Meese III, his nominee for attorney general, for more than a year while investigators researched charges that he had abused his office as a White House aide. Reagan also supported his Secretary of Labor, Raymond Donovan, until he was officially indicted on charges arising from actions prior to his appointment. (He was later acquitted.) In contrast, President Eisenhower dismissed his aide, Sherman Adams, rather abruptly after learning that Adams had accepted illegal gifts.

Turn Away Critics with a Joke. A useful response for the politician who can pull it off is to deflect a mildly serious incident with humor. The model is President Franklin Roosevelt's famous speech, "And now these Republicans are picking on my little dog Fala." Some Republicans accused Roosevelt of sending a military plane back to Alaska to fetch his scottie, inadvertently left there. Roosevelt, slowly and with the timing of a Jack Benny or Bob Hope, reeled off how the Republicans had attacked him, his wife Eleanor, each of his children, and now his little dog. He went on to describe how Fala's Scotch dander was up at being accused of wasting tax funds. Each phrase brought a bigger wave of laughter as he moved to the climax. Roosevelt defused the issue and even turned it against his critics. Notice, though, that Roosevelt chose to make this defense before a very partisan labor union audience, who relished every word and every quip.

Ronald Reagan several times has used a joke to turn aside criticism. During presidential debates, his aside, "there he goes again" deflated President Carter's claim that Reagan planned to dismantle Medicare.

The Worst Response. The worst way to react is any act showing that the politician is off balance and on the defensive: confusing language, belligerent behavior, or breaking down into tears, as Senator Edmund Muskie did on the campaign trail in New Hampshire. Ronald Reagan, under fire in the Iran–Contra investigations, changed his responses twice and then said he could not remember when he authorized the shipment of arms to Iran — a performance that left even most reporters somewhat skeptical.

Muskie later withdrew from his campaign because some journalists asked whether he was stable enough to be president. Journalists and others questioned Reagan's mental and physical ability to cope with the pressures of the job.

Committing a "Media Crime"

Some politicians seem to be in hot water with journalists almost continually. Any story that can be turned against them gets that treatment. Their negative public image seems unshakable. The punishment is severe: general contempt or merciless ridicule.

Such attacks, politicians claim, are unfair, hitting below the belt.

Journalists blow up a minor incident far beyond its importance. Reporters tag their victim with a label that the politician cannot shake off. For politicians caught in the web of "media crimes," the record seems forever to trail them as it does those lesser mortals who bear a criminal record.

In President Reagan's administration, one such victim was presidential adviser and later Attorney General Edwin Meese III. President Reagan claimed that journalists were creating a "lynch atmosphere," with charges that "were later revealed as having no foundation." A special prosecutor cleared Meese of all criminal charges, but the journalistic sniping continued. What fuels such journalistic behavior?

Violating Accepted Norms. In a candid column, "Is the Press Out to Get Ed Meese? Yep." Richard Reeves explains that the traditions of journalism require that journalists report the words and deeds of public figures without comment — even when journalists think they are "a danger to the Republic and small children in school yards." He said that journalists "must wait for an opening — a mistake made by a public figure — to say, indirectly, what they really think." Reporters lie in wait for the event that they believe reveals the person's true character as a politician.[9]

One type of "crime" is violating the social norms to which reporters and many other middle-class Americans subscribe: the media's social bias. Reeves says the "crime" Meese committed was being one of those "hardhearted millionaires and would-be millionaires who could not care less about the poor, the weak, or the hungry." Meese, as the 1983 Christmas season approached, had told a group of reporters he had never seen "any authoritative figures" showing that there are hungry children in the United States. And he also thought that a great many people go to soup kitchens just because they are looking for free food. Then he made a few jokes about what a good fellow the unreformed Scrooge of Dickens's *Christmas Carol* really was.

The attitude that earned the reporters' contempt, said Reeves, was the social Darwinist approach to political issues that Meese's comments exposed. *The New York Times* and other papers began running stories comparing Meese's comments with those of food and welfare specialists, using such headlines as "True Hunger and Malnutrition Cases Are Growing Problems, Experts Say." And reporters highlighted some of Meese's actions, such as appointing to public office people who had helped Meese solve some of his financial problems. During the 1984 campaign, Democratic candidate Walter Mondale dubbed this "the sleaze factor" of the Reagan administration.

We can add the case of James Watt, President Reagan's first Secretary of Interior. Environmentalists disliked his policies. Perhaps reporters were unsympathetic to his fundamentalist Christian views. But the statement that drove him from office referred to the members of a special coal commission advising him as including "a black, two Jews, a woman, and a cripple." In one phrase he managed to offend four groups with whose demands for equity reporters and many other Americans generally sympathize.

Earl Butz, secretary of agriculture under Nixon and Ford, ran into similar troubles because he told ethnic jokes in the hearing of reporters. When journalists reported the first incident, President Ford made him apologize. Later, a similar episode led to his resignation.

Others too have fallen afoul of these norms. Governor Richard D. Lamm of Colorado generated a loud outcry when he seemed to suggest that older people with terminal illnesses had a "duty to die." The Rev. Jesse Jackson finally apologized after referring to New York City as "Hymietown" in a comment he assumed was off the record to a black *Washington Post* reporter he had invited to breakfast. Even more intemperate, and generally dealt with more harshly, were the anti-Semitic remarks of Jackson's political ally, the Muslim minister, Louis Farrakhan.

Questionable Competence. Journalists can send out indirect suggestions about a politician's competence. But reporters apply the tactic columnist James Kilpatrick calls "the bonehead play" only to politicians they have concluded are too dull to be in positions of great power. [10]

Reeves points to the many stories about the awkwardness of All-American athlete Gerald Ford, how he would hit his head getting out of planes and tee off golf balls that hit spectators. Chevy Chase's standard opening to *Saturday Night Live* mimicked the president's stumbling over himself and falling down. The indirect message was the same that Lyndon Johnson gave more directly when he said Ford had played football too often without a helmet.

Journalists still fondly recall such revealing anecdotes as the defense Senator Roman Hruska of Nebraska gave for a Nixon nominee to the Supreme Court who was described as mediocre. Hruska said, apparently in earnest, that there are a lot of mediocre people out there and they too deserve representation on the Supreme Court.

A series of major policy failures that generates direct questions about a politician's competence also inspires indirect suspicions. The event that summarized the media view of President Carter's competence was the "killer-rabbit" incident. Unwisely, press secretary Jody Powell told a reporter that while the president was fishing in Georgia, a crazed rabbit started swimming toward his boat as if it wanted to get in. Carter warded it off with an oar. Powell considered the incident a joke, without realizing the story's implications. The television evening news on every network ran it. *The Washington Post* headline read "President Attacked by Rabbit." The story came to symbolize the political weakness of a president who needed to be defended from bunny rabbits. [11]

If journalists had more regard for President Carter's competence, the rabbit story might have received different treatment or perhaps not been published at all. Perhaps reporters' questioning was set off by Carter's *Playboy* magazine interview, in which he talked about having "lust in his heart."

Lying. Being caught regularly in or suspected of lying, is a major "crime" to reporters. Journalists wrote about Lyndon Johnson's "credibility gap," jokingly asking, "How can you tell when the president is lying? Is it when he tugs his ear like this, or when he rubs his hair in the back or when he touches his nose? No. Then when is it? It's when Johnson moves his lips."

Exploiting the Position. Politicians who use their public office in ways that are blatantly exploitive — a conflict of interest, vacation travel with family to other countries at public expense, unabashed nepotism, high living — are also likely to bring on journalistic scorn and negative publicity.

Teflon Politicians. In a prebroadcast radio warmup, midway in his reelection campaign, Ronald Reagan said in "testing" his mike: "My fellow Americans, I'm pleased to tell you today that I've signed legislation that will outlaw Russia forever. We begin bombing in five minutes."

A furor erupted immediately; Democrats, our European allies, and even leaders of the Soviet Union were harshly critical. "How could anyone joke about nuclear war?" they asked. "Is this what goes through his mind when he thinks about negotiating with the Soviet Union?" But the furor died and the criticisms failed to stick despite the wide coverage given this off-the-record joke.

Every politician can expect to make some gaffes. Reagan has made many more, including an off-the-record Italian joke during his 1980 campaign through New England. Some politicians seem able to walk unharmed through the barrage of criticism such remarks inspire. Like Reagan, they are held up to scorn but usually deflect the criticisms. Dwight Eisenhower shared this trait, as did William Milliken, Michigan's longest-serving governor.

What Is the Secret of Teflon? On President Reagan's overwhelming re-election, columnist William Raspberry wrote, "His [Reagan's] continues to be, in Rep. Patricia Schroeder's apt phrase, a 'Teflon presidency,' to which nothing seems to stick: not wrongheaded policies, not meanness, not factual distortion, not out-to-lunch inattention to his job, not even what, if told by anybody else, would be just plain lies."[12]

President Eisenhower also easily survived accusations of not taking his job seriously enough. A joke about Eisenhower that circulated during his presidency said, "As usual one day he was out playing at the exclusive Burning Tree Golf Club. A foursome was playing ahead of him at the sixteenth hole. An aide rushed up to them and pleaded, 'Could you let the president play through? We just got word that the Russians are bombing Washington.'"

Few theories explain the phenomenon of "Teflon politicians." Journalists may report the gaffes or the inattention to the job. Yet the voters seem neither permanently upset nor angered by the substance of the reports.

Eisenhower could perhaps shrug off criticism because he seemed a kind of nonpartisan or bipartisan president, a grandfatherly figure somehow above politics. His reputation as a great military leader during World War II also carried over to his presidency. Michigan's Governor Milliken brushed off criticism by always seeming sincerely to follow the suggestion by professionals in the field: creating the appearance of being nonpartisan. But President Reagan was clearly partisan and often at variance with professional advice.

Observers usually explained his ability to sidestep criticism as an attribute of personality. All three of these politicians with pleasant personalities carried nice guy-images. Peggy Noonan, a speechwriter for Reagan described him as "a genuinely decent, optimistic, kind-hearted, and fair person."[13] Probably the average citizen would say the same about the other two. But that phrase would also perhaps describe a good many other politicians including Ford and Carter, both of whom were less artful in dodging criticism.

Others suggest that it is a matter of luck. Citizen's approval reflects a thriving economy. With a recession, the ability to deflect criticism lessens or disappears.

After Reagan's sweeping win in 1984, television commentator Sander Vanocur theorized that one the quality Reagan could be credited with was bringing back civility to political discourse. After a twenty-year period of nastiness characterized by Vietnam and Watergate, citizens were disgusted and worn out. Reagan's pleasantness was a relief. Each of the other two Teflon leaders also had this quality of being above political infighting and of not holding political or personal grudges.

Garry Trudeau, in his comic strip, *Doonesbury,* offered a thought-provoking explanation. A journalist explains to a fellow journalist that when President Reagan says or does something that seems the opposite of what he says he believes, "He doesn't know he's being hypocritical. . . . He seems sincere. And he seems sincere because he is. . . . When Reagan says, 'they didn't do it,' people actually believe it, or at least they believe he believes it, which removes personal responsibility, so they forgive him."[14]

If Trudeau was correct, then finding the Teflon worn down by the Iran–Contra scandal became understandable. For the first time the president was found to be doing something he said he would never do — bargain for the release of hostages. And worse, he was sending arms to a deadly enemy of the nation — Iran — again an action difficult to explain. People no longer believed he believed what he said. The incident roughed up his impervious coating and left him significantly less immune to criticism. His public-approval rating plummeted (but not to record levels) and some citizens even suggested he should consider resigning.

CONTROL OF JOURNALISTS

Politicians attempt to exploit the advantage they have when they are the only source for a major news story. They may try to prescribe rules for reporting the news they have to give.

What Can Be Reported?

Franklin Roosevelt set out four ways in which reporters had to handle the information he gave them at his press conferences. (1) Some comments could be quoted directly and attributed to the president. These were on the record. (2) Some statements could only be quoted indirectly but could be attributed to the president, enabling him to claim later that he had been misunderstood. (3) About 20 percent of Roosevelt's comments at his press conferences were "background" — the information was on the record, but reporters could not say whom they were quoting. (4) Finally, some information President Roosevelt said must be "kept in the family" — it would be off the record and could not be used at all, at least not until he or his press secretary gave permission.

Background Rules. In a "backgrounder," reporters get information they would not get if everything were on the record. Some politicians distinguish between the more informal "background meeting," which allows reporters to indicate the source by a vague phrase, and "deep background," in which reporters may not indicate any source for the news story.

Reporters use code phrases such as "an informed source close to the White House," "informed circles," "a usually reliable source," or a "highly placed official." President Coolidge invented "a White House spokesman," and reporters continue to use the phrase to mean that the White House stands behind that information. The "highest authority" is used to signal that the president is the source. When we see terms such as "a source high in the administration," "sources close to the administration," or "authoritative sources," we know the president or a cabinet official is successfully getting a reporter to cooperate with the background rule.

Off-the-Record Rules. Politicians, even presidents, have some trouble in enforcing their off-the-record rules. John F. Kennedy discovered a truth that Theodore Roosevelt had known fifty years before. In both cases stories leaked out because a reporter who had attended the off-the-record session told what had transpired to another not attending. The second reporter did not feel bound to keep the story out of print. Kennedy ended off-the-record sessions. Roosevelt gave a stern warning about confidentiality but continued the sessions.

Sometimes information gets out because reporters say they did not know the comment was off the record. Some refuse to honor the rule if a politician on the record makes a comment and then declares it off the record. At other times reporters try to persuade a politician to put a comment on the record. A few refuse to participate in off-the-record sessions and others argue that nothing is ever off the record, regardless of what the politician says.

During the 1984 election, *Newsweek* assigned a team of reporters to both presidential campaigns for a full year of off-the-record observation. The reporting teams were allowed to read private memoranda and attend party planning sessions. They agreed not to publish any of this information or pass any information on to colleagues until after the election. Then *Newsweek* issued an "Election Extra," a special edition in which appeared, "Exclusive: The Untold Story of Campaign '84." Predictably, other journalists said they would not have participated in such an arrangement.

Even though off-the-record rules or understandings are more unstable today, important politicians generally can dictate their terms. Lesser politicians must take their chances.

Flattery and Harassment. Theodore Roosevelt was the first to understand the value of "massaging" reporters. He noticed reporters standing in the rain outside the White House gates waiting for stories. Realizing that they would appreciate having their own press room within the White House grounds, he set one up for them. He turned reporters, his critics said, into "Roosevelt worshipers." The famed Kansas editor William Allen White said, "Teddy bit me and I went mad."

Figuring that journalists would like a president who could occasionally joke with them, Roosevelt dropped in on reporters traveling on his train to watch their poker games. He would extend mock sympathy to other travelers who had joined the games and called the veteran players the "Charley Thompson Finger Club," after one of the reporters who regularly traveled with him. The president described this club as "a very exclusive organization devoted to the study of financial problems, psychology, and the relative and varying values of certain pieces of paper."

Roosevelt also understood how to apply sanctions. He invented another organization for a few reporters that he called the "Ananias Club." The biblically trained among the journalists recognized the allusion to Acts 5: 1–11. Ananias and his wife Sapphira held back part of a gift to the early Christian church and then lied about it. Peter scolded them and they fell dead. The president was gently but also publicly scolding journalists who wandered too far from the truth as he saw it.

But Roosevelt also angrily cracked the whip if he believed the occasion demanded it. During his unsuccessful 1912 campaign, the editor of a weekly, the Ishpeming (Michigan) *Iron Ore* wrote, "Roosevelt lies and curses in a most disgusting way; he gets drunk too, and that not infrequently, and all his intimate friends know about it." Indignantly announcing that he did occasionally take "just a glass or two of white wine or champagne at public dinners, no beer or cocktails," Roosevelt sued. He brought thirty-seven associates to Michigan's Upper Peninsula to testify. The editor apologized and Roosevelt asked for nominal damages. The jury awarded him just six cents, but he made his point.

Franklin Roosevelt also had this light touch with reporters, calling them by their first names and inviting those on regular assignment as well as a few columnists to Sunday night family suppers of scrambled eggs at the White House. On one occasion, though, he awarded the German Iron Cross to a journalist whom he viewed as not totally in sympathy with the Allied cause.

Kennedy used many of these techniques as well. He concluded that *Time* magazine was most influential with "middle America." To gain as much favorable coverage in *Time* as possible, Kennedy gave Hugh Sidey, *Time*'s Washington correspondent, almost unlimited access to White

House offices. It gave Sidey at least the appearance of being very well informed and Kennedy got extensive coverage.

Kennedy also visited journalists in their homes. As president, he began the custom of inviting publishers and editors separated by interest or region to White House dinners. At first he provided excellent cuisine with five wines. When he found some publishers overindulging, he cut the wine list to one but kept the food the very best.

On campaign trips Kennedy joked with reporters. At every whistle stop he gave the same speech, referring in passing to a "Colonel Davenport." After reporters had heard the speech several times, with a glint in his eye he dropped the "Davenport" and began inserting the reporters' names. It was an in-house joke that few aside from the reporters caught. But those named were subtly flattered.

Even more flattering were his chats with reporters about technical points in stories they had recently written. He discussed knowledgeably how the stories might have been handled differently, as if he were a fellow journalist. Reporters learned that the president read their stuff and also that he cared enough about what was written to read it with care, a subtle form of compliment.

But President Kennedy could also show displeasure. He once publicly canceled every White House subscription — there were 22 — to the *New York Herald Tribune.* Later, he put *Time* in the doghouse for two weeks. All White House sources dried up for the magazine's reporters, including Sidey. And Kennedy attempted to get the editors of *The New York Times* to transfer David Halberstam out of Vietnam because Kennedy considered his reporting too critical.

Less adept politicians have tried to buy or force favorable treatment. Lyndon Johnson entertained journalists and their spouses lavishly, smothering them with stories and trying to trade exclusives for favorable treatment. But he also gave Saturday-morning briefings at which reporters knew he was purposely dawdling as the wire service deadline got closer and closer. He meant to punish them, but the message they got was that he enjoyed tormenting reporters.

And Johnson could be rough on individual journalists. Dan Rather describes a typical LBJ "put-down": "A reporter posed a complicated question. LBJ gave him 'The Stare,' then said flatly, 'Well, first of all, I don't think you can even repeat that question.' And the guy couldn't. He just froze. The room erupted with laughter."

And Rather himself caught the back of LBJ's hand at least once, when LBJ refused to recognize Rather at a news conference. Rather had dismissed as "politics," a "presidential" speech for which Johnson asked for and got free air time. Johnson thought he should get better treatment from fellow Texan Rather, and accused him of having "gone eastern."[15]

But one politician made a calculated policy of intimidating journalists. Richard Nixon put reporters on the defensive by suggesting they would not give him a fair break because of his role in the Alger Hiss case early in his congressional career. The press room was moved farther from the center of activity and the White House became off limits to reporters. He refined the stonewall technique, separating himself as much as possible from the journalists except for staged appearances. Reporters who might write favorably about the president were given exclusives and favored in other ways.

Newsweek quoted a White House source as saying, "Big mouths mean little careers." With Nixon's blessing Vice President Spiro Agnew attacked "liberal" journalists and their instant analyses following the president's televised addresses. The FBI investigated Daniel Schorr and other reporters, telling those interviewed that the journalist was being considered for a federal job. The reporter's sources may have suspected otherwise and began avoiding Schorr. Reporters were also subjected to harassing income-tax reviews.[16]

A minor and somewhat pathetic case and we will say no more on intimidation. Dan Rather describes how the day after his televised confrontation with President Nixon, White House aide Pat Buchanan passed on to reporters some White House social notes. Rather writes, "Then he [Buchanan] sort of stood on his tippy-toes, raised his voice and over the heads of the other newsmen threw out the word, 'Oh, yes, and Arthur Taylor, the president of CBS, was there.'"

This jab was aimed at the journalist who wrote that the best advice he got from his favorite journalism professor was, "Don't let the bastards scare you."[17] Sometimes attempts at intimidation bring a response the opposite of that the politician hoped for.

DRYING UP LEAKS

Journalists such as Jack Anderson prefer to label those who leak governmental information with the flattering appellation "whistle-blowers," implying that the leaker's motives are altruistic and not self-serving. Periodically, Anderson writes columns defending whistle-blowers and detailing how politicians "isolate, intimidate, and hassle them once they are detected."[18]

Perhaps the best-known whistle-blower is Ernest Fitzgerald, who in 1968 told a congressional committee that development of the C-5A military transport would cost $2 billion more than expected. "I was asked a question and just told the truth," he said. Fitzgerald lost his job, sued, won, was given a lesser job, sued again, and was reinstated in his original job — after fourteen years and $1 million in legal fees.

Others wrestling with the question of whether to blow the whistle on their bosses occasionally call Fitzgerald for advice. "I always tell them," he says, "they need a good free lawyer and another job unless they are independently wealthy or ready to retire. . . . You never recover. . . . It ruined my career. . . . And I came out better than anyone I know of."[19] Admiral Hyman Rickover observed that the Good Lord will forgive, but a bureaucracy never does.

In 1978 Congress passed new safeguards for whistle-blowers, establishing the Office of Special Counsel to defend whistle-blowers harassed despite the law. And since 1979 the General Accounting Office, responsible to Congress, has operated a hotline for whistle-blowers. It has handled

© The Boston Globe, 1987 by permission of the Los Angeles Times

45,000 calls, involving everything from welfare fraud to illegal contracts and kickback schemes. Even this protection has proved to be of doubtful service for would-be whistle-blowers.

But most of Jack Anderson's leakers and those of other reporters are not whistle-blowers who leak because they are outraged with government waste or corruption. Most are self-serving, out to gain political advantage for themselves, to impress journalists with their importance, or to further political viewpoints not being advanced by higher-ups. These motives infuriate political executives.

President Nixon gave the nation the White House "plumbers," a group whose job was to dry up leaks. Their tools were intimidation, spying, wiretaps, and any other means they thought necessary to track down leakers. Lyndon Johnson was so incensed with a leak that he refused to appoint Lloyd N. Cutler as Undersecretary of Commerce because news of the appointment had leaked. And he held up Walter Washington's appointment as mayor of Washington D.C. because *The Washington Post* carried a story that said he was about to make the appointment.

Jimmy Carter threatened to fire anyone caught leaking stories. And after two years in office, Ronald Reagan angrily told reporters "I am up to my kiester in leaks." He was burned up because newspapers reported that the administration would not sell advanced fighter planes to Taiwan.

Classifying Information. The standard method for reducing leaks is to classify documents. National-security matters get a "Top Secret Sensitive" label. Less sensitive materials are stamped "Limited Official Use," or "Administratively Confidential." The labels at least give a warning. But since the Pentagon Papers case, reporters generally print or publish anything they get. And though editors may have second thoughts about publishing classified information, they often say, "If our reporter knows, perhaps others do as well. Why let someone else have a scoop?"

But the courts have made it clear that it is the leaker who takes the risks, not the journalist. It is difficult to prove that an official is punishing an employee for leaking information. And the justices hesitate to let a leaker profit from the leaks. In February 1980 the Supreme Court ruled that Frank W. Snepp III, a former CIA agent who wrote a book criticizing the agency's work during the fall of Saigon, had to turn over his profits to the government. He had not obtained prior agency approval for the disclosure, as the law covering the CIA required.

The Reagan administration expanded the classification categories, reduced the number of officials who could handle classified information, and made it more difficult to get information under the Freedom of

Information Act. As we saw, employees who plan to discuss classified information with a reporter must get prior approval and file a report on what was discussed.

The Reagan administration also proposed a national security directive requiring all federal employees and applicants to sign a form that says, "I shall not publish, nor reveal to any person, either during or after my employment, any classified or administratively controlled information." The directive would also require them to submit to a government board, before publication, anything written about things they learned in office. If suspected of leaking, they could be asked to take a lie detector test, with "appropriate adverse consequences" for those who refused to take the test.

The administration decided to exempt top administration officials from the rules, though reporters claimed they were the source for many leaks. And the administration also announced it was "rethinking" the directive, suggesting that it might be limited to top people in Defense, the National Security Council, the CIA, and related agencies. The Democratic Congress put this directive on hold.

Following the invasion of Grenada, journalists bitterly criticized the Department of Defense (DOD) for excluding them. The DOD then agreed to new arrangements on such expeditions in the future: each major news bureau in Washington, D.C. would be permitted one reporter in a news pool. In 1985 the DOD secretly tested the system. Reporters were to be ready to leave Andrews Air Force Base at 4 A.M. Journalists failed the test — before the proposed departure hour, the DOD got more than a dozen calls from uninvited media organizations. Pentagon officials told journalist representatives that they would have to come up with a new plan for covering military stories.[20]

Some tightening of regulations against leaking has been done, but the politically damaging disclosures continue.

A Closing Note

Incumbent politicians, both elected and appointed, have become more calculating and aggressive in their efforts to get favorable stories.

Especially since 1970, politicians have gone to journalistic technicians for help. They are more than press agents, advising politicians on how to gain the best advantages from electronic media, especially television. During the 1980 presidential campaign, observers began noticing that television coverage of the Reagan campaign made the crowds seem bigger than they really were. They discovered that Reagan's media technicians at each stop placed the raised platform for the cameras closer than usual to the speaker's rostrum. The crowds, unable to see from behind the camera platform, jammed themselves between the cameras and Reagan. His crowds appeared to overflow the meeting area.[21]

Today's aggressive journalists face more astute and aggressive politicians. Because the primary media focus of the political battle is the president, we turn next to president–media relations, beginning with the campaign for office and continuing with interaction between reporters and president while the president attempts to govern.

NOTES

1. James Deakin, *Straight Stuff: The Reporters, the White House, and the Truth* (New York: William Morrow, 1984), Chapter 1, pp. 13–37.
2. "Washington Whispers," *U.S. News and World Report* (June 18, 1984), p. 16.
3. Daniel Boorstin, *The Image: A Guide to Pseudo-Events in America* (New York: Harper, 1961).
4. Louis Kilzer, "Clean Air Drive: Try Again, Excuses, Excuses, Excuses," *Denver Post*, Nov. 16, 1984, p. 1.
5. *National Journal* (June 2, 1979), p. 898.
6. Frank Cormier, *Presidents Are People Too* (Washington D.C.: Public Affairs Press, 1966).
7. "Hodding Carter Tells Almost All," *Columbia Journalism Review* (November/December 1980): 36–37.
8. Mike Royko, "It Takes a Lot of Courage to Admit You're Right," syndicated column, March 8, 1987.
9. Richard Reeves, "Is the Press Out to Get Ed Meese? Yep." Universal Press Syndicate, Dec. 22, 1983.
10. James Kilpatrick, "Bonehead Theory," syndicated column, Feb. 19, 1984.
11. For Powell's mea culpa see Jody Powell, *The Other Side of the Story* (New York: William Morrow, 1984) pp. 103–108.
12. William Raspberry, "The Incredible President Teflon," Washington Post Syndicate, Nov. 7, 1984.
13. Robbie Vorhaus, "Peggy Noonan, Presidential Speechwriter," *Northwest Orient* (October 1984), p. 53.
14. Garry Trudeau, *Doonesbury*, Nov. 4, 1984.
15. Dan Rather, *The Camera Never Blinks: Adventures of a Television Journalist* (New York: Ballantine, 1977), p. 10. George Reedy, one of Lyndon Johnson's press secretaries during the 1960s, said that Johnson regarded every news story about him as either for or against; none could ever be neutral. Perhaps Johnson was right, for many politicians seem to agree with him.

16. See especially the discussion in Timothy Crouse, *The Boys on the Bus: Riding with the Campaign Press Corps* (New York: Ballantine Books, 1972), Chapters 8–13, pp. 191–317.
17. Dan Rather, *The Camera Never Blinks*, pp. 13, 37.
18. Jack Anderson, "No Reward for Whistle-blowers" (Jan. 14, 1982); "Ganging up on a Whistle-blower" (Feb. 19, 1982); "Energy Whistle-blower Hounded" (Sept. 29, 1984); and "Fed Worker Gets 'Treatment,'" (Oct. 29, 1984). Alan F. Westin in *Whistle-Blowing: Loyalty and Dissent in the Corporation* (New York: McGraw-Hill, 1981) examined ten cases in private industry and found that the whistle-blowers "have been paying for it ever since."
19. Rebecca Nappi, "Whistle-blower: You Never Recover," *USA Today* Oct. 11, 1983.
20. Associated Press, "Pentagon Press 'Pool' Springs a Leak," April 23, 1985.
21. Joel Swerdlow, "The Decline of the Boys on the Bus," *Washington Journalism Review*, 3 (January/February 1981). Noted in Dan Nimmo and James E. Combs, *Mediated Political Realities* (New York: Longman, 1983).

5

The Presidency: Getting Nominated and Elected

As they go through the trial of seeking nomination, party professionals' career goals collide head-on with those of journalists. Party professionals generally prefer stability; journalists like change.

Milton Rakove describes what party professionals in Chicago look for when they "slate" or choose local candidates:

> If he can win and can't do the party any good, who needs him? If he can win and can do the party harm, who wants him? In other words, the interests of the party and the ability of a candidate for public office to serve the interest of the party come first in building a ticket.[1]

Nationally the attitude is much the same. Party professionals may disagree over which candidate can best serve their own careers. But they are generally united in rejecting the unpredictable outsider, the candidate who will bring "amateurs" or his own crowd of home-state, non-Washington cronies to positions of power.

Reporters are less interested in the established professional, about whom much has already been written. They prefer the unknown and unpredictable mavericks who make a journalist's stories crackle. They seek colorful and dramatic copy. They like upsets. And they also prefer to concentrate on the mechanics of winning, rather than stands on issues. They want to report conflict between personalities, changes in strategies, who is ahead.

CHAPTER OVERVIEW

We discuss how television, especially, has been a driving force in the sweepstakes for presidential nomination and election. We begin by considering how party professionals once managed the nomination process to achieve their goals. Next we see how television discovered political conventions and how professional politicians changed conventions to cope with new circumstances brought about by television coverage. We then discuss how in recent decades increased journalistic attention to presidential primaries revived their part in the nominations. In the fourth section we consider how politicians sought to control or limit journalists' influence in the primaries. In the fifth section we review how political campaigns are designed to attract free television coverage, supplemented by paid ads. We close this chapter by briefly reviewing election-night coverage.

The four presidential debates of 1960 established the importance of media technicians and other advisers in utilizing television for successful political campaigning. As Vice President Richard M. Nixon debated John F. Kennedy, viewers remarked on Nixon's apparent "five o'clock shadow," due in part to his heavy beard and refusal to wear makeup. The debates helped determine the election outcome and gave politicians something to think about and work on — namely, their telegenic qualities.

THE OPEN PRESIDENTIAL NOMINATION PROCESS

Three political career routes have traditionally led to the presidency. An ambitious politician might become governor of a major state, as did Ronald Reagan, governor of California, and Theodore and Franklin Roosevelt, both governors of New York.

Or a candidate might run from the U.S. Senate, a position that now can provide national exposure through television. The third route may be through the vice presidency, although sitting vice presidents have not often been able to gain the presidency by election.

But none of these have ever been sure bets. Some have captured the nomination from outside these recognized career ladders, among them William Jennings Bryan in 1896 and Abraham Lincoln in 1860. Dwight Eisenhower and Wendell Willkie became presidential nominees without having held elective office — politicians were even in doubt about which party the two supported.

Before 1956, party professionals usually were able to dominate the nomination process. Candidates courted professional politicians, not the voters in presidential-primary states or the journalists who reported the primaries. Before we see how journalistic coverage changed nomination politics, let us examine the former procedure briefly.

How Party Professionals Chose Nominees

Party professionals want a candidate who is predictable, someone with a record of government service. A Republican choice in 1980 might have been Senator Howard Baker of Tennessee, who had served ably as Senate minority leader, rather than the relatively unpredictable Ronald Reagan.

Party leaders also wanted a candidate who would win. They anticipated that most presidential candidates would carry their home states. Therefore party professionals screened out candidates from small or "safe" states and picked nominees from marginal states with a large number of electoral votes, like New York. Although the system for nomination has changed, candidates still do well of course in their own states. In 1984, Mondale carried only one state and that one with only ten electoral votes — his home state, Minnesota. Reagan's home state, California, had forty-seven electoral votes.

Party professionals then bargained over candidates who met these requirements and who, in running, might also help the professionals' own political careers. Most of the bargaining was done at the party's national convention, which was thus called a "brokered convention."

Convention support was traded for prizes ranging from the vice presidency and cabinet offices to local patronage, such as postmasterships. John Nance Garner threw his strength in the Texas and California delegations to Franklin Roosevelt in return for the chance to be FDR's running mate. Perhaps the baldest trades were made by southern Republican delegates in the days when no Republican could win in the South — their votes were for sale to the highest bidder.

Issues and public-works projects were other forms of convention currency. We asked a Democratic national committee member from a prairie state why his delegation had supported the South on a civil-rights plank. His answer was, "Garrison Dam. The southerners in Congress support us on that and we support them in the convention." Support might also be exchanged for promises to farmers, civil-rights groups, or business and manufacturing interests. In fact, any issue considered important by a group that had delegate support to trade was acceptable merchandise for barter.

Convention Rules Favored Bargaining. Past rules encouraged trading and brokering. The "unit rule" required a delegation to cast all its votes as a unit, even if some members favored a different candidate. And the "two-thirds rule," in Democratic conventions through 1936, meant a person had to get two-thirds of the delegates votes to be nominated. The bloc of southern states thus had a veto. Perhaps even more important, local party professionals strengthened their own bargaining power by shaping state laws and party procedures determining who could become a national convention delegate.

The Early Presidential Primary

Progressives in both parties invented the presidential primary as a way to change this system. The primary voters would show whom they favored as candidates and also would choose delegates to the national convention. Newspaper publicity was to make it difficult for politicians to deny nomination to the successful primary candidates.

The first test came in 1912, when Theodore Roosevelt challenged William Howard Taft for the Republican nomination. Roosevelt won the primaries but in the convention some of his primary-elected delegates were denied seats, allowing Taft to be renominated. Roosevelt then left the party and established a new one — party professionals would say he acted like a typical unreliable maverick.

Primaries Become Irrelevant. In 1916, twenty-six states had presidential primaries. But professional politicians were beginning to recognize that primaries need not be a threat to their power. By 1920, the Republicans nominated Warren G. Harding, who had lost all the primaries he entered. Party professionals chose him in "a smoke-filled room" at the Blackstone Hotel in Chicago. He won in a landslide. Journalists stopped paying much attention to presidential primaries, for they seemed irrelevant to the real decision making.

By 1936, only eighteen states had presidential primaries. Sometimes candidates, usually those outside the party mainstream, used specific races to demonstrate to party professionals that they would be effective nominees. The successful ones eliminated competitors as well. But party professionals remained unimpressed. Tennessee Senator Estes Kefauver, a politician with a reputation for independence, in 1952 won twelve of the fourteen primaries he entered. Adlai Stevenson, governor of Illinois, entered only the Illinois primary, and lost. But Stevenson still got the nomination.

The professionals could disregard the presidential primaries because they were often held in small states, such as New Hampshire, Nebraska, or Oregon. And light voter turnout cast doubt on the results. Moreover, some states had open primaries that permitted supporters of the other party to "invade" an election and skew the outcome.

Professionals also found ways to subvert the primaries and remain free to bargain. They entered "uncommitted slates," or had the governor run as a "favorite son," so that the state delegation could be used as a bargaining chip in the convention. And even when the voters did choose pledged delegates, it was not clear for how many convention ballots such delegates had to stay with their candidate. Little could be done if a delegate failed to honor that pledge even on the first ballot.

HOW TELEVISION CHANGED PARTY CONVENTIONS

Television made 1952 a pivotal year for presidential nomination politics. Viewers for the first time could *watch* convention politics, and television journalists learned that convention bargaining could be attractive media entertainment. With television, the conventions themselves and the role of party professionals began to change.

Covering the National Conventions

The Republican party nomination produced an especially dramatic script in 1952. Supporters of five-star general, war hero, and then NATO commander Dwight "Ike" Eisenhower, began a write-in campaign for him in Minnesota. Friendly election officials agreed to count every scrawl, including "Ike," that vaguely suggested his relatively difficult-to-spell name. Former Minnesota governor Harold Stassen won narrowly. But the "Minnesota Miracle" convinced Eisenhower that he should run for the nomination.

The Taft–Eisenhower Battle. Republican leaders for Eisenhower took full advantage of the novel television coverage. Conscious of television's need for drama, they turned the convention maneuvering into a replay of 1912, when party regulars disqualified Theodore Roosevelt delegates and nominated Taft. This time (1952), the party regulars favored Taft's son, Ohio's conservative Senator Robert Taft. The convention became a great morality play — "Ike against the party bosses." "Fair play" was the slogan. Appropriately for the drama of it all, Eisenhower won.

Almost immediately television coverage began to change the convention itself. When delegates filed in, they found a card on each of the folding chairs. The national committee reminded them that they could expect cameras to pan the audience during speeches, looking for someone yawning, eating, talking to neighbors, or sleeping.

Further Changes. In subsequent conventions, the television cameras grew restless if dead spots came up. They switched away from the rostrum where candidates up for election were orating: radio had covered these fully. But television audiences wanted entertainment and considered political speeches boring. Thus the television commentators gave their own analysis or conducted human interest interviews with especially colorful or knowledgeable delegates. Soon speeches had to be limited and strictly tailored to suit the television schedule, and "spontaneous" demonstrations were given time limits. After a few disastrous experiences, politicians tried to schedule actions that could lead to fights, such as proposing platform planks or seating a delegation, at times when television cameras would not be covering the convention.

No longer were podium activities directed to delegates who were choosing a presidential nominee: television viewers became the audience for whom the politicians were expected to perform. And as that audience became critical of some material that they saw, the parties began to make basic changes. Reformers insisted that the parties clean up their act — the issue was again "fairness."

Changes in Party Rules

We find that party professionals began sanitizing the rules to make political conventions and politics itself appear less "political" to the viewing American public. The underlying theme was to make the nomination process more "democratic."

The new rules, which usually benefited the winners of presidential primaries, removed much of the entertainment and excitement that nominating conventions had once provided. As we will see, the changes, to the journalists' chagrin, produced a convention that was no longer the best show in town. Few would watch, and as a result the networks gradually cut back on their coverage.

Conventions in the 1960s. The 1964 and 1968 Democratic national conventions gave impetus to those who advocated change in convention rules. A group of blacks, calling themselves the Mississippi Freedom Democrats, challenged the regular delegation in the 1964 convention. Friendly delegates smuggled a few of them to the convention floor. Television journalists found it an exciting story in an otherwise dull convention — President Lyndon Johnson's renomination was a certainty.

Faced with a television spectacle that would suggest to black viewers in the North that Democrats condoned racism, party leaders compromised by giving the freedom delegates two seats. And in 1968, they said, any state that discriminated against blacks in choosing its delegation would not be seated.

The 1968 Democratic convention was a public-relations disaster. Television journalists focused on street fights and bloody battles in the darkness of Grant Park on Chicago's lake front. Mayor Daley's police struggled with supporters of "Peace in Vietnam" candidates. Daley argued that the journalists encouraged the riots by their coverage. Meanwhile inside the hall, cameras focused on delegates with plastic cards at their necks filing through security checkpoints, disturbing images suggesting a totalitarian society. Fistfights broke out on the floor and the cameras of all networks followed as Daley's aides forcibly ejected Dan Rather from the convention floor.

Conventions in the 1970s. To make conventions suitable for public viewing, Democrats agreed to establish the McGovern-Fraser commission to revise its delegate selection rules for 1972. The new rules were designed to make it clear to television viewers that rules of fair play would be followed. They cut back the power of local party leaders. Officeholders — governors, state legislators, or members of Congress — would not automatically become delegates. Delegates had to be chosen at properly publicized meetings held according to written party rules. No longer could delegate selection votes be cast by proxy. Most important, delegations must include women and "minorities" such as blacks, Spanish Americans, and the young according to their ratio in each state's population.

The rules for 1972 backfired on the television screen. Journalists took delight in panning their cameras across the hall in search of unusually dressed delegates, leaving the impression with some that "hippies" were in control of the Democratic party. The cameras and commentators followed closely as Mayor Daley's delegation was refused seats and ejected because they had not followed the new rules.

To prevent embarrassing delegate challenges, some state party leaders opted for choosing delegates in primaries. By 1976, thirty states, representing 75 percent of the delegates, were chosen in primary elections. In 1968, only seventeen states, with 40 percent of the delegates, chose delegates in that way.

The party professionals sanitized political conventions even more in 1976. The unit rule, a major reason for charges of bossism, was abolished, again to avoid political fighting on the screen. No longer would a primary winner get all the votes. A candidate receiving 15 percent or more of the votes would get a proportional share of the delegates.

Rule changes were especially pronounced in the Democratic party but affected the Republican party as well. In both parties leaders and convention delegates had less say in choosing the nominee; the need to appear fair and democratic became overriding.

By the 1980s, the "contest" element had been eliminated. Most would-be viewers already knew who the nominee would be. Convention managers therefore provided commercial entertainers for the viewers — in 1980 pop singers Donnie and Marie Osmond sang and danced for appreciative Republicans.

But the networks had better use for prime time. In 1984, the ABC network cut back its convention coverage to the highlights. The other major networks had also abandoned gavel-to-gavel coverage, henceforth available only on CNN, PBS, and C-Span.

TELEVISION DISCOVERS THE PRESIDENTIAL PRIMARIES

Not until 1960, did politicians and journalists begin to realize the media potential in the presidential primaries. Theodore H. White, then a magazine journalist, followed Senator Kefauver through some of the 1956 primaries, later stating that only four other journalists from outside New Hampshire covered the final day of that primary; two from the wire services, one from a Boston newspaper, and a stringer for *The New York Times*.[2]

White decided to examine the 1960 race more profoundly, from primary elections through national conventions and the election. His book awoke journalists to the entertainment possibilities in presidential primaries. In 1980, White estimated that 450 reporters covered the final day of the New Hampshire primary, with 500 or so technicians to aid them.

With the rise in television coverage, politicians — a few at first and more later — began to look intently at primary races as a way to the party nomination.

The Making of the President: 1960

The race for the 1960 Democratic nomination pitted Massachusetts Senator John F. Kennedy against Senator Hubert H. Humphrey of Minnesota. As the first Catholic presidential candidate since 1928, Kennedy decided he had to show that he could attract more than Catholic and urbanite votes. He challenged Humphrey in West Virginia, a nonurban state in which the depressed conditions seemed made to order for Humphrey. Kennedy won the primary and crippled the Humphrey candidacy.

Events in Ohio were equally influential. Governor Michael DiSalle planned to lead an uncommitted delegation slate to the national convention. But public opinion polls showed that Kennedy could beat a DiSalle favorite-son slate in the Ohio primary. DiSalle decided he would head the Kennedy delegation from Ohio.[3]

The story of the West Virginia campaign and events in Ohio make an absorbing section in journalist Theodore H. White's *The Making of the President, 1960*. His book unexpectedly became a bestseller because of his way of presenting the clash of political personalities in the primaries. White wrote a president-making book for subsequent presidential campaigns, further heightening media interest.

Growing Importance of the Primaries. In 1964, journalists began covering the primaries in depth, in print and with late Tuesday-night television reports. Party professionals had to begin taking seriously candidates who did well.

The 1968 Democratic convention in Chicago may have been the last of the old-style conventions. The Democratic nomination went to Vice President Hubert Humphrey, even though he had not entered primaries against candidates such as Eugene McCarthy, Robert Kennedy, George Wallace, or George McGovern. Opponents charged it was a boss-dominated convention.

Politicians recognized that failure to participate in the primaries handicapped Humphrey in the general election. The idea gradually spread that no one should be chosen who had not proved himself or herself in the primaries. In 1972, Humphrey entered the primaries and fought McGovern through to the final one in California, where McGovern's victory pretty much clinched the nomination for him.

From there, the presidential primaries gained significance: they, instead of the party conventions, not only tested the candidates, but chose the nominee as well. We next review the steps in this procedure and the role journalists played.

How Journalists Cover the Presidential Primaries

The journalists' influence on the nominations stems from which candidates they focus upon in the presidential primaries, as Jimmy Carter and his campaign manager, Hamilton Jordan, realized. They figured out how the procedures journalists follow would help Carter win the nomination.

The Primary Story as Journalists See It. In the early days of the primary season, most citizens have not yet figured out who is running, and they pay little attention. Journalists act as a surrogate to sort things out for them, interpreting what is happening in small and unfamiliar states, explain results that may be ambiguous, and telling the public who appears to be winning and which are the serious candidates. This is the journalist's winnowing-out function, the period when reporters can deeply affect the nominations.

But reporters, especially on television, also want to show the drama and human interest in these contests — their value as entertainment. Inevitably they play up the horse-race character of primaries. They also are attracted by the unexpected, such as an upset of the frontrunner: Jesse Jackson as the first serious black candidate and Republican John Anderson in 1980, when he appeared not only to be more liberal than other Republicans but even to the left of Jimmy Carter, the Democratic frontrunner.

When they first seriously cover the presidential primaries, television and print journalists realized that they needed a set of guidelines to help them winnow out weak candidacies, rules of thumb that party professionals sometimes consider bizarre. But reporters and editors are not interested in finding candidates who will help the party win the general election; they focus on candidates who make interesting copy. If journalists' rules, built around the need for drama and human interest, assist individual candidates or damage party leaders, it is an unintended side effect.[4]

Winnowing Before Any Votes Are Cast. Journalists feel that a candidate can be taken seriously who is able, without too much effort, to get people to give money. Their test is whether the candidate qualifies early for federal funding. Many little-known candidates waste time raising $100,000 in amounts no greater than $250 in twenty states. More importantly, as Rep. Pat Schroeder (D-Colo.) noted in withdrawing in 1987, is whether a candidate can raise huge amounts and hire competent staff well before primaries begin.

Reporters also zero in on any show of strength in any preprimary popularity contest, no matter how minor or silly the effort. Thus, Carter and Kennedy vied for delegates' support in a Florida state convention at which party leaders in the Carter camp had already chosen half the delegates. Others competed by seeing who could raise most for the Iowa Democratic party organization.

Reporters seek out gaffes; the politicians say they try to make minor mistakes into major issues, especially important when voters know little about the candidates. In 1987, Senator Joseph Biden was found to have "borrowed" phrases and even whole paragraphs from the speeches of Bobby Kennedy and British Labour party leader Neil Kinnoch. Reporters argued that such plagiarism gave an important clue to his political character.

Finally, reporters encourage their own type of media event — sponsors label it a candidate debate. They hope that candidates will create drama by attacking each other; perhaps the frontrunner will make a misstatement. Then journalists broadcast and rebroadcast highlights.

Such debates put the candidate in the lead at a disadvantage. Jimmy Carter in 1980 agreed to debate with Edward Kennedy in Iowa, but backed out when Kennedy began slipping in the polls, claiming that the press of government duties kept him away. Reagan in 1980 stayed away from the Iowa debates among Republican candidates. George Bush took away Reagan's frontrunner position by capturing the Iowa caucus vote. Reagan then went on to New Hampshire and a debate in which he bested Bush and won that crucial first primary.

Professional politicians regard these journalistic measures as of questionable value.

Picking Primary Election "Winners." The journalists' way of defining news tells us a great deal about how they pick winners. The unexpected is news.

When underdogs lead or even do better than expected, that is news. When frontrunners do worse than journalists expect them to, that too is news: they are losers according to journalistic standards no matter how great their lead in the voting. Politicians sometimes argue that journalists are so zealous to uncover the unexpected that the situations they claim to find such stories in are highly doubtful.

A harmless illustration of how the unexpected becomes news was Senator Fritz Hollings's sweep of Dixville Notch, New Hampshire in the 1984 primary. The village gathers its twenty-seven voters in the Balsam Hotel for an election night party and is always the first precinct to report, right after midnight. Hollings made two visits to Dixville Notch and won with three votes in its Democratic primary and also got five votes in the Republican primary. Those votes did not suggest that Hollings would carry New Hampshire, but the story got national media coverage.

In 1968, Senator Eugene McCarthy of Minnesota challenged President Johnson in the New Hampshire primary, attacking the president's Vietnam policies. Johnson received 62 percent to McCarthy's 37 percent. Journalists reported a stunning McCarthy victory (Johnson was expected to do better). Yet in 1976 another incumbent president, Gerald Ford, "won" New Hampshire with only 50.5 percent over Ronald Reagan with 49.5 percent. Ford was declared the winner because at first he had not campaigned and everyone expected Reagan to win — his own aides had released a poll shortly before the voting showing him eight points ahead.

Senator Edmund Muskie beat George McGovern 46 to 37 percent in the 1972 New Hampshire primary. But that was heralded as a McGovern victory because Muskie was a native of nearby Maine and, journalists reasoned, should have done better against his South Dakota opponent. In assessing who "won," journalists also observe how much a candidate spent or how hard he or she campaigned.

Washington Senator Henry "Scoop" Jackson's sweeping 1976 wins in New York and Massachusetts, states with large electoral votes, were given little journalistic attention, for they were expected. But George Bush's 1980 victory in the Puerto Rico primary received respectful media attention, perhaps because of its offbeat quality. Puerto Ricans, though, do not vote in American presidential elections.

Plurality Wins. If no other interpretation can be arrived at, the candidate who receives a plurality is declared the winner, even though the margin

of victory may be just a percentage point or two and the winning vote less than a third of the total. Professional politicians question the validity of such minority "victories." A win may be declared even though more votes were cast for uncommitted delegates. Jack Anderson totaled Carter's percentage in all the 1980 primaries and found that more Democrats voted against him than for him, indicating to Anderson that the major story was that his own party voters had rejected an incumbent president.

The "Big Mo" and Reporting. Candidates who do well in the Iowa precinct caucuses, the New Hampshire primary, and the other early contests are described, in sports lingo, as picking up momentum. Candidate George Bush, winner in Iowa in 1980, called it the "Big Mo."

Such momentum pays off handsomely in news coverage. Carter in 1976 received 28 percent of the Democratic vote in New Hampshire, leading by 4,500 votes. Thomas E. Patterson measured the media response: front covers of both *Time* and *Newsweek* and 2,600 lines inside. Morris Udall received 23 percent of the votes and got only ninety-six lines of coverage in these magazines. Carter's opponents, sharing 72 percent of the vote, got only 300 lines total.[5]

A Patterson analysis of the thirteen-week campaign in 1976 found that on the average each week's primary "winner," even if leading by only a plurality, received roughly 60 percent of the primary coverage on network evening newscasts, in *Time* and *Newsweek*, and only a little less in selected newspapers. Those in second place got from 14 to 29 percent, those in third place about 15 percent, and those in fourth place usually less than 10 percent.[6]

With such unbalanced coverage, most of the candidates whom journalists tag as weak are eliminated after a month of primaries. And the first runner-up is often groggy and hoping for a second wind.

The Carter Media Breakthrough. Politicians in the mid-1970s were aware that coverage of the primaries was gaining influence but they still anticipated that a brokered convention would choose the nominee. Only one, Hamilton Jordan, saw clearly how journalists in pursuit of stories could be used to help a candidate capture the nomination even before the convention gathered.

He demonstrated that a candidate from a southern state that had relatively few electoral votes and little support from professional politicians could capture a major party's presidential nomination. He also showed that Carter, a politician nearly unknown to voters, with no national experience, could become a media celebrity and make it impossible for the professional politicians to deny him the nomination.

Jordan concluded that Carter would get national media coverage by coming out slightly ahead in the early races. These early pluralities would make the candidate the frontrunner, at least in the media, and a major contender in the eyes of the public. The unexpectedness would bring massive media coverage.

Georgia's constitution prohibited Carter from running for reelection when his term as governor ended in 1974. He volunteered to be campaign chair of the Democratic midterm campaign, a position that gave him reason to travel around the country and meet with newspaper editorial boards as well as party politicians.

In November 1974, he focused his main efforts in three states with early nomination decisions; the precinct caucuses in Iowa and the primaries in New Hampshire and Florida. Carter, his wife Rosalynn, and sometimes their children campaigned endlessly from fall 1974 through early 1976. Almost every week one or more of them visited Iowa, New Hampshire, and Florida, seeking support for Jimmy Carter.

As the Iowa precinct caucuses were about to meet, the Gallup poll reported that Carter had 4 percent national support for the nomination. Almost every other declared candidate was ahead of him. People outside these states hardly knew who Jimmy Carter was. Indeed, in 1974, he had appeared as a guest on "What's My Line?" a popular television quiz program. Panelists could not guess that he was then governor of Georgia.

The Iowa precinct delegates were cautious — 37 percent remained uncommitted. Carter came in second with 26 percent, but Roger Mudd of CBS declared him the "clear winner." And soon after in New Hampshire, Carter got 28 percent, enough, Walter Cronkite said on the evening news, to give him a "commanding head start." Critics pointed out that he was billed as "conservative" and that the three leading Democrats who opposed him were all "liberals" and together had received more than double his vote. But Carter had the Big Mo and novelty value as well.

A part of the Jordan strategy was to enter every primary, hoping for at least one win every week. Carter would show confidence without raising media expectations by simply predicting each week that "we will do well," and let reporters figure out what that might mean. The reasons given for primaries he lost was that he had not campaigned hard or spent large sums of money in those states.

Carter won seven of the first nine primaries. Momentum was less important in subsequent primaries. Austin Ranney mentions that in the later stages of the campaign, Carter won eight primaries that neither Idaho Senator Frank Church or California Governor Jerry Brown, then his chief rivals, entered. But he lost six of eight in which one or both challenged him. Journalists paid little attention to these losses, because they considered the race over. Ranney writes, "Carter's mediocre performance in stage two of the campaign did not appreciably damage his chances for the nomination."[7]

And although Carter either lost or did not run in major states such as Massachusetts, New York, and California, party politicians, among them Mayor Richard Daley of Chicago, scrambled to get on his bandwagon. Nelson Polsby reports that before Carter had won even a third of the convention delegates, the overwhelming consensus among journalists was that the "magic number" had been reached.[8]

As Carter pushed down the aisle to accept the nomination at the 1976 Democratic convention, he came to Mayor Daley and the Illinois delegation. As a symbol of party unity, he was supposed to greet Daley, but Carter cut Daley dead. He thought it more important to symbolize for television viewers that he did not owe his nomination to professional politicians.

Other Changes Traceable to Televised Coverage

Several political extravaganzas on television led to its supremacy. The Kefauver crime hearings in 1951 made that senator a national figure. Coverage of the John F. Kennedy assassination in 1963 showed television potential as a provider of breaking news. Almost immediately, CBS lengthened its evening news to a half hour, and the other networks followed shortly. News broadcasts moved from public-service to profit-making operations. Competition for viewers became intense.

But few televised political offerings attracted as great a national audience as daily coverage of the Watergate hearings that resulted in resignation by President Nixon. These hearings brought on further "fair-play" rules that weakened professional politicians by encouraging presidential primary contenders.

Campaign Finance Rules. The "dirty-tricks" and laundering of campaign funds revealed in the Watergate hearings encouraged Congress to amend the 1971 campaign finance law. One change was that federal funds could be used to finance candidates in the presidential primaries. Public campaign funding encouraged maverick candidacies, something professionals deplored while journalists applauded.

Candidates who accepted funding faced further rules on contributions and spending. Overall limits were set as well as individual state limits, according to a state's size. States might set additional limits. A significant outcome of these rules was that candidates became more reliant on their own resources and less on party organizations for funds.

But these were not the worst of the changes from party professionals' perspective. Just before the 1976 primary season, the U.S. Supreme Court, reviewing these finance-law changes, ruled that the government could not restrict the amounts candidates could contribute to their own campaigns. It also held that candidates who refused federal campaign financing were not bound by the spending limits. The third and most important part of the ruling was that the act could not limit the money spent by groups independent of a candidate's campaign organization. The court said such a restriction deprived persons of the right to free expression.

These independent groups have come to be known as political action committees (PACs). In 1975, 608 PACs were registered with the government; by 1980, 2,010. Of course, PACs could raise funds in some states and spend them lavishly in others. Some became very sophisticated in gathering political monies, relying heavily on direct-mail campaigns, computerizing memberships of organizations that reflected their liberal or conservative political bias.

Political Consultants in Campaigns. Candidates appreciated what television could do for their campaigns, allowing them to "enter the voters' living rooms." But most were uncertain how to exploit television's potential. Media consultants, using techniques from the advertising world, moved in to fill this need.

The consultants took over direction of whole campaigns. They advised how to use the "paid media," that is, campaign advertising, to best effect, as well as how to get maximum coverage in the "free" or "unpaid media" of campaign reporting.[9]

The media consultants could promise two advantages over traditional party organizations. First, they would produce a bigger bang for the buck, a greater return on each dollar spent. They were efficient in using resources. Literature that was printed would get distributed. Broadcast time would be used where and when it would do most good. Public appearances would be arranged to produce greatest media coverage. They would not waste money on local organizing activities.

The media firms also offered scientific polls to help the candidate create a favorable image and give him or her accurate information on which appeals to stress. They could seek out the potential switchers in the electorate and find out which appeals would be effective.

Media firms entered national campaigns with sixty-second "I Like Ike" radio and television spots in 1952. The Democrats countered by broadcasting speeches of their candidate Adlai Stevenson "talking sense to the American people," but were no match. By 1956, Democrats also had their consulting media firms. Soon all major campaigns were guided by consultants.

Underdog candidates in the presidential primaries needed name recognition in a hurry, and media consultants devised television strategies to help. The goal was to separate their candidate from the rest of the pack, generally by painting "their" candidate as an independent, one who owes no favors to party leaders or to the party's associated interest groups.

PARTY PROFESSIONALS COUNTERATTACK

Party professionals in both parties began to devise strategies to offset media influence in presidential nominations. Democrats were most upset perhaps because media coverage had so often unhorsed their political strategies.

Controlling the Primaries

The first Democratic party response was relatively weak: they clamped down on open primaries, which permit voters to decide in the voting booth whether they will vote in the Democratic or Republican primary. In 1976, party officials told Democrats in four open-primary states to adopt closed primaries or find another way to choose delegates. By 1980 Michigan and Wisconsin still had not complied. Michigan Democrats were persuaded to switch to the precinct caucus method. But Wisconsin fought the party mandate in court, and conceded to party wishes only much later.

Ten states also gave up their presidential primaries. By 1984, delegates chosen in presidential primaries dropped from 75 percent of the national convention to 55 percent. The move to party caucuses for choosing delegates also strengthened the hand of party leaders and their interest-group allies. Persons attending the caucuses would know each other and, it could be assumed, would challenge non-Democrats. Votes in many caucuses would be announced openly, allowing local shop stewards to know how their union members voted.

The Democratic leadership encouraged bunching up of primaries early in the year, "front-loading" rather than stringing them out over the whole spring. This timing, they reasoned, would handicap maverick candidates and those who campaigned for two years before the Iowa caucuses. It would also lessen the effects of media coverage. The biggest delegate prize of 1984 was awarded on "Super Tuesday," when nine states chose delegates. But Iowa and New Hampshire politicians refused to give up their early contest dates.

Democratic professionals also created a new group of "superdelegates," who would constitute 14 percent of the delegate seats. These seats would go to party professionals — United States representatives and senators and state party leaders and activists. Also delegates chosen in primaries would no longer be bound to vote for the primary choice even on the first ballot. Finally, the Democrats reinstated the unit-rule or winner-take-all elections at the district level, favoring party organizations in large urban centers.

The Test of the Counterattack. In 1984, the Republicans, with a popular incumbent president, had little to worry about. Still, Ronald Reagan delayed until the last moment announcing that he would run again. His strategy made it difficult for other potential candidates to raise funds, and his popularity discouraged opposition candidacies.

Long before the first primary, Democratic party organizations and allied interest groups — labor unions, blacks, and women's groups — began screening possible candidates. Senator Edward Kennedy announced he would not be a candidate. The choice landed on Walter Mondale, Carter's vice president. Before the first primary he had received major endorsements and built up a substantial campaign chest. As a nonincumbent politician, he was also able to campaign for Democratic candidates and appear at party rallies for several years before the primaries.

The party leaders hoped to head off a media candidate by making it seem the race was over before it had even begun. Party strategists most feared the candidacy of Senator John Glenn of Ohio, America's first astronaut to circle the globe, whose exploits were detailed in a Hollywood movie scheduled for release during the primary season.

The strategy seemed to work: Mondale won the Iowa precinct caucuses. But Senator Gary Hart of Colorado, relatively unknown, took second place. Hart was photogenic and attracted media attention, whereas Mondale often appeared wooden and uncomfortable on the screen. Hart added to his attractiveness by deliberately aping mannerisms of the late President Kennedy, as by placing his right hand in his suitcoat pocket while speaking.

And then the worst happened for the party leaders — Hart won the New Hampshire primary. Suddenly a candidate separated himself from the field of seven who opposed Mondale. He portrayed himself as a person with a new look and fresh ideas; he captured the momentum. Here was a candidate made for television stories, an underdog battling against party professionals who were trying to get the public to accept their hand-picked candidate. Meanwhile, Jesse Jackson also promised he would stay in the race until the end.

Many primaries later, Mondale managed to fight his way back into the lead. But Hart and Jackson threatened to carry the fight to the convention. They shouted "fair play," claiming they were not receiving as many delegates as their primary showings merited. In the end they conceded and did not make a convention fight. But Democratic leaders were left with a divided party and a damaged candidate.

After the election, Hart supporters implied that he would have won the nomination and gone on to beat Reagan, were it not for the party bosses and lavish spending by the Mondale camp. Later, the U.S. Elections Commission fined the Mondale campaign for overspending in the primaries, a small consolation to his primary competitors. Hart and Jackson vowed they would run again in 1988.

Party leaders now understood that if they were to control nominations, they would have to recruit candidates with skill in playing by the media rules. From President Reagan they learned the value of an attractive television image.

Strategies for the Future

A number of southern states vowed they would create their own superprimary for 1988. Their goal was to amass a large group of conservative Democratic delegates to offset the "liberal" wing of the party in the early Iowa and New Hampshire races. By early 1987, fourteen southern states plus six outside the South and Washington, D.C. had elected to hold their primaries or precinct caucuses on the same "super Tuesday" in early March. Only nine did so in 1984.

The strategy was likely to favor candidates already known, but not necessarily those party professionals would favor.

Candidate Strategies in the Media Age. Candidates continued to follow the Carter strategy of campaigning long before the first primaries, but with mixed success. Senator Howard Baker, majority leader, decided not to run again in 1984, presumably so that he could spend years campaigning in the early primary states. His candidacy made little headway and he gave up campaigning to become the president's chief of staff. Senator Hart gave up his Colorado senate seat in 1986 to devote full time to campaigning, but his candidacy collapsed in 1987 following media exposure of meetings with a model, Donna Rice.

But the relatively unknown "seven dwarfs" remained in the Democratic race while the vice president and Senate Republican leader appeared as frontrunners on their side.

Incumbent presidents can be expected to follow the "Rose Garden Strategy," avoiding primary conflict. Carter opposing Ford in the general election described the strategy: "As you know, he [Ford] would come out from the White House into the Rose Garden, memorize a 90-second speech, make his speech, go back into the White House and that's all the evening news had to put on the television. And it looked like he was very much in control of things. Or he would sign a bill in the Oval Office, that he had opposed for the last two years, take credit for it, and look like he was managing the nation's business." The strategy has also been used in primary races.

In 1980 Carter used a variation of this technique, claiming that the Iran hostage problem kept him from the promised debate with his primary challenger in Iowa, Edward Kennedy. On the day of the Wisconsin primary, he announced a break in the hostage crisis, six months prematurely. Jody Powell claimed the announcement was genuine, even if politically fortuitous.[10]

MANAGING THE ELECTION CAMPAIGN

As media coverage reshaped the nomination process, so too has it changed the way in which the major party candidates campaign against each other. They attempt to attract free media coverage but to supplement it with paid media attention in a way that results in a harmonized campaign.

The Paid Media

Political advertising offers a number of advantages and disadvantages. The advantage is that of control — no journalist need be depended upon to interpret information that is presented. Every detail can be carefully planned. Nothing need be left to chance. But the disadvantages are those of expense and credibility. That which appears in news reports is more likely to be believed than what the viewer sees in a paid message. An added disadvantage for some is so much dependence on media consultants that candidates are told how to comb their hair, what to wear, and so on. But this regimenting is an irritation that now goes with running for office, particularly at the presidential level.[11]

Planning an Advertising Campaign. Media consultants recognize that their campaigns must be tailored to the candidate, to the competition, and to the voter constituency.

The facts that matter about the candidate are the tightness of the race, the candidate's personality and strengths and weaknesses, and whether the opponent is better known. The first step is to gain name recognition, a goal sometimes even in presidential races and particularly in presidential primaries.

The main effort at winning votes is to get the public to perceive the candidate favorably — image making. Finally, research has shown that political advertising differs from consumer-product advertising in that voters pay closer attention and demand a reason beyond name recognition for supporting the candidate. That reason can be a favorable image, but it also helps if it is reinforced with some approach to issues. The Patterson and McClure study showed that television viewers learned more about a candidate's stand on issues from ads than from news broadcasts.[12]

The common steps are to take a poll to determine the candidate's popularity and to test the importance of issues for groups who may provide support. The themes to be stressed in both the paid and free media are then chosen. But no consultant stays completely wedded to those themes. As the campaign develops, the candidate may have to react to claims and issues raised by events or the opposition. Sometimes reaction has to be on short notice.

The actual approach in paid advertising varies somewhat depending on the consultant. They all agree that a major portion of funds available, from 40 to 70 percent, should be spent for television advertising, particularly for candidates who are lagging behind their opposition.

Other media outlets can be used to target specific audiences. Radio ads can be aimed at the young, blacks, and the freeway crowd returning from work. Magazines have their specialized audiences. Newspaper advertising is confined to weeklies and ethnic or specialized publications. Billboards give name identification. And money may be spent in nonmedia efforts such as literature for more detailed discussion of issues, or phone banks or direct mail for organization and fundraising.

The consultants are well versed in the technology of advertising — how long the spots or longer ads should be, when and where they should be broadcast to reach targeted audiences, whether the campaign should build up gradually to election day or wait until the final weeks for a saturation blitz — all decisions on how best to spend the funds available.

Consultants vary most in packaging the paid media message. Some prefer media events such as candidate Reagan grabbing the microphone at the Nashua, New Hampshire debate in 1980. Others prefer candidate interviews, person-on-the-street comments, talking heads, humor, and even statistics.

Most give lip service against using negative advertising that directly attacks the opponent by name or implication. But when candidates are trailing, they and their media consultants often turn to such appeals. And some stoop to deception. Advertisements have been designed to simulate network "newsbreaks." John Connally used a news clip of Iowa's governor implying that the governor was supporting him in the Iowa precinct caucuses, which he was not.

Campaign Appeals — The Image Counts. Campaign consultants generally agree that voters vote on the basis of image, the kind of a person voters think the candidate is. Television news and commercials have reinforced this reliance on image.

When Jimmy Carter first appeared as a candidate in 1976, he blurred the issues. One of his most widely quoted comments was that he wanted to make government "as truthful, capable, and filled with love as the American people." He made a point of looking directly into the camera and speaking in a positive way. He was widely viewed as both compassionate and capable, but events in the last two years of his term damaged this image. He appears to have convinced many voters that although he remained compassionate, he was not capable.

In 1980, he tried to switch this image by focusing his campaign against Ronald Reagan on the issues that divided them, but without success. Many analysts argued that in 1984 Mondale, Carter's vice president, suffered a similar fate. It became a truism among Democratic party professionals that 80 percent of the voters who supported Reagan disagreed with him on the issues. But they admired a man who, after being shot, could joke about forgetting to duck.

In creating image, consultants generally agree that surrogates, not the presidential candidate, should attack the opposition candidate. The vice presidential nominee often gets to take the low road of negative campaigning in the attempt to damage the opponent's image.

Some consultants suggest, however, that a presidential candidate can use a positive–negative technique, attacking the opponent's image indirectly. When Senator Kennedy ran against Carter in the 1980 primaries, Carter strategists devised an ad to emphasize Carter's image as a moral family man, also reminding voters, not too subtly, about Kennedy's playboy image, his marriage problems, and the Chappaquiddick incident.

The ad shows Carter helping daughter Amy with her homework while wife Rosalynn looks on. Carter says, "I don't think there's any way that you can separate the responsibilities of being a husband and father and a basic human being from that of being a good president. What I do is maintain a good family life which I consider crucial to being a good president." Invisible announcer voice then adds, "husband, father, president. He has done these three jobs with distinction."

Consultants also argue against too close an association with the party label; it may suggest an image of party hack. Walter Mondale was thought to have been harmed in 1984 by being too closely identified with party officials and with Democratic labor leaders — those whom opponents could characterize as "the party bosses." Voters seem to prefer the image of independent and underdog versus the organization — an image cultivated by mavericks from Teddy Roosevelt onward.

Campaign Appeals — The Issues. Joel Bradshaw, Hart's campaign consultant in his successful 1980 senate race and his 1984 Democratic nomination campaign, advised other Democratic campaign managers, "Issues are the vehicle by which you create your image."

When Reagan began his 1980 campaign, his choice of issues put him well on his way to creating an image of "right-wing extremist and demagogue." He implied that Carter was sympathetic to the Ku Klux Klan because Carter opened his campaign seventy miles from where the Klan was founded. He cast doubt about the value of the Nixon-Kissinger policy on Communist China and he dragged out the issue of evolution, all within the first week of the campaign.

Reagan abandoned this early scattergun approach and focused his campaign on a few popular issues such as government spending and taxation. Later during the televised debates, when Carter attempted to pin the extremist image on him, Reagan deflected it in a visual that would remain in the viewers' memories, a half-forgiving, half-put-upon response of, "There he goes again." He also reinforced an image of Carter as acting less than presidential.

The growing body of campaign consultants argue that issue appeals can be tailored to the electorate's wishes — within limits. The public-opinion poll is a basic tool, but it is only a tool, not a guide to be followed slavishly. A candidate who suddenly shifts a basic position because of polling data may ruin a hard-won image by appearing opportunistic, a political wimp, ready to say anything for votes. Consultants say a major problem is that many candidates want everyone to love them. Trying to win over those least inclined to support them may injure their image and may also waste resources.

The consultants advise candidates to concentrate on a few issues thought out well in advance of the campaign. Those chosen should reinforce rather than blur the candidate's image.

But candidates cannnot avoid some issues. Overriding issues which directly affect the voter negatively, and which can be blamed on the incumbent president or party, cannot be dodged. An economic recession, even one that affects only a segment of the voters, such as farmers or small-business people, can override image. So too will a drawn-out war or unsettling international conflict such as Korea and Vietnam. Single issues are also important for some groups — pro and antiabortionists, for example. Presidential candidates, feeling they may only antagonize some voters, frequently do as Carter did, blur these issues.

Utilizing Free Media — The Campaign Rituals

Every presidential campaigner wants to gain maximal free media coverage. They have two opportunities. One is the campaign events that have become almost rituals. Reporters can be expected to cover these in some depth. The candidate's performance will be analyzed and the visuals will, in two cases, be presented live. All will be repeated on television newscasts for those who missed the event.

The other opportunity consists of events the candidate or running mate can create by campaign appearances. We deal with the campaign's ritualistic events first.

The Acceptance Speech. Until 1932, a presidential nominee would wait at home for a committee of party officials to appear with the news that the party had chosen him as standard bearer. Sometimes as much as two months would pass before the official notice would be delivered. The nominee would then pull a speech of acceptance out of his pocket and read it to the small crowd of party officials, neighbors, reporters, and stray dogs.

Franklin D. Roosevelt changed that musty tradition. As soon as he was nominated, he told party leaders that he would travel from the governor's mansion in Albany to Chicago to address the convention and accept their nomination in person.

Roosevelt's speechwriter, Sam Rosenman, later wrote that most people expected Roosevelt to take a train. "But Roosevelt would have none of such prosaic arrangements. He knew the value of drama in public office and in public relations, and he understood the psychology of the American people in 1932. He felt that the dismayed, disheartened, and bewildered nation would welcome something new, something startling, something to give it hope that there would be an end to stolid inaction . . . that his approach was going to be bold and daring; that if elected he would be ready to act — and act fast."[13]

Roosevelt's flight aboard a Ford trimotor Tin Goose was eventful. They ran into strong headwinds. With scheduled refueling stops in Buffalo and Cleveland, the planned six-hour flight was two and a half hours late, a fact that did little damage to the drama. The delegates and the radio mikes patiently waited amid growing anticipation.

Few candidates have used the media as skilfully to kick off an election campaign. Roosevelt set the stage for a dramatic news event that included party delegates, his flight symbolizing his approach to the nation's problems. And in a radio speech that many citizens heard, he opened his campaign by outlining a program of "bold, persistent experimentation." In that speech was the sentence, "I pledge you, I pledge myself, to a *new deal* for the American people." It was the first time he used the phrase identified with his administration ever after.

Other candidates have been less successful. In 1972, because of fights on the convention floor, George McGovern did not get to deliver his acceptance speech until 2 A.M., long after even political junkies had gone to bed. One observer noticed that he hit prime time in Guam. For some, it also symbolized his disastrous campaign. And Carter, in a statement that was supposed to be a conciliatory reference to a rival for the nomination, former Vice President Hubert Horatio Humphrey, called him "Hubert Horatio Hornblower." Humphrey supporters immediately recognized this slip of the tongue as the way the Carter entourage referred to Humphrey in private and took the reference as an insult to their leader.

Most nominees prepare carefully to reach some of the effectiveness Roosevelt achieved. And party leaders help by tailoring convention proceedings to schedule the speech as a prime-time climax. But a candidate seldom sways the uncommitted. At best, the acceptance speech may hearten party loyalists, soften disappointment among those who had been supporting losing candidates, and unite the party for the fight against a common foe.

Kickoff on Labor Day. Choosing where to make the Labor Day speech that opens presidential campaigning may involve a conflict between political strategy and media strategy.

Political strategists know that many voters will pay little attention until the last weeks before election day, and so many candidates start campaigning in their home states. They can gracefully thank partisans and homefolks for support given during the nomination struggle. Later, when they are campaigning in the large competitive states, the homefolks will not feel they were neglected.

But Labor Day may also be an opportunity to make a dramatic gesture that results in media coverage. Democratic nominees such as Roosevelt, Truman, and Kennedy opened in downtown Detroit. Democratic union leaders were then able to turn out large crowds in the area now called Kennedy Square. Recently, they have been less able to produce such crowds. In 1980 therefore, Carter opened his campaign with a barbecue in Alabama. His choice emphasized that he was not forgetting his southern roots.

Reagan took the opening that Carter left and kicked off his campaign in downtown Detroit, thus suggesting that Carter was neglecting his labor-union supporters. Reagan urged his blue-collar listeners to follow him into the Republican party, which still believed in such values as patriotism and resistance to Communism and opposed abortion, affirmative action, and busing.

Reagan also dramatized a major campaign appeal, telling blue-collar union workers that he was a former Democrat and labor leader, but that Democratic party liberals had deserted their basic principles and so he had switched.

Opening in the opponent's area of strength also may stir up trouble, but at the very least eliminates the need to visit it later.

The Presidential Debates. The first presidential candidate debates occurred in 1960 with Kennedy against Nixon. Neither was the incumbent, though Nixon was ending his term as Eisenhower's vice president. The importance of image was nicely demonstrated in the analyses of voter response. Radio listeners picked Nixon as the winner, television viewers thought Kennedy had the edge. The television audience particularly noticed Nixon's heavy growth of beard and poor makeup.

Presidential candidates did not debate during the next three elections. Then in the Carter–Ford race of 1976, the League of Women Voters revived the idea. Carter faced Jerry Ford, and they faced each other uncomfortably in silence for twenty-eight of those minutes because the television audio went dead. Since then the debates have become a standard feature in every election, another example of how television's needs have reshaped American campaigns.

Because these debates can be crucial, candidates and their staffs insist on setting conditions before they agree to debates, which, of course, are not really debates. The candidates do not talk directly to each other except rarely. Instead, a panel of journalists and a moderator ask the candidates questions in turn.

Among details to be settled are candidates' vetoes over members of the questioning panel; as many as a hundred names have been vetoed before agreement is reached. Candidates also want limits on followup questions, restrictions on time limits, approval of location, and understandings on broad topics for each meeting, such as foreign policy and domestic policy. Finally, they agree on the number of times they will debate and on such details as whether the candidates will stand or sit.

Pitfalls of Debates. The debates can help or hurt a campaign by affecting the candidate's image. When Carter in 1980 illustrated a point about atomic policy with a remark that his daughter Amy made, the point was lost. The image that was not lost was that of a president turning to his grade school daughter for advice on nuclear warfare.[14]

Again in 1984 the major question in the first debate was not the candidates' views but whether Reagan was showing advanced age. He stumbled over the word "progressivity," rambled, seemed unclear in his answers, and never finished an involved story about traveling down the California coast. The "issues" question was whether Reagan was competent to be president.

The Reagan forces claimed he had been overbriefed. In the second debate he came back more precise and confident and turned aside citizens' doubts with a joke, saying he would not raise the age issue by dwelling on Mondale's youth and inexperience. Thus reassured, voters reelected him almost by a landslide. Few who saw the debates between Reagan and Mondale would be able to recall any policy issues that the candidates discussed or the later analyses that the television critics made. Memorable for most was a visual, the image the two candidates presented as they parried the questions.

Utilizing Free Media — Campaign Events

A well-planned campaign is meant to do two things: create favorable visuals for television at each campaign appearance and maximize the influence of campaign appearances.

Campaign Media Events. The candidate wants appearances that result in good visuals for the national evening news. Every day a candidate's managers strive for a visual better than a wave from a moving limousine or handshaking along an airport fence. Other clichés are pictures of candidates putting on a hard hat with construction workers or bending down to speak to a shy child. Not only do the managers want to be more imaginative — they seek visuals that will symbolize an issue the candidate has been stressing.

The Reagan team in his first term discovered that image is created most readily by television visuals, rather than by the spoken or written word. They realized they could overcome negative comments by television commentators if the visuals showed the president favorably. Thus, one critic remarked, the photo opportunity might show Reagan sympathetically handing a torch to a young person in a wheelchair at the handicapped Olympics. The visual would be remembered longer than the reporter's comment that the president had cut budget funds for handicapped programs.[15]

More than most other campaigners, the Reagan team in the 1984 campaign appreciated the value of visuals. They concentrated on photo opportunities because they recognized that many voters disagreed with their candidate on specific issues and reporters' comments might well be negative.

Maximizing Effects of Campaign Appearances. Politicians believe that the most effective way to campaign is personal contact. The voter who touches the candidate in some way is much more likely to vote for him or her. Because presidential candidates cannot press the flesh or smile directly into the eyes of every voter, they use secondary contacts. Once party workers called on the voter on behalf of the candidate. Now televised appearances close to where the voter lives symbolically substitute for the candidate's handshake.

The technique is to appear where population is concentrated, so as to increase the local television coverage given each campaign appearance. Media consultants calculate that they can reach 85 percent of the citizens of Illinois by campaigning in just five metropolitan areas, which advertising professionals call media markets.[16] Candidates carefully target appearances to get maximum media exposure, both local and nationwide. Except as an occasional media event, they no longer whistlestop through small-town America, as Harry Truman did in 1948.

In a day a candidate can fly to three or more media markets: march in an Italian parade in New York at 10 A.M., speak at a business luncheon in Knoxville, appear at an afternoon labor-union rally in Flint, have dinner with a veteran's group in Indianapolis, and address a conference of senior citizens in Dayton later in the evening. And then fly back to Washington.

Small towns and rural areas get visits only when they provide a special opportunity to emphasize a point with vivid imagery. Carter wanted to show he cared about rural poverty and visited a depressed coal-mining area in southern Illinois late one afternoon. It helps also to find such a location near to a major media market: he held a town-meeting question-and-answer program in St. Louis that evening.

Planning Campaign Appearances. In 1960, Richard Nixon promised to campaign in every state to symbolize his feeling for all the nation's citizens. A minor injury threw him off schedule and as the campaign came down to the wire, he felt obliged to keep his promise. That meant taking time to go to Alaska instead of campaigning in states with large electoral votes.

Most campaign managers agree that visiting every state is unnecessary under the electoral-system method of tabulating votes. As a McGovern campaign aide said in 1972, "McGovern couldn't carry the South with Robert E. Lee as his running mate and [former University of Alabama football coach] Bear Bryant as his campaign manager."

Hamilton Jordan, Carter's campaign manager in 1976, approached the problem systematically. He recognized that Carter had to capture 270 electoral votes to win. He decided that the Carter–Mondale team members should campaign where they would likely to do most good — Carter in the South and the more conservative states and Mondale in the East and in labor-union areas.

Then he calculated a numerical value for each state, based on its electoral votes, likelihood for voting Democratic based on data from previous elections, and finally on the effort required to win it. The effort factor was determined by support for Carter in the presidential primary period, the resources Democrats or the Carter campaign had already expended in the state, and how close the two candidates were in the local polls. Jordan's formula gave California 5.9 points and New York 5.1. Alaska and Wyoming each received 0.6.

Jordan then devised a point system for campaign appearances. Carter was given 7 points, Mondale 5 points. Rosalynn received 4 points and Joan Mondale 3 points. Finally the Carter children and any spouses, received 2 points each.

Campaign spending and personal appearances were allocated by these formulas. Some flexibility was allowed in expenditures or appearances in October as new information or unexpected events dictated.

But the formulas provided a rough system for keeping the campaign on track.

ELECTION-NIGHT REPORTING

Journalists influence the choosing of the president from the very beginning in the winnowing out through the election campaign. A vital question on election night is whether journalists' reports and predictions about who will win directly affect the outcome. At issue is whether predicting winners in the East, sometimes before the polls are closed elsewhere, causes some citizens not to vote. In the West, polls commonly stay open three hours after the first results are reported.

Network Battles to Be First

On election night the networks pool the collecting of election results through News Election Service, a consortium of the three major television networks and the two wire services. It sends out the raw vote totals to all members. They do not, however, pool their exit polling surveys, which are the basis for the network competition to be first in predicting — and equally important, predicting accurately — the state-by-state results.[17]

Each network selects "bellwether" precincts in every state. For instance, CBS claims to base its predictions almost entirely on the raw vote totals reported in these key precincts. But each network has interviewers in selected precincts asking those leaving the voting place how they voted. These exit polls have proven very reliable for predicting election outcomes.

Do Predictions Influence the Outcome? The controversy over network predictions became acrimonious in 1980 when, using early predictions, Carter conceded several hours before the polls had closed in the West. One prominent Democratic member of Congress in Oregon was defeated, he suspected because discouraged Democrats stayed home. California's Field Poll reported that 10 percent of those who had not voted had skipped the election because of network projections.

A number of proposals have been made to limit network predictions. One was to have all the voting places stay open for twenty-four hours and open and close at the same time. The networks instead agreed not to predict the outcome in a state until its polls closed and to make no national predictions until the first results came in. In 1984, NBC predicted

© Alabama Journal, by permission of John Crawford

at 8:15 EST that Reagan would win; ABC predicted the same at 9:52 and CBS at 10:32. Throughout election day, however, newscasters hinted that a landslide for the president was in the making.

A Closing Note

Observers agree that nowhere does television coverage so shape the political process as in the choosing of a president. Little else in politics offers as much potential for easily understood entertainment — the clash of personalities, the testing of character, the drama of the horse race. And in few other instances are important politicians as powerless in manipulating the journalists.

A truth that is less commonly recognized is that even campaign politics cannot compete with the other forms of entertainment it plays against. The nonbrokered convention has become a bore that cuts out lucrative prime-time programs in favor of politicians. Campaign advertising is not always welcome because it cuts into prime-time revenues. And primaries and the debates as well have their long stretches of dullness. An election at midterm without the presidential race draws too little interest to give full election-night coverage.

Ironically, just as politicians have come to depend on television to get nominated and elected, the networks, facing competition from alternative channels on cable television and video recorders, are cutting down their campaign coverage. If this withdrawal continues or accelerates, American campaign politics will take new forms. And professional politicians may yet regain their lost influence in the presidential nomination process.

NOTES

1. Milton Rakove, *Don't Make No Waves, Don't Back No Losers: An Insider's Analysis of the Daley Machine,* (Bloomington: Indiana University Press, 1975), p. 96.
2. Theodore H. White, *America in Search of Itself: The Making of the President, 1956–1980* (New York: Harper & Row, 1982), p. 27.
3. Nelson W. Polsby, "The News Media as an Alternative to Party in Presidential Selection," ed. Robert A. Goldwin, *Political Parties in the Eighties* (Washington, D.C.: American Enterprise Institute, 1980), p. 55.
4. Donald R. Matthews, " 'Winnowing' the News Media and the 1976 Nominations," ed. James David Barber, *Race for the Presidency: The Media and the Nominating Process* (Englewood Cliffs, N.J.: Prentice-Hall, 1978), pp. 55–78.
5. Thomas E. Patterson, *The Mass Media Election, How Americans Choose Their President* (New York: Praeger, 1980), pp. 44–45.
6. Patterson, *The Mass Media Election,* p. 45.
7. Austin Ranney, *Channels of Power: The Impact of Television on American Politics,* (New York: Basic Books, 1983), pp. 97–98.
8. Polsby, "The News Media as an Alternative," pp. 50–66.
9. Larry J. Sabato, *The Rise of Political Consultants: New Ways of Winning Elections* (New York: Basic Books, 1981).
10. Jody Powell, *The Other Side of the Story* (New York: William Morrow, 1984), pp. 209–222.
11. Sabato, *The Rise of Political Consultants.*
12. Thomas E. Patterson and Robert D. McClure, *The Unseeing Eye: The Myth of Television Power in National Politics* (New York: G. P. Putnam's Sons, 1976).
13. Samuel I. Rosenman, *Working with Roosevelt* (New York: Harper, 1952), p. 74.
14. Myles Martel, *Political Campaign Debates: Images, Strategies, and Tactics* (New York: Longman, 1983), p. 26.

15. Quoted from a 1984 CBS News broadcast, Dean Alger, "Television, Perceptions of Reality and the Presidential Election of '84," *PS* 20 (Winter 1987): 52.
16. James Dunlap Nowlan, *Television Charts a New Campaign Map for Illinois* (Urbana: University of Illinois, 1981); "Occasional Papers in Illinois Politics, Number 2."
17. Joan Bieder, "Television Reporting," ed. Gerald Benjamin, *The Communications Revolution in Politics* (New York: Academy of Political Science, 1982), pp. 37–41.

6

Governing in the Television Age: The President

George Reedy, press secretary for Lyndon Johnson, argued that the presidency was no longer just "a bully pulpit," as President Theodore Roosevelt described it. Now, he said, it is "a great stage."

He wrote: "A pulpit is a platform for persuasion and exhortation. A stage is a setting for a presentation which may or may not carry a message. It can be an instrument for education and leadership or an attention-getting device for entertainment."[1]

Reedy and others imply that politics has become major entertainment on television. And the president is the greatest political entertainer of all. As President Reagan observed, "You'd be surprised how much being a good actor pays off in politics."[2]

CHAPTER OVERVIEW

We examine how presidents, as they govern, have dealt with the changes in journalistic coverage, particularly network television. We begin by looking at the phases in president–media relations. We observe different media styles that presidents use. We examine the other major participants: the Washington press corps and major aides to presidents such as the press secretary and press office, speechwriters, and media technocrats. We then look at the presidential press conference, where president and journalists face off. We end by observing how television has changed presidential policy making.

PHASES IN PRESIDENT–JOURNALIST RELATIONS

President watchers say that patterns are recognizable in the interplay between the president's and the journalist's career goals and the kinds of stories each considers newsworthy. Michael Grossman and Martha Joynt Kumar distinguish three phases: the honeymoon, the competitive alliance, and detachment.[3]

The Honeymoon

When a president is first elected, his popularity with the voters and with other politicians is generally as high as it will ever be. He has just won an election, a formal indication of citizens' approval, with which public-opinion polls cannot compete.

This euphoria lasts from the evening of election day to several months after inauguration. President Kennedy suggested that the end comes by August in the first year, or sooner. Jarol Manheim, examining the presidencies of Kennedy, Johnson, Nixon, and Ford, argues that a turning point occurs in late March, about two months after inauguration day.[4]

During the honeymoon, president and journalists test and learn from each other. Despite an occasional probing and pointed question a journalist may ask in a press conference, it is generally an amicable period.

A new president means a new division of benefits, a filling of offices in the executive branch, and new policies. Why antagonize the new president before it is absolutely necessary or risk being on the wrong side of public opinion? Members of Congress do not provide news stories challenging the president. Even the opposition party is willing to wait and see. Interest-group leaders also hesitate to criticize before new policies take hold.

Reporters and the new president generally agree on what is newsworthy. People want to know what the president is really like, and his staff tries to dig out revealing biographical anecdotes. Journalists found copy in minor items and speculated on whether President Reagan dyed his hair.

Grossman and Kumar call the honeymoon "an expository period," when the president explains what he hopes to do. Only later can reporters write stories comparing such rhetoric with the president's record of achievement. During the honeymoon, the president's rhetoric itself is the story.

Reagan took advantage of the honeymoon period in a way that is

In the past, the element of "contest" and uncertainty about who
would win attracted the public to tune in to political conventions.
Convention delegates too would thrive on the competitive drama.
More recent political conventions, however, have had to devise new
forms of entertainment, especially in the 1984 Republican convention, when Nancy Reagan introduced a large-screen presentation of
the highlights of President Reagan's first term in the White House,
including his personal reflections televised "live" from his hotel
room.

likely to be a model for other presidents. He did not offer, as both Carter and Truman had, so many proposals that no clear-cut program took form. Rather, Reagan and his aides orchestrated the transition news to prepare the public and Congress for tax reduction and budget cutting. From the day of his election, through his inauguration speech, and into the transition period beyond, the president stressed just these two issues.

When Reagan first proposed these ideas in the early days of the campaign, candidate George Bush called them "voodoo economics." But by the time the president's proposals went to Congress, the truly abrupt change in policy had lost much of its novelty. After the careful news buildup, the proposals became "Reaganomics."

And so journalists report favorable images of the new president along with his rhetoric, generally appending little critical comment. And both the president, who is achieving his career goals, and the journalists, who are getting stories heaped on them, are pleased with the relationship.

The End of the Honeymoon. When the president and reporters begin to disagree over what makes a good political news story, a new relationship begins. Usually a major political controversy signals the change.

Carter's honeymoon ended as he defended his budget director, Bert Lance, from charges of improper banking activities. Ford's ended when he pardoned Nixon. Reagan ended his when he started budget and tax proposals through Congress.

No longer is the president's rhetoric the only story. Now conflict and controversy claim the reporters' attention. For Reagan, the criticisms by economists, the opposition party, governors and mayors, and beneficiaries of social programs became part of the Reagan stories. Sometimes the criticism became the major story of the day.

The Competitive-Alliance Phase

After the honeymoon, reporters and president need not become openly hostile. But journalists no longer are as cooperative in getting out the stories presidents wish to see in print and on television, and presidents become more cautious.

Conflicts Within the Administration. Reporters are now attracted to conflict within the president's administration. President Reagan's first year was hardly complete before feuding between two top-ranking cabinet members — Secretary of Defense Caspar Weinberger and Secretary of State Alexander Haig — was out in the open, culminating with Haig's firing. Reporters began interpreting every Reagan action to see whether he was leaning toward the moderate or hard-line conservatives among his advisers and cabinet.

Conflicts Within the Family. For a president who stressed the values of home and family, dissension within his immediate family become the meat and potatoes of a journalistic banquet. Wife Nancy Reagan, explaining why all the Reagan children except Michael came to the family Thanksgiving gathering at the ranch, admitted that Michael and the president were estranged. Reporters recalled earlier charges that Michael had traded on his father's position in a business dealing. The press pointed out that the president had never seen his nineteen-month-old grandchild.

Michael, at his in-laws' home in Omaha, responded that Nancy's remarks "shocked" and "hurt" him. He went on to suggest that the knock she received on the head during the campaign may have been more serious than at first thought. Then Michael's wife Colleen, his sister Maureen, and even the president's brother, Neil, gave statements to inquiring reporters. And Michael appeared on two morning talk shows. He suggested that Nancy should think more about her own grandchildren than the foster grandchild program, which was one of Nancy's projects. The president did not comment, but as we will see, took action to counteract this negative image making.

Guarded Cooperation. News-management, as described in previous chapters, becomes standard procedure. In response, reporters become more skeptical, especially when, as with Carter, the polls show the president's prestige steadily plummeting. The relationship becomes one of guarded cooperation because the president is the source of major news, and he in turn wants favorable coverage.

This competitive-alliance relationship, described earlier, is the common one and generally characterizes most of a president's term in office.

Detachment

Presidents become detached when they are clearly lame ducks, unable or unwilling to take on further policy initiatives. A major unresolved issue such as the Vietnam War for Johnson, the Iran hostages for Carter, or the Iran-Contra scandal for Reagan tend to hasten the passage to ineffectiveness. So too does loss of party control of Congress at the midterm elections.

The president begins to avoid press contacts except for formal occasions and works through surrogates. Grossman and Kumar describe the relationship as latent antagonism masked by structured formality. The mood is one of stalemate and resignation. Fortunately, in most administrations, the period of detachment, if it occurs at all, is short.

PRESIDENTIAL MEDIA STYLES

Presidents do not govern by exercise of legal powers alone. Presidential prestige with the voters is a necessary part of the president's ability to persuade members of Congress and interest-group leaders to accept his policy leadership. Each month, for more than thirty-five years, the Gallup poll has assessed the president's popularity.

And presidential popularity is also an important aspect of media relations. When a president is popular, editors are less likely to demand critical stories and reporters are more restrained. In 1972, when Nixon's prestige was high, Gore Vidal's *An Evening with Richard Nixon* was produced on Broadway. He writes, "my revelations about shoe boxes filled with money, and break-ins, and illegal spying and other high capers were not only premature but they were the one thing no American journalist can abide — bad taste." He remembers that *The New York Times* accused him of saying "mean and nasty things about our President."[5]

Preserving popularity through the long competitive-alliance phase is a great part of being an effective president. Yet every recent president except Eisenhower has left office less popular than when he entered it.

Swings in Presidential Prestige

Elmer E. Cornwell claims every president who tries to govern inevitably loses prestige.[6] John Mueller hypothesized that this fall occurs because those who benefit from the president's policies do not feel as intensely as those who are harmed. The disgruntled, even though they disagree among themselves, unite in opposing the president. This group in time becomes sizable — even a majority — who never stop criticizing.[7]

Samuel Kernell argues instead that shifts in the president's prestige usually are gradual and do not occur inevitably but in response to specific events such as war, inflation, or recession.[8] If Kernell's view is correct, and most politicians act as if it were, presidents can hope to preserve and perhaps even increase their popular support. They need to avoid unpopular situations, have a little luck, and also receive a favorable press on their handling of the job.

But all presidents will face some unfavorable events. Students differ on whether presidents, even with the best media relations, can overcome the effects of a recession or an unpopular war. But presidents and their aides try.

The techniques they try, the ways in which presidents present themselves to journalists, depend in part on the personality of the president. Still, four media styles are visible. They range from cooperation to open warfare to the president's losing control of his media relations and of journalistic respect as well.

Cooperation-Control

Theodore Roosevelt pioneered the media approach that most successful presidents in modern times have adopted. He was cooperative with reporters, providing them with stories and dealing with them in a friendly, personal manner. He did not hold them at arm's length. But, as we have seen, both sides knew there were limits to that cooperation based on his own political career needs.

His "reporter's cabinet" best illustrates Roosevelt's success. He succeeded in getting reporters, off the record, to advise him on how to handle breaking stories, just as if they were a part of his administration. Seldom have journalists been so effectively co-opted.

But reporters could argue that they also gained from this exchange. They could prepare for future stories. They knew how the president would be likely to act and what some of his innermost thoughts were. And they could use these ideas if they did not directly attribute them to the president.

Only two other presidents have succeeded as well: Franklin Roosevelt and John Kennedy. They too had their worshipers among journalists. Columnist Jack Anderson wrote that rapport between Kennedy and reporters was so great, it was difficult to write unfavorably about him.

The two Roosevelts and Kennedy usually were their own best representatives to the media. They approached reporters with disarming friendliness and confidence rather than suspicion. Franklin Roosevelt began his first press conference in 1933 with the words, "They say it won't work but I'm going to try it." He told reporters he would take them into his confidence. At the end of that first press conference the reporters spontaneously broke into applause.

Other presidents such as Truman and Ford tried to achieve this relationship but were less successful. Truman's natural scrappiness and need to prove himself at every opportunity introduced friction where it served no political purpose. Ford was personally liked but just partially successful, perhaps because of his general lack of skill in media relations and his choice of a particularly abrasive press secretary.

Open Warfare

Woodrow Wilson began his administration saying he was for "pitiless publicity," but soon expressed disappointment with reporters. He used the United States entry into World War I as an excuse for walling out journalists. At the high point of his administration, the fight over the Versailles treaty incorporating his League of Nations idea, he tried to bypass the media with a speechmaking tour through the nation. At the same time some reporters were feeding to senators, hostile to Wilson, data with which they could defeat his treaty. And Wilson was describing reporters in letters to friends as "those who observe no rules, regard no understandings as binding, and act always as they please."

Lyndon Johnson too began with the media solidly behind him, amid the tragedy of the Kennedy assassination and his promise to carry on the Kennedy policies. But Johnson was overly sensitive to criticism. He thought every story he considered unfavorable was so written because the reporter wanted to embarrass him. He could not treat reporters as professionals doing a job. Relations deteriorated quickly into open warfare as journalists filed critical stories about Vietnam.

Richard Nixon campaigned against Johnson's media practices, promising an open administration. The political cartoonist Herblock, who had always drawn Nixon with a growth of beard to suggest Nixon's seediness, drew an inauguration day cartoon that caught the honeymoon mood — he offered the president "one free shave," a chance to let bygones be bygones. But shortly the "New Nixon" faded away and the "Old Nixon," distrustful of all journalists, reappeared.[9]

The President Loses Control

As we have seen, politicians have the advantage over journalists. And the politician with supreme advantage is the most powerful one in the nation and perhaps the world, the president.

How then can a president lose control of his media relations?

Part of the problem is inadequate understanding about the journalist's professional career motivations. President Carter naively confided to a reporter from *Playboy* magazine that he had sometimes looked at women with "lust in his heart." Whatever Carter's motivations, he made at least one basic error.

The mistake was to assume that journalists will not report an item because of personal friendship or liking, because of their own political preferences, or because it was gained in an informal and relaxed meeting. Politicians, including presidents, generally learn that journalists are really professionals first. Politicians may feel hurt and betrayed and sometimes may become vindictive, but they learn to respect the professionalism of reporters.

A second mistake some presidents make is demonstrating ineptitude to reporters. Timothy Crouse writes, "The private vocabulary of journalists reeks with obscenity, but the dirtiest word it contains is 'lightweight.' A lightweight, by definition, is a man who cannot assert his authority over the national press, cannot manipulate reporters, cannot finesse questions, prevent leaks, or command a professional public relations operation. The press likes to demonstrate its power by destroying lightweights."

Reporters appear to assume that presidents who are inept in handling reporters, in spite of all their advantages, will also be inept in office. They are professionals who respect other professionals.[10]

Warren G. Harding, once publisher of the *Marion Star*, liked to mingle with journalists. Soon, though, his ineptitude was revealed. He crumbled as reporter Paul Y. Anderson of the *St. Louis Post-Dispatch* began digging out the facts about the Teapot Dome oil-reserves scandal in Wyoming.

William Howard Taft, faced with the Payne-Aldrich tariff and the Ballinger-Pinchot affair over disputed Alaskan land claims, threw up his hands in helplessness. He appeared to quit trying to influence what the journalists wrote. Herbert Hoover, with the depression growing steadily worse, became petulant and largely ineffective.

All these presidents, especially Hoover, suffered calamity. But all made bad news worse by their own reactions. More successful presidents too have experienced calamities. Franklin Roosevelt survived the surprise attack on Pearl Harbor that crippled our navy, and the criticism and failures following his "packing" of the Supreme Court and his 1938 efforts to "purge" some members of Congress. Kennedy, early in his presidency, absorbed blame for the botched Cuban invasion. Eisenhower not only had to face up to the Russians' capture of our U-2 spy plane and pilot, but also reporters, who caught him lying about it. Reagan had to explain the loss of 218 marines in Lebanon, a good many more than the eight lost in Carter's Iran rescue attempt.

Would these incidents have unraveled the media influence of a Taft, Harding, Carter, or Hoover? We think it probable.

The Public-Relations Style

Presidents Johnson, Nixon, Ford, and Carter all failed in trying to apply old techniques of cooperation and conflict in a media scene now dominated by television.

If Michael Robinson and Margaret A. Sheehan are correct, television network news began in 1963 to change citizens' way of looking at politics and politicians. Robinson and Sheehan argue that television news has "made us all more presidential, more political, more volatile, and more cynical than we were in the era of traditional print, or even traditional radio."[11]

The Reagan administration, during its successful first term, developed a style suited to the television age, which we call the public-relations style. The Reaganites attempted to use some characteristics of television news reporting to their advantage while playing down the elements that put the president at a disadvantage.

Developing Policy. One of Jody Powell's conclusions after serving as a major Carter aide was that he spent too much time putting out fires — dealing with the daily crises — and not enough time on long range planning.[12] The senior aides in Ronald Reagan's first term did not make that mistake. Assisted by deputy press secretary Larry Speakes, they planned future as well as daily strategies. They knew they had to plan ahead to maximize good news, and also, if possible, to bury bad news.

Reagan had recruited a politically balanced team, rather than one tilted to one wing of the Republican party. His chief of staff was James Baker, a moderate from the George Bush campaign. Baker was offset by senior aide Edwin Meese, a conservative. Michael Deaver, skilled in public relations, became Reagan's communications adviser and chief implementer of what was decided.

They concentrated on actions consistent with announced Reagan policy initiatives. When polls showed that the public disapproved by 2 to 1 of the Reagan education policy because of cutbacks in federal aid, the aides had Reagan unearth an obscure report on merit pay for teachers and begin a series of speeches on school discipline. Opinion on education policy now was 2 to 1 in the president's favor, without, Deaver said, changing the basic policy of cuts and thereby appearing inconsistent.

The president's senior aides decided on a "theme" for each day, what idea would be stressed and how best to present it in one or more newsworthy events. Some of their efforts evolved by trial and error. Press secretary James Brady initially persuaded the president to hold a weekly session with a small group of reporters. The aides wanted stories emphasizing the president's position on the budget and taxes. Instead they got news reports on Reagan's harsh words about the Russians and his criticism of Carter's hostage negotiations. The Reagan team abandoned this approach.

Reagan was also prone to answer off the cuff, but the aides found that these comments also detracted from "the theme for the day." Thus the staff began to limit opportunities for such quotes. Reporters were kept at arm's length. Every press contact was, when possible, carefully planned and staged. Reporters were allowed to cover some events but not others. The pool reporters found that the Secret Service sometimes kept them out of hearing range. Some claimed the helicopter motors were revved up purposely to drown out their questions.

Where possible the news stories presented a president dealing with overall policy but separated from controversy. He was positioned as a mediator above the contestants. At the beginning of the second term, Treasury secretary Donald Regan, as instructed, prepared a tax-cut plan. It was described to the media as "the Treasury plan," rather than "the administration plan." On television the Treasury secretary plaintively asked, "Am I not part of the administration too?"

Media Strategy. Reagan's senior aides decided that the prestige press set the national news agenda. But the visuals on the evening news rather than stories in the prestige press were the average citizen's source of information and there the president must get his message across. But the stories the prestige press emphasized were those featured on the television evening news.

Part of their strategy then was to provide stories for the prestige print media. Just before a summit conference, Hedrick Smith, *The New York Times* chief Washington correspondent, had lunch with Michael Deaver. A few days later a front page story in the *Times* told of the president's vigorous preparations for the summit, how hard he was studying, and how he planned to take detailed notes. All the televised coverage then showed him in that role. Especially gratifying to Deaver was ABC's twice showing the president studiously taking notes.[13]

Photo Opportunities. Visuals were carefully planned in settings that seemed less rigidly posed. The Reagans made a surprise trip to Thomas Jefferson's home, Monticello, in Charlottesville, Virginia. The president was photographed sitting in the dugout of the world-champion Baltimore Orioles on opening day, biting into a hot dog. Television commentators could make deprecating comments when these visuals were broadcast.

But to the Reagan "spin doctors" the important fact was that millions saw pictures that buttressed the president's favorable image. The team assumed, and were probably correct, that viewers would remember the image and forget the spoken criticism.

The Reagan aides also designed media events to show a president on the job. Deaver is also credited with transforming the First Lady's image from one who buys expensive new china and donates old gowns to charity for a tax break, to a woman who frequently appears with handicapped children and is involved in fighting drug abuse.

Technical Expertise. The visuals were of high technical quality. The Reagan aides were fortunate in that Reagan was a media professional. As a former actor he appreciated how minute details can affect photographed images. Before the crucial second debate in 1984, he and Michael Deaver went into the Kansas City studio to check the lighting. Deaver stayed up in the camera area while Reagan stood at the microphone. "Mr. President," said Deaver, "there's a reflection in your left eye." Reagan removed his contact lenses. "It's still there, Mr. President," Deaver shouted down. The president looked carefully up at the lights using technical skills honed in Hollywood. He shouted back to Deaver and pointed, "Block out that klieg light there!" When it went out Deaver shouted down, "It's gone now, Mr. President."

Handling Reporters. At state dinners reporters and photographers were required to appear in black-tie dress, or they were barred from the affair. The aides believed it inhibited somewhat the spirit of irreverence.

Reporters complained that they were being cut off from Ronald Reagan, that they were being effectively stonewalled. But Reagan without prompting adopted a major feature of the cooperative-control style — in public he maintained friendly, confident, and nonconfrontational personal relations with journalists. He called reporters by their first names. To the television viewer he did not seem isolated from journalists. Even when confronted with critical questions, as he sometimes was in press conferences, Reagan sidestepped pleasantly. Viewers then wrote in criticizing the lack of manners and boorishness of the reporters asking the questions.

The Reagan technique of creating a friendly public image on television by planned visuals had a secondary purpose as well. Daily ceremonial activities in which he congratulated some Olympic wrestler on behalf of the nation kept him in the public eye. Though reporters claimed the president was isolated, again he did not appear so to the average citizen who every night saw him on the evening news, going about his duties.

DOONESBURY

Reporters attempted to break through the shield surrounding the president. Sam Donaldson of ABC developed the technique of shouting questions while the president was in transit. Reagan, cupping his ear while ducking under helicopter blades and good-naturedly motioning that he can't hear, became almost a symbol of his friendly but distant media relations.

Sara Fritz of the *Los Angeles Times*, president of the White House Correspondents Association, complained, "What I find absolutely revolting about the whole situation — and it was introduced by President Reagan — is that policy is now communicated by three questions shouted over the roof of a car. I have actually heard reporters yell, 'What about the Middle East?' Is that any way to discuss foreign policy?"

Handling Failure. Does the public-relations planning always work? No, not when the policy itself is questionable. Withdrawal of the marines from Lebanon was a major public-relations botch. Five days before he pulled the marines out, the president responded to House Speaker Thomas P. O'Neill with, "He [the Speaker] may be ready to surrender, but I'm not." Three days before the withdrawal he promised in his weekly radio speech that he would never "cut and run." Later he said the administration had already decided "in principle" to redeploy the troops. But Defense Secretary Weinberger and the chair of the Joint Chiefs of Staff said they weren't aware of any such decision. Then others added their versions. It was like the catastrophes that follow in football when a play is broken up and a back tries an unexpected lateral.[14]

Reagan's second term, almost from the start, was a public-relations failure. Every member of the senior-aide team of the first term went to a different position, Deaver leaving government service altogether.

Donald Regan, as chief of staff, headed a new team of senior aides heavily weighted with conservative Republicans.

Part of their lack of success was due to faulty execution. But more to blame was the choosing of faulty policies to implement. Chief of staff Regan deferred to the president when the earlier team would have presented alternative arguments. The basic mistake, perhaps, was the assumption that all the White House team need do was "let Reagan be Reagan."

The Iran–Contra scandal of the second term points up the dangers inherent in the PR style. First it requires competent aides. The president cannot plan all the activities required. He needs aides who will warn him away from compromising situations and hasty actions. Second, the president may become too detached from the policy making, too "laid back" and dependent on aides to make the policy decisions. One of Reagan's journalistic supporters, columnist George Will, bluntly criticized Reagan in his second term for becoming "slothful" and "lazy."[15]

The situation improved slightly when skilled politician Howard Baker became chief of staff and created a better-balanced team of advisers.

Public Relations and the Future. The public-relations style is likely to be adopted by some future presidents, especially if the media continue their aggressive, Mike Wallace style, adversarial approach to politicians. Not all presidents will have the pleasant media manner of a Ronald Reagan, but party managers will be looking for that telegenic quality. And not all presidents will be as competent a media professional as the former Hollywood actor-president. But they will all have media technicians with those skills to advise them.

OTHER ACTORS IN PRESIDENTIAL MEDIA RELATIONS

Besides the president and his chief aides, White House media relations involve four other groups. The president interacts most frequently with a select body of journalists, the White House press corps. Presidents also have three types of media assistants; the press secretary heading the press office, speechwriters, and specialized media technocrats.

The White House Press Corps

At one time the White House was the most prestigious news beat. Still rated high, it is now considered a somewhat lower assignment than the State Department or general politics.

More than 1,700 reporters are accredited to cover the White House, but only about sixty or so "regulars" are full time. Another hundred or so check in from time to time depending on events in the news.

Of the regulars, like other Washington reporters, many are in their thirties and early forties, most white and male. They differ from other Washington reporters in that most represent prestigious media outlets. They include a contingent of old-timers and a few representing foreign media, and more often than other journalists their media sponsors rotate them to fit the characteristics of the incumbent president. Thus CBS sent Dan Rather, a fellow Texan, to the White House when Lyndon Johnson became president. Often the reporter who covered the president during his primary and election campaign becomes White House correspondent, as did Ed Bradley of CBS when Jimmy Carter took office and Bill Plante when Ronald Reagan moved in.

Reporting the President. The White House press corps gathers most news at the daily briefing that the president's press secretary gives, and from news releases the press office prepares. They also get some information by phoning members of the White House staff. Presidential interviews are relatively rare, but the White House corps attends all the president's speeches and travel with him everywhere.

They form the core group of the 500 or so reporters of the capitol press who attend the presidential press conferences. They have the seats up front. They are the group from whom the president chooses most questioners, though not the sole journalists to be called upon. The senior White House wire-service reporter, for many years Helen Thomas of UPI, has the first question, and closes these sessions with the customary words, "Thank you, Mr. President."

Press-Corps Problems. White House correspondents much of the time are prisoners of the press secretary and the press room that they inhabit. Columnist Russell Baker of *The New York Times* said he felt like a sycophant or courtier to a king, like men and ladies in waiting. No longer can these reporters roam freely through the executive office building digging out stories. And as we have seen, presidents and their aides have become very adept at news management with these standby journalists.[16]

White House press-corps members complain that much of the news they are given is inconsequential. Rosalynn Carter's press secretary set up a photo opportunity for the press to talk to daughter Amy, who had spent all night in her new tree house. Ed Bradley of CBS commented, "This is the sort of thing that eats up our time. Photo opportunities, briefings, releases, more photo opportunities. Most of it doesn't mean a damn thing. But the White House grinds it out and we eat it up. The network wants everything we can give them on the President. It's like *Jaws* over there. The jaws are always open."[17]

But the corps had a new complaint under Ronald Reagan — lack of contact with the president. They found the on-the-run "door stoppers," the quick question and answer sessions, resulted in one-liners when they got any response at all. *Newsday* correspondent Susan Page concluded, "They're communicating right over our heads. We're just vessels carrying their message."[18]

Timothy Crouse voiced a different complaint, pointing out how easily intimidated and co-opted the White House corps were during the Nixon years. They did not uncover or pursue the Watergate story, perhaps, he suggests, because many preferred to think of themselves "as part of the White House, and they proudly identified themselves as being 'from the White House press' instead of mentioning the paper they worked for."[19]

The Press Secretary

Herbert Gans, in his ten-year study of news stories, found that the president is the source of 20 percent of the nation's domestic news.[20] Much of that information comes to the public through the president's press secretary, his official media representative.

Presidents may hire and fire press secretaries without asking anyone else's permission. Generally the secretaries are journalists or from public relations. But Jody Powell, whom journalists regarded as effective, was a political-science graduate student and Carter campaign aide. Bill Moyers, a secretary for Lyndon Johnson, was trained as a Baptist minister.

Mutual Trust. The most important quality for a press secretary is to have the president's trust. Reporters suspected that Lyndon Johnson had the press room bugged while George Reedy was secretary, lest Reedy give out news that Johnson felt he should not. Reedy denies it was. Jerry terHorst resigned after a month on the job because President Ford did not tell him about the Nixon pardon until one day before he announced it.

In some administrations the press secretary has been only a technician who channels the president's views to journalists.[21] Some, as Powell was to Carter, and Hagerty to Eisenhower, were among those presidents' closest advisers. But all are necessarily involved in much presidential decision making, if only as observers, for they will have to explain or defend that which is decided. They generally attend cabinet and National

Security Council meetings, and are present at White House strategy sessions.

The secretary meets with the president four or five times a day and has a direct phone to the president and a nearby office in the west wing of the White House. The secretary travels everywhere with the president, a closeness that had tragic consequences for Reagan's press secretary, James S. Brady. An unsuccessful assassin severely wounded him following a speech the president made at the Washington Hilton.

The Press Office. The press secretary heads the press office and organizes it, subject to presidential approval. Some deputy press secretaries may be specialists, as in foreign affairs. Another may serve as communications director, planning and coordinating public-affairs activities of the president with executive agencies. The Office of Media Liaison, headed by an associate secretary, prepares news releases on specialized topics, particularly for reporters who do not attend the briefings. Press-office aides prepare the White House News Summary for the president, a daily digest of news and comment from around the nation, and a weekly digest of magazine articles. Nixon had a special office of telecommunications. In all the press office may employ up to 500 people.

News Briefings. The secretary's principal duty is the daily briefing that occurs around 11 A.M. and other briefings as the news warrants. As Ford's press secretary, Jerry terHorst observed that for every briefing the press secretary has to have some idea which headlines and television stories he or she hopes will come out.

Every day, the press secretary has to answer or parry the questions reporters ask, including those in the group of five or six who often dominate these sessions, described by fellow reporters as "the zanies." The banter back and forth may reach a tone that reporter Richard Reeves described as "Washington testy."

It helps if the press secretary has a sense of humor. Jody Powell, Carter's press secretary was asked about a note in a *Washington Post* gossip column stating that Hamilton Jordan, Carter's chief aide, "never wears — in fact, has never owned — a pair of underwear in his whole life." Powell answered that "Hamilton Jordan does not wish to respond to questions about his underwear. It is his position that the author of that piece will be the last one to know, one way or the other."[22]

Other Duties. The secretary may pass along the president's criticisms of the press or of individual reporters. Kennedy also instructed his press secretary, Pierre Salinger, to be on the lookout for "hidden bomb" questions from reporters about matters which were troubling them and which might surface in news stories later. In turn, the press secretary may also become the reporter's advocate to the president, arguing that certain information should be released or that the president should hold a press conference soon.

In several administrations the secretary has also prepared the president for questions that may be asked in press conferences or following speeches. This task includes supervising the preparation of briefing books out of reports from the various departments and rehearsing the president with mock questions.

White House correspondents occasionally complain that the secretary too often is unavailable. A five-minute uninterrupted interview is a rarity. At the same time journalists want a secretary who is involved in what the president is doing. At one of his first press briefings, Reagan's press secretary Jim Brady was unable to answer a question requiring inside information. A reporter growled at Brady, "The question is, Jim, why don't you know?"[23]

The Success of James Hagerty. Hagerty, who had been a working journalist, skilfully aided the president, saving up stories to release when Eisenhower was on vacation or golfing so that it appeared the president was on the job. He also showed compassion for the White House correspondents. He invented the press pool, the small rotating group of correspondents who ride on the president's plane and report later to the others. He also devised the "lid," a flat guarantee that no routine announcement would be made during lunchtime or after 5 P.M. The lid is now a star in the press room that lights when no news is to be given, and two stars when no more routine news is to be expected for the day.

Hagerty also made friends for the president. A Michigan editor and political columnist told our students that his first national assignment was covering President Eisenhower's trip to the Philippines. On the long flight back, Hagerty sat down beside him and asked if he had gotten any special stories for his chain of eight Michigan papers. The reporter ruefully admitted he had not. Hagerty then suggested that the reporter interview him. The editor told the class, "I had an exclusive story to send back to my papers and I never forgot Hagerty's kindness."

Dan Rather went on the same trip, also, he says, "a nobody from nowhere." And on the way home Hagerty also gave him an exclusive interview so that he too would have a special story that might justify the trip to his sponsors. Hagerty clearly took care of more than media stars. Rather writes, "Of all the men who have spoken, and misspoken on behalf of the presidents of the United States, the model for the job ought to be Ike's man, James C. Hagerty."[24]

Presidential Speechwriters

The president and his aides know that a broadcast speech may be the best opportunity he has to discuss his proposals and present his reasons for making them. He can highlight the issues he wants on the national agenda. He is not facing questioning reporters who skip from subject to subject and who are trying to trap him into a slip.

His aides know that the electronic and print analyses that follow the speech will focus on the implications of the policy proposed rather than its content. A speech on reforms in Medicare will be analyzed by its effect on senior citizens or the medical profession and less on its rationale.

Such speeches are also political entertainment. Television and radio will carry some in full and may excerpt highlights from others. Print media give detailed summaries.

In a televised speech, the president has a chance to create a nationally shared experience. Franklin Roosevelt's radio broadcasts, the Fireside Chats, achieved this intimacy.

The Reagan Technique. Skill in making speeches earned President Reagan the title "The Great Communicator." He gave the same careful attention to preparing a major speech that Roosevelt did. Franklin Roosevelt was perhaps the first to admit without apology that he had help in writing his speeches, including the Pulitzer prize-winning playwright and author, Robert E. Sherwood. But like most other presidents, Roosevelt edited and put his own mark on every speech he gave.

A major Reagan speechwriter, Peggy Noonan, had worked at CBS as writer of Dan Rather's radio spots and some of his television news comments. She says, "I continually stop and mouth what I've just written, and say it to myself, to see if it's got the right sound . . . . What I learned to do in radio is to write for the ear . . . . A speech is not for the eye."

And she fits her prose to the speaker's personality. She says, "Dan [Rather] is direct. Blunt, terse, straight in his prose approach: 'Good morning. It's five o'clock. The sun is up. Let's have fun'. While with President Reagan, there is a more ambling quality. I sometimes imagine a sailor ambling along the deck of a ship on the rolling sea. That's more President Reagan's style."[25]

Reagan received drafts from his major writers and then revised them. Stuart K. Spencer, long a political aide, says, "The stuff that cranks up the crowd, the stuff that gets him sailing, that's his stuff. And he works at the pauses, the applause lines, the sequence." Reagan then would take "a meticulously honed, well-rehearsed script" and put it on a TelePrompTer. He found that using cards, as he had before he was president, sometimes made him lose eye contact with the audience.

Reagan's TelePrompTer reflected the speech onto two glass shields. The audience saw clear glass; the president, on three directions, saw the half-inch-high words moving across the mirrored surfaces. And as he read, the president watched for cues from the audience. Says Spencer, "he really is sensitive to the vibrations he picks up, to the looks in people's eyes as he speaks."[26]

President Reagan hoped to get across a positive image of his character and personality. Franklin Roosevelt did the same. He began all his speeches with, "My Friends." Many listeners responded as if they knew him personally. An admiring Spencer claimed about President Reagan, "there's a whole other aspect to this guy that's not verbal. It's the comfort-factor. He's a comfort for the listeners. That's not just developed, but what the man is all about inside. If you're mean, nasty, it comes out. If you're an upbeat, sincere, happy person, that comes through. So a great part of his communication skill is that these things, over time, have come through to the people."[27]

Media Technocrats

All these aides to the president are technical specialists who help him in his media relations. But television and polling techniques have added others from the advertising or entertainment industries. Critics often dismiss them with the faint contempt associated with the word "technocrat."

George Reedy discusses the changes these technocrats have brought to the presidency: "As a stage, the White House has no equal in the electronic age. It is equipped with props that cannot be matched by Hollywood, Broadway, and Madison Avenue combined. It is staffed by technicians capable of solving the most difficult electronics problems in the wink of an eye."[28]

How important is this technical advice? When vice-presidential candidate Geraldine Ferraro answered journalists' questions about her income taxes, she did two things that disturbed technocrats expert in television communication. She sat down. And she wore a blouse that blended with the brick wall behind her. When Walter Mondale spoke in the presidential debates, he had white papers on the stand before him that reflected on his face, accentuating the bags under his eyes. Were these details important? The Reagan senior aides thought so.[29]

The other experts presidents depend upon are the opinion pollsters. Their techniques may be equally esoteric. But the political value of the results they produce is easier to understand than that of the television technocrats.

THE PRESIDENTIAL PRESS CONFERENCE

Presidents, like the rest of us, avoid situations in which they risk being put on the defensive. They may face them in election campaigns and less frequently after giving a speech. But aides can help out, and a quick escape is generally possible. Even spouses may provide the needed protection. Nancy Reagan was caught on camera supplying words to the president in such a situation.

But once a televised press conference has begun, the president is alone and vulnerable. Custom allows the journalists to decide when the questioning will end, though if the conference lasted much more than the half hour the networks allot the president could probably end it. Since President Kennedy, press conferences have been televised live. As Dan Rather correctly observed, it is the only time the president is stripped of all protection.[30]

Still, the president sets most of the rules. He decides how often, when, and where to have a press conference, whom to call on, and whether his response has answered the question.[31]

Journalists get restive if the president lets more than a month go by without a press conference. They agree with Jody Powell that when the period between conferences stretches to two or three months, "There is no way for any human to keep at his fingertips all the information that might be needed."[32]

The Informal Press Conference

Woodrow Wilson held the first presidential press conferences. He was a political-science professor who admired the British parliamentary system, particularly the "question period." Four days a week while Parliament is in session, the prime minister or other members of the cabinet must submit to an hour or so of questions from other members of Parliament. Wilson hoped his press conferences would serve as an American substitute, a time in which the president would be questioned seriously about his proposals.

But Wilson was disappointed. Reporters did not behave as the president had wanted. They asked questions that he regarded as frivolous and sometimes even insulting. The war gave Wilson the excuse he was looking for to end the conferences.

Warren Harding, who succeeded Wilson, revived the press conference, but was not very good at it. He made a major blooper on an impending four-power treaty. His Secretary of State, Charles Evans Hughes, demanded that thereafter questions be written in advance so that the president could be instructed what to say.

Calvin Coolidge held two press conferences a week, more than any president before or since. But they were, one observer said, "a transparent political hoax." Coolidge made the sessions almost meaningless by answering the questions only when he wished to. But he stonewalled with finesse. One day the dozen or so reporters in attendance conspired to corner him: all submitted the same written question on an important issue. Coolidge thumbed through the stack reading each card until he came to the last one. Looking up, he blandly said, "A writer wants me to state my opinion about the condition of children in Puerto Rico," a question no one had asked. He then began a dry speech on that topic lasting fifteen or twenty minutes. The reporters got the message.

Herbert Hoover, a shy man, dutifully held about sixteen press conferences a year. The low point came when reporters detected him in a lie. Hoover turned to giving out important news to a few sympathetic reporters ("the trained seals"), rather than in press conferences.

The Roosevelt Press Conferences. Franklin Roosevelt was especially adept at using the press conference to keep himself and his policies in the news. The informal and partly off-the-record press conference reached its prime under his skilful direction. The handicapped president was seated at his desk as reporters filed into his office at two regularly scheduled times each week, once in a morning session and once in the afternoon, thus giving neither morning nor afternoon papers an advantage. Roosevelt knew that editors would hold open a news hole for his news, and used the sessions to influence what went on the national agenda.

At the White House from 100 to as many as 200 reporters gathered around his desk, and the president fielded questions just as the reporters asked them. But he insisted that they play by his rules. A few questions he would not answer at all, especially hypothetical questions that Roosevelt called "iffy" questions. As we have seen, he set down guidelines on how his information could be reported.

Roosevelt clearly enjoyed these sessions. He held 998 press conferences, an average of 82 a year up to his death. He chatted with reporters as they filed in around his desk; those new to the beat received a handshake and a comment, and he joked and talked seriously about questions he was still wrestling with. He prepared the journalists for stories coming up, spiked rumors, and helped them check leads.

Mrs. Roosevelt also held press conferences, which she limited to women reporters; she had her own affirmative-action program, designed to give these often discriminated against journalists some exclusives.[33]

Press Conferences Become Theatrical Spectacles

By the end of World War II, the number of reporters attending had so increased that they no longer fit in a White House office. Truman moved the conference to the Indian Treaty Room at the State Department.

The Truman Conferences. Presidential news conferences became formal and impersonal. The president strode in after the reporters had found their places in rows of theater seats. He mounted a raised platform. They now called out for the president's attention. Soon it was found both he and the reporters needed microphones. Truman introduced recording equipment to keep the record straight, later allowing parts of the recordings to be rebroadcast. Presidential press conferences were now on the record.

The press conference also took on a more confrontational character. Sometimes Truman retorted with just a "yes" or "no." Or he would give his unflattering opinion of the questioner rather than answer the question. He dismissed one press conference in seven minutes, as though the reporters had been bad boys and girls.

And he got into trouble with his public off-the-cuff answers. Asked if use of the atomic bomb was being considered in the Korean War, he snapped back that "the atom bomb is always under consideration." In some reports he was quoted with the word "always" left out.

The Eisenhower Conferences. Truman's successor, Dwight Eisenhower, disliked press conferences and held them out of duty or because Hagerty told him he had to. He was distant with reporters but stayed outwardly friendly. He called on reporters, not by name, but by pointing and saying things like, "the young man with the glasses next to the lady with the red hair." And when a conference ended, he rewarded himself by taking the rest of the day off at the Burning Tree golf course.

Under Eisenhower, one further step in formalization occurred — video recording. Hagerty insisted on reviewing the tapes before their release for broadcast. But his cuts were minor and only to correct what he called "bloopers."

The Kennedy Conferences. John Kennedy handled the 400 reporters he faced masterfully, much as a skilled conductor draws music out of a symphony orchestra. At the suggestion of his press secretary, Pierre Salinger, he authorized live broadcasts. He memorized the names of reporters, knew where the regulars would usually sit, prepared carefully for expected questions, and added touches of light humor.

Kennedy turned the conference into political entertainment for the television audience. He campaigned over the heads of reporters to the citizens watching on television. And the reporters also started campaigning — they wanted their bosses to see them on television asking questions and advertising the media outlet. Under Eisenhower, the reporters had been asked to state their name and affiliation. Kennedy dropped the practice because he thought it encouraged self-advertisers.

Kennedy skillfully manipulated the sessions. He would avoid some reporters. He had ordered a North American Air Defense Command (NORAD) alert involving Canadian planes under his command rather than that of their own prime minister, John Diefenbaker. A Canadian reporter said about the session that followed, "The president knows me all right. I was on my feet six times, but he passed me by every time." And when Kennedy was being pursued too closely, he called on specific reporters, especially Sarah McClendon, who represented several small Texas papers. She could be depended upon to change the subject with a question that no one else had thought to ask. And in his responses he sometimes made her the target of his humor, a practice more accepted in those days than today.

David Schoenbrun of CBS wrote about Kennedy, "No one could think more quickly on his feet, with spontaneous wit . . . . All of us reporters looked forward to his news conferences every other week . . . . His quick sallies, his deft way of turning questions back, had us roaring throughout the conferences. He was the first great performer of the television age."[34]

Post-Kennedy Press Conferences. Since Kennedy, press conferences have gone downhill. Journalists believe that the number of press conferences drops off in direct ratio to the trouble a president is in. But presidents may avoid them simply because they do not perform well.

Johnson avoided press conferences because he hated being compared with Kennedy. He invented the "snap press conference," called at a moment's notice so that the number of reporters would be small and the questions not too well prepared. Some of these he held as he strode around the Ellipse on the White House grounds. Television cameras couldn't easily follow and reporters had trouble keeping up, writing down answers precisely, or even hearing what he said.

Nixon, Carter, and Reagan reduced the number of conferences held as their terms advanced. Carter devised a substitute that he called "televised town meetings." Citizens rather than reporters asked the questions, often underhand set ups.

The Reagan Press Conferences. Press conferences are a special problem for a public-relations style like Reagan's. They allow journalists to grill the president on prime-time television. And a public-relations style president is at his worst in this kind of unstructured situation, which requires unprepared thoughtful arguments rather than one-liners.

Reagan's press-conference style provides examples of the possible pitfalls and how they might be lessened. He made major problems for himself by proneness to gaffes. His aides often had to explain later "what he really meant." Few politicians are as quick on their feet as Kennedy was. Reagan's uncertainty was perhaps most clearly revealed by the habit that Jack Germond and Jules Witcover called his "disjointed, uncertain ramblings."[35]

How then could Reagan's aides structure press conferences so that they would do least damage, and perhaps occasionally offer an advantage? Like all recent presidents, Reagan was thoroughly briefed on expected questions. But also from another room, he scanned the audience ahead of time on a television monitor to find out who was there and where they were sitting, presumably so that he could turn to a friendly questioner if he felt cornered.

One technique he used was filibustering in order to eat up time. Reagan sometimes opened the session with a long statement. At one conference the statement took five minutes. Helen Thomas of UPI then extended the conference an extra five minutes before shouting out her "Thank you, Mr. President." Reagan's reaction was in character, "Helen, I was beginning to think you'd never say that this evening!"

And his sometimes long responses to questions wandered from the point. These "broad generalities," Lesley Stahl of CBS believed, were not accidental but were part of an overall strategy that believes a successful news conference is one that makes no news. [36]

Reporters claimed Reagan's favorite way of sidestepping was to say he could not speak out because the matter was under study. He would hold up his reply until a cabinet member reported back, or until some future cabinet meeting had a chance to discuss the question, or until a commission on the subject reported its findings.

Reagan also attempted to keep sessions from becoming confrontational by making small jokes, like his response to Helen Thomas. And he called correspondents by their first names. Lars-Erik Nelson of *The New York Daily News* says it made him feel like "Ron's prop." He wrote, "He [Reagan] pointed at me and said 'Bob Thompson.' I looked at him. My look said 'Harpo Marx.' He looked at me. His look said, 'oh-oh.' " Then the president pointed his finger at Peter Brown of Scripps-Howard and called out 'Al.' " Nelson wrote, "Peter is smarter than I am. He got up anyway and asked a question."[37]

In Reagan's second press conference, questioners were chosen by lot. The aides perhaps thought this tactic would defuse the big guns of the capitol press corps, who are those normally called on. These reporters objected strongly, and aides realized at the same time that a lottery was a big gamble for the president — it opened up the possibility that a very peculiar questioner might be chosen. The experiment was dropped.

The president's aides were more successful in other "reforms." They worked out an entrance and exit arrangement to the East Room, cutting off the possibility of questions to the president in transit. And from the beginning Reagan insisted that reporters not stand and bellow to be called on. Rather they would sit, or more realistically, half crouch, and hold up hands. The aides hoped this procedure would add a measure of decorum, put some reporters off balance, and perhaps reduce the confrontational atmosphere.

But the results were still far from satisfactory from a public-relations point of view. The president still was at his most unprotected. The Reagan team then appeared to have decided that the best strategy was to avoid press conferences as much as possible. Ronald Reagan set the record among recent presidents for infrequency of press conferences.

Informal Meetings. The Reagan White House devised another technique to allow some press contact, but under more control. Beginning in 1983, President Reagan once again began meeting with selected reporters, late in the afternoon, in backgrounder and off-the-record sessions. He created the cozy kind of informal and friendly mood that had characterized Roosevelt's press conferences. As with Roosevelt, staff aides could also be present to help out. And the reporters found that the relaxed atmosphere without the television cameras encouraged follow-up queries and presidential candor.

But the Reagan conferences differed from Roosevelt's in several ways. The meetings lacked continuity of participants, because the president rotated those invited. And he could screen out the mob of journalists from minor or foreign enterprises, the zanies, and anyone who published

"...COMING TO YOU LIVE FROM THE PRESIDENT'S LARGE INTESTINE!"

© Universal Press Syndicate, 1985 by permission of Universal Press Syndicate

material that was off the record. Also, if he wished (but there is no evidence he did so), he could punish some reporters by not including them often or at all.

Reagan also granted a few individual interviews. But journalists remarked that during the first three and a half years in office, Reagan granted no personal interviews to a representative of *The New York Times*, another record.

Future of Press Conferences. For reporters the press conference has become a game of hounds chasing a fox, of reporters trying to corner the president before a national audience. In 1987 Senator Alan Simpson (R-Wyoming) accused reporters of being "sadistic" for forcing Reagan into a conference on the Iran–Contra scandal. The purpose of the conference, he implied, was not to gather information but to destroy the president.

For most presidents, the press conference is a trial. It can be a way to inform the country on matters he thinks important, but most presidents probably think there are better ways, and so they try to sidestep embarrassing questions gracefully. Dan Rather says Eisenhower avoided answering by applying his peculiar syntax, Kennedy with humor, Johnson with the stare and the blowtorch phrase, and Richard Nixon waffled.[38]

Some argue that the tradition should be discontinued or changed back to off-the-record informal sessions. They say a theatrical performance may be entertaining but it generally reveals little news. President Reagan's press secretary, Larry Speakes, said just before he resigned, "The press conference in its present form is...an East Room extravaganza . . . a battle of wits . . . too much of it boils down to: How can we get 'em to say what they don't want to say? Somehow we need to get away from this 'I gotcha' syndrome."

But columnist William Safire disagrees: "The press conference tradition is not merely to put on a lively show, which it does, or to help the people understand their leaders, which it also does. The regularity of a formal press conference disciplines an administration and makes a better president."[39]

Some presidents perhaps do not welcome being disciplined.

MEDIA INFLUENCE ON PRESIDENTIAL GOVERNING

Television-age coverage has affected presidential governing in at least three ways: changes in the style of governing, the content of policy, and the new constraints it imposes.

Style of Governing

Charles Peters, editor of *Washington Monthly*, contends that much of what passes for news is make-believe that politicians and journalists create for each other. Reporters, he says, no longer look behind the public-relations hoopla to find out what is really happening. They care about style — images rather than reality.[40]

A president announces a bold new policy with fanfare. Is this reality? Politicians know that journalists usually are not very good at follow-through. The nitty-gritty of carrying out a policy lacks the drama in the gesture of announcement. Two weeks later, matters other than the "massive war on crime" or whatever have captured their attention. Six months later, only in an occasional think piece will a reporter try to assess the results.

Television encourages a public-relations style of politicking — exploiting the presidential personality and creating other gimmicks and stunts. Presidents and their aides provide these gimmicks as a form of self-promotion. One may almost say that the duties and responsibilities of being president today require being the nation's chief political entertainer.

But should we be wholly disdainful of all make-believe? Our great presidents generally have been able to symbolize their policies in gestures that we would now call part of public relations. And presidents who accomplished a great deal but lacked these skills, as James K. Polk did, are the poorer in our memories for it. And we note that our mediocre presidents have generally also been those who lacked color and a sense of the power in symbolic actions. Presidents represent our nation and its aspirations in such gestures; we expect of them actions that Russell Baker calls making "music to lift the weary spirit."

But now we have come to expect these gestures almost daily for the evening news. In the future all presidents, the great as well as the mediocre, will need to exercise these public relations skills to survive comfortably.

Reagan's team defused the feud with son Michael by applying these skills. An ordinary public-relations group would have been content with Michael prominently displayed at the second inaugural, perhaps having a long chat with the president. That scene was arranged. But the media image, the one tugging at the hearts of all parents and grandparents, was put across by the pictures of a president out on the back lawn helping his grandchild build a snowman.

The Policy Content. Some, observing the political make-believe, conclude that all content has disappeared from policy making, that anything left is only show.

The Reagan administration's public-realtions sense during his first term was among the finest tuned. Its goal was to alter public perceptions of policies that were needed. It would be difficult to argue that this effort was lacking in policy content. The policy shifts, both foreign and domestic, which President Reagan accomplished were substantial.

We are left, though, with a question: Did the public-relations techniques of the Reaganites allow a president to push through programs that Americans unwittingly supported? If they had known what they were getting without the make-believe, would the public have supported these policies?

This is a perennial question with which defenders of democracy must struggle. As long ago as the Revolutionary War we have had media events such as the Boston Tea Party, which the patriot Sam Adams engineered, and which we celebrate fondly today. Bostonians, dressed as Indians, boarded British ships and dumped tea into Boston harbor. Perhaps this make-believe stampeded some citizens of the day into feeling that a war with the British was inevitable.

One either has the faith that eventually the citizens will see through public-relations gimmicks to their own best interest and that of the nation, and agree or disagree with the policy, or one does not. Abraham Lincoln resolved the issue with the now-hackneyed statement, "It is true that you may fool all the people some of the time, you can even fool some of the people all the time, but you can't fool all of the people all the time."

The New Constraints on Presidents

The clearest influence of television-age coverage is that every evening the president is on trial to prove himself.

Measuring Performance. The media are now armed with statistical measures — of the president's popularity, of economic indicators from unemployment to inflation, and of innumerable other indices that suggest failure or success in policy initiatives, such as the crime rate and infant-mortality rates.[41]

Journalists are quick also to search out any hint of scandal and will highlight members of Congress who investigate. If President Reagan thought that, by admitting his administration had sent arms to Iran, he had defused the issue, he was wrong.

The president is always running. During his first term it is for reelection. During his second it is for what the history books will say about him. But if neither of these matters, he has to run just to stay in place, to preserve the popularity and therefore the power to influence policy; otherwise he is a lame duck.

Making Decisions. The attention drawn by television increases the pressure for action — quick action. During the Iran hostage crisis, each night the network news announcements giving the "days-in-captivity-count" was like a steady drip, drip, drip on Jimmy Carter's head. Something had to be done. And the hastily conceived and inadequately planned rescue attempt was the answer the president gave. Television wants action now to light up the screen.

Television also allows outside interests to penetrate presidential decision making more easily. An event that once appeared as a small item in the inside pages of newspapers now takes prominence when announced over the national network news. Ralph Nader or the National Audubon Society or the plight of the nation's farmers as their representatives describe it, cannot as easily be brushed aside. Some defenders of President Reagan argued that the pressure caused by television interviews with relatives of hostages in Beirut led to the policy of trading arms for hostages. George Will commented that this was a softhearted president who cried while watching episodes of *Little House on the Prairie.*

The danger in television pressures is that the president will lose control of the national agenda, he may have a policy forced on him much as the peace groups used television coverage to force the government to alter policy during the Vietnam War.

And this increased interest in presidential decision making is combined, in the eyes of all our presidents since Kennedy, with the need to tighten government security. Each television-age president has become more intent than his predecessor on keeping executive-office information confidential than previous presidents have.

The Media Alliance with Bureaucrats. Austin Ranney suggests that television has caused presidents to lose power over policy implementation and that government bureaucrats have filled the vacuum. He argues that public-relations demands on the office leave the president less time for "the Herculean task of trying to get the executive agencies to do what he wants them to do."[42]

He points out, as we will see again in Chapter 8, that media coverage of the bureaucracy is minimal compared to the coverage given elected officials. Bureaucrats do not desire publicity for themselves and the issues they raise rarely result in the kinds of visuals that television desires. And the bureaucrats, the most frequent leakers of information, are thereby doubly protected from scrutiny.

A Closing Note

As you review the parts of this chapter you may be struck with the degree to which television has brought to the surface tendencies that have been part of our American system of governing from the beginning. American politicians have always brought an element of theatrics and symbolism to the political stage, and television merely increases their opportunities.

More important, the Founders designed a government that would counter career ambition with career ambition and thus preserve freedom. Creating a government that could act efficiently and with dispatch was their lesser priority. Television reinforces the decentralization and frag-mentation that the Founders sought for the American system of governance.

In a sense, television reporting is also the logical outcome hoped for by those democratic theorists who wanted the people to have more influence over their governors. It not only legitimizes opposition but encourages criticism of the president and the others who govern us. Television also, more than other media, encourages groups of citizens to attempt to wrest control of the political agenda from officials.

NOTES

1. George E. Reedy, *The Twilight of the Presidency* (New York: New American Library, 1970), p. 105.
2. *U.S. News and World Report* (May 14, 1984), "Current Quotes," p. 16.
3. Michael B. Grossman and Martha Joynt Kumar, "The White House and the News Media: The Phases of Their Relationship," *Political Science Quarterly* 94 (Spring 1979): 37–53.
4. Jarol B. Manheim, "The Honeymoon's Over: The News Conference and the Development of Presidential Style," *Journal of Politics* 41 (1979): 55–74.
5. Gore Vidal, "Nixon Without Knives: Even the Most Skeptical Must Admit: He Knew the Way to China," *Esquire* (December 1983), pp. 66–71.
6. Elmer E. Cornwell, Jr., "The President and the Press: Phases in the Relationship," *The Annals* 427 (September 1976): 53–64.
7. John Mueller, *War, Presidents and Public Opinion* (New York: Wiley, 1973).
8. Samuel Kernell, "Explaining Presidential Popularity: How ad hoc Theorizing, Misplaced Emphasis, and Insufficient Care in Measuring One's Variables Refuted Common Sense and Led Conventional Wisdom Down the Path of Anomalies," *American Political Science Review* 72 (1978): 506–522. See also Richard A. Brody and Benjamin I. Page, "The Impact of Events on Presidential Popularity: The Johnson and Nixon Administrations," in Aaron Wildavsky, ed., *Perspectives on the Presidency* (Boston: Little Brown, 1975), pp. 136–148; and Charles W. Ostrom, Jr., and Dennis M. Simon, "Promise and Performance," *American Political Science Review* 79(1985): 334–358.
9. Timothy Crouse, *The Boys on the Bus* (New York: Ballantine Books, 1972), p. 196.
10. Crouse, *The Boys on the Bus*, pp. 257–290.
11. Michael J. Robinson and Margaret A. Sheehan, *Over the Wire and on TV: CBS and UPI in Campaign '80* (New York: Russell Sage Foundation, 1983), p. 262.
12. Jody Powell, *The Other Side of the Story* (New York: William Morrow, 1984), "White House Flackery," pp. 297–314.
13. Jaroslovsky, "Manipulating the Media Is a Specialty for the White House's Michael Deaver," *Wall Street Journal*, Jan. 5, 1984, p. 42.
14. Rich Jaroslovsky, "White House Trips Over Its Words: Great Communicators?" *Wall Street Journal*, Feb. 16, 1984, p. 54.
15. George Will, "Tower Report Kind to Slothful Reagan," Washington Post Writers Group, March 1, 1987.

16. The material in this section is from Stephen Hess, *The Washington Reporters* (Washington, D.C.: Brookings Institution, 1981), pp. 51–55, 59–60.

17. J. Anthony Lukas, "The White House Press 'Club,' " *New York Times Magazine*, May 15, 1977, p. 22.

18. Jane Mayer, "How Reagan Staff Manages News," *The Wall Street Journal*, Oct. 12, 1984, p. 50.

19. Crouse, *The Boys on the Bus*, Chapter 9, "The Old Squeeze Play," and Chapter 10, "Divided They Fall," pp. 203-256.

20. Herbert J. Gans, *Deciding What's News A Study of CBS Evening News, NBC Nightly News, Newsweek, and Time* (New York: Pantheon Books, 1979).

21. Ron Lovell, "Keepers of the Flame," *The Quill* (February 1981), pp. 9–14.

22. Charles Mohr, "The Not-So-Cool Jody Powell," *New York Times Magazine*, May 15, 1977, p. 68.

23. "Life in the White House Fish Bowl — Brady Takes Charge as Press Chief," *National Journal*, Jan. 31, 1981, pp. 180–183.

24. Dan Rather with Mickey Herskowitz, *The Camera Never Blinks* (New York: Ballantine Books, 1977), pp. 181–184.

25. Robbie Vorhaus, "Peggy Noonan — Presidential Speechwriter," *Northwest Orient* (October 1984), pp. 48–57.

26. George Skelton, "Reagan at Best with Well-Honed Script," *Los Angeles Times*, Oct. 28, 1984, pp. 1, 10–11.

27. Skelton, "Reagan at Best," p. 11.

28. Reedy, *The Twilight of the Presidency*, p. 105.

29. We are indebted for insights and illustrations in this chapter to Ken Bode, NBC correspondent and former colleague in the Department of Political Science, Michigan State University.

30. Rather, *The Camera Never Blinks*, p. 280.

31. The literature on press conferences includes James E. Pollard, *The Presidents and the Press* (New York Macmillan, 1947); Elmer E. Cornwell, Jr., "The Presidential Press Conference: A Study in Institutionalization," *Midwest Journal of Political Science* 4 (November 1960): 370–389; and by the same author, *Presidential Leadership of Public Opinion* (Bloomington: Indiana University Press, 1965); Jarol B. Manheim, "The Honeymoon's Over: The News Conference and the Development of Presidential Style," *Journal of Politics* 41 (1979): 55–74; Jarol B. Manheim and William W. Lammers, "The News Conference and Presidential Leadership of Public Opinion: Does the Tail Wag the Dog?" *Presidential Studies Quarterly* 16 (1986): 177–188; and Kenneth W. Thompson, ed., *Three Press Secretaries on the Presidency and the Press, Jody Powell, George Reedy and Jerry terHorst* (New York: Lanham, 1983.)

32. Powell, *The Other Side of the Story*, p. 306.

33. B. H. Winfield, "Franklin D. Roosevelt's Efforts to Influence the News During His First Term Press Conferences," *Presidential Studies Quarterly* 16 (1986): 189–199.

34. David Schoenbrun, "Great People Who Have Known Me," *Parade Magazine* (Oct. 7, 1984), pp. 8–11.

35. Jack Germond and Jules Witcover, "Reagan Fails Press Meet Test," Gannett syndicated column, Aug. 10, 1981.
36. Leslie Phillips and Karen DeWitt, "Chief Goes in Well-Rehearsed," *USA Today* May 23, 1984.
37. Lars-Erik Nelson, "It's a Privilege to Be Your Prop, Ron," *New York News* syndicated column, Jan. 10, 1983.
38. Dan Rather, *The Camera Never Blinks* p. 292.
39. Quoted in John W. Kole, "Reagan's Silence, Uninformed Aides Leave Reporters Irked, Frustrated," *The Right to Know,* (January–February 1982), p. 47.
40. Charles Peters, *How Washington Really Works* (Reading, Mass.: Addison-Wesley, 1981), Chapter 2, "The Press," pp. 17–34.
41. This section is based in part on insights of Austin Ranney, *Channels of Power: The Impact of Television on American Politics* (New York: Basic Books, 1983). See especially Chapter 5, "Governing in the Television Age," pp. 123–155.
42. Ranney, *Channels of Power*, p. 153.

7

Congress Meets
the Press

When Theodore Roosevelt invited reporters out of the wet and cold and set up a press room for them in the White House, his kindness turned out to be symbolic. Since the beginning of this century, print journalists have regarded the president as the primary source of political news.[1] The president fits the structural needs of today's national media, especially those of television. The president creates reportable political events.

One member of Congress concluded that "Congress, by fulfilling its proper function, just studies and deliberates. Its only easily reportable actions are the final votes taken at the end of a long drawn out process."[2]

CHAPTER OVERVIEW

In this chapter we first compare the print and electronic coverage of the Senate and House of Representatives and assess the Congress as a source of news. Next we focus on the correspondents who report on the Congress and their impact in creating congressional celebrities. We then examine the efforts of legislators to gain favorable press coverage and conclude with a look at the functions of the media during election campaigns.

CONGRESS AS A SOURCE OF NEWS

Journalists understandably treat the president as the center of a political solar system. Measured by newsworthiness, Congress circles the presidential office like a lesser planet caught in its gravitational pull.

The president receives twice as much national television coverage as Congress, in number of stories and air time. Presidential stories are usually placed earlier in television newscasts, a measure of their importance, and are more frequently illustrated with visuals.[3]

The media dominance of the president presents members of Congress with a major media role: for national journalists they become the primary reactors to and critics of presidential initiatives. They represent so many opinions and interests that one can almost always find a legislator who disagrees with what the president does or says.

The work of journalists is greatly simplified if they can present the president as proposing programs to deal with a national problem, report how representatives and senators disagree, and thereby create news of conflict. That conflict and its creators get journalistic attention.

This style of presentation encourages citizens to believe that Congress the institution is significant only if what it does affects presidential prestige. And this attitude influences more than just citizen viewers. Michael Robinson suggests that television coverage has affected members of Congress as well, reshaping their view of opposition as their major role because that is what gets national news coverage.[4]

Regional journalists, though, see the role of a member of Congress differently. For them, individual legislators defend local interests — they are errand runners or skilled politicians who bring benefits back to the locality. The stories that regional journalists report deal with what the representative or senator does on issues affecting the community or state, and often making the legislator out to be something of a celebrity.

CONGRESS: THE INSTITUTIONAL SETTING

Several constitutional provisions shape congressional behavior and contribute to differences in media coverage of House members and senators: the length of terms of office, the number elected to each house, and the special legal powers of the U.S. Senate.

Congressional Behavior

Senate seats are preferred over House seats. Senators serve six years, representatives just two. The Senate has only 100 members, the House, 435. Senators have two distinctive powers they can use to check a president — before a treaty takes effect, they must ratify it, and they must confirm major presidential appointees. Nelson Polsby observes that these differences determine the kinds of legislative activities in which each branch engages.[5]

The House. Leaders of the House of Representatives use numbers to maximize that body's political influence. House organization decentralizes decision making into many specialized committees and subcommittees. Representatives get only a few committee assignments and are encouraged to become expert in a subject.

Representatives advance to positions of power slowly, by their specialized knowledge, by gradually gaining respect of party colleagues, and by seniority. House rules and custom also permit power and influence to develop slowly. The chance to speak on the floor about a bill is limited and often reserved for the relevant committee specialist and those in leadership posts. Maverick behavior is not welcomed.

Many members of Congress have established themselves as household names across the land through televised congressional investigations. Most have become national heroes: Estes Kefauver, Sam Ervin, Peter Rodino, and others. None has used television and other techniques so ruthlessly as did Senator Joseph McCarthy. The tactic eventually brought about his own political demise, as his unbridled and unfounded accusations of Communist sympathizers in federal agencies became apparent when he unjustly accused an attorney in the law firm of Joseph Welch, the army's chief counsel, in 1954. This act shocked and later dismayed millions of viewers, who saw his unethical methods acted out in televised hearings. Indeed, his reputation has lived far beyond his own lifetime — "McCarthyism" is still the label for such unsavory tactics.

© Universal Press Syndicate, 1986 by permission of Universal Press Syndicate

The Senate. Senators are fewer and have longer to develop their influence. Each receives a larger number of committee assignments and usually has unlimited floor time to speak on any topic.

A senator thus has the opportunity almost immediately to go in his or her own way, whether by being a party loyalist or a maverick. Senators are encouraged to deal with topics that are broad in scope and national in their implications. The special responsibility in foreign policy as well as the legal duty to check on major presidential appointments suggest to senators that they are responsible for monitoring the whole range of presidential, and indeed national activities. Moreover, because they represent an entire state, senators are less likely to be controlled or intimidated by an interest group.

The Senate deals less with the nuts and bolts of legislation. Its members are more likely to float new ideas, to debate over the great issues, to publicize demands of groups who do not otherwise get a hearing.

These differences generate competition between the houses and encourage members to feel loyal to their own body. Journalists of course treat the two bodies differently.

House vs. Senate Coverage. Stephen Hess found that network television reported on the Senate about twice as often as the House, by 66 to 34 percent. In newspapers the breakdown was 54 to 46 percent for the Senate. And 73 percent of members of Congress mentioned on network television were senators. The greater expertise of representatives received more play in the printed media. Passing mentions slightly favored senators, also by 54 to 46 percent.[6]

THE CONGRESSIONAL PRESS CORPS

From 1789 on, the House permitted journalists to cover its sessions from the galleries (unlike the British House of Commons, which well into the nineteenth century evicted journalists spotted among the spectators). The Senate resisted this intrusion until 1800. At that time it opened its doors to journalists, giving them freedom of the floor and a special position near the podium, privileges that they no longer enjoy.

The Press Gallery

Journalists were first provided a congressional press gallery in 1838. Because of the long procession of weak presidents during the 1800s, floor debates in Congress dominated national policy making and national news.

Reporters rarely use the press galleries now because floor debate is usually a minor source of news. Floor speeches rarely are very important. Press secretaries inform interested reporters and provide the text when their bosses are about to say anything worthy of special notice.

Correspondents in congressional press rooms, especially those of the wire services, daily receive overflowing baskets of press releases from congressional offices. They gather other news at committee hearings, press conferences, and individual interviews with legislators, press secretaries, and sometimes staff. And fellow journalists themselves are a major source of news.

Stephen Hess, in his study of Washington reporters, classed Congress as a medium prestige beat, less desirable than covering the president or state department but preferred over most bureaucratic agencies.[7]

Governance of the Press Gallery. Admission to the congressional press corps was left to a committee of newspaper reporters. Because print journalists refused to admit radio journalists, Congress in 1939 established a Radio Correspondents' Gallery, which was later expanded to take in television journalists.

Presently about 2,500 reporters, about equally divided between print and electronic media, are accredited to Congress. But the numbers do not necessarily indicate the extent of coverage. For Washington journalists, accreditation has become a badge, like a social climber's invitation to the country club. Of those registered, perhaps only four to five hundred are regulars who have a major assignment covering some aspect of Congress.

Diversity Among Congressional Reporters

The events that reporters cover depend on the audience they are writing for and the medium that will carry their stories.

Print Coverage. Comprehensive coverage of day-to-day events is left to the wire services, the Associated Press and United Press International. Each has a staff of fifteen to twenty. The wire services provide almost every daily paper and radio and television station with a daily log of congressional activities. Wire-service reports may stress regional as well as national stories. They are usually factual, objective, and bland.

Interpretive stories are provided in the *New York Times News Service* and the *Washington Post-Los Angeles Times News Service* and occasionally in syndicated political columns.

Large city newspapers subscribe to all these and also have their own bureaus, some of them just one reporter, assigned, perhaps only part time, to cover Congress. The major newspaper chains and the newsmagazines also have correspondents.

Correspondents representing metropolitan papers often write up major news stories not covered elsewhere. But these reporters complain that their stories are not reported nationally, even by the wire services, until one of the prestige newspapers — *The New York Times, The Wall Street Journal,* or *The Washington Post* takes an interest.[8]

Specialized journalists cover Congress for religious, economic, civil-rights, trade and business, and other groups. Some issue newsletters, others report for association publications.

Much print reporting, however, has a regional slant, which is called "localizing the national news." These localized stories play up the activities of a state's senators or representatives and government projects or topics of special interest in the circulation area, such as forestry policy and effect on the lumber industry in places such as Oregon. Many small Washington bureaus and freelance writers specialize in this kind of reporting. They receive a retainer from their clients plus a fee for each story used.

The prestige newspapers serve also as part of the regional media for east-coast legislators. Members of Congress from these states realize that coverage in the prestige press has local as well as national significance.

Electronic Coverage. The networks and a few independent stations have their own congressional correspondents, but they are severely hampered because they cannot report directly from the floor. Network television reports the Washington stories that the prestige newspapers emphasize.

Congress has not excluded commercial television entirely, however. The House permits coverage of state occasions such as the president's State of the Union address to Congress. The Senate for some years has permitted coverage of committee hearings, and recently the House has also done so. Members of the committee, though, may restrict such coverage, but as the Iran–Contra hearings suggested, they welcome such media exposure — at least initially.

Since 1979, the House has provided gavel-to-gavel coverage through C-SPAN on cable television. It is available to an estimated 16 million homes, but has a daily audience of roughly 200,000. House personnel control the cameras with minimal editorial comment, usually focusing only on the speaker and not on reactions by other legislators or observers in the galleries. Commercial television stations as well as representatives may use clips from these broadcasts.

The Senate until 1986 allowed no televised coverage of its sessions, except for the 1974 swearing in of Nelson A. Rockefeller as vice president. In 1986, it experimented with C-SPAN televised sessions, with procedures similar to those of the House. The experimental coverage is expected to become permanent.

Commercial television journalists criticize C-SPAN coverage because congressional staff rather than reporters control the cameras. But Brian Lamb, C-SPAN president, pointed out that journalists often are no more open than Congress. Journalists, he said, do not allow C-SPAN or anyone else's cameras inside the *Washington Post* editorial-board conferences, the Gridiron Club, or the White House Correspondents' dinners.[9]

HOW JOURNALISTS REPORT CONGRESS

A member of the House of Representatives reported that after an exhausting trip to his district, he stopped to freshen up in a men's room at Chicago's O'Hare airport. Looking around for a towel, he spotted a hot-air drier on the wall. As he approached it he found a graffito above it that read, "For a message from your congressman, push here."

The graffito writer singled out no particular legislator for ridicule; the salvo was directed against Congress in general. Polsters find the same feeling: Congress as an institution is held in contempt, the polls typically reporting less than 20 percent approval. Yet citizens hold their own representatives in high regard.

Part of the reason for this divergence is that the national prestige media cover Congress as an institution but home-state or district newspapers cover the individual members. The former coverage exhibits more cynical assessments — PBS reporter Hodding Carter calls the activity "caricaturing Congress." Local coverage of home-state legislators is seldom critical.

Local Coverage of Members

A study by a Ralph Nader task force showed that almost three-quarters of the nation's dailies had no Washington correspondent or contract with an independent stringer. They depended on the wire-service regional reports for unbiased coverage. These reports generally concentrate on a region's U.S. senators. Individual House members are mentioned only if they have done something exceptionally newsworthy. Wire-service coverage of these legislators too is usually factual and uncritical, not analytical or interpretive.[10]

Metropolitan papers, which may have a Washington correspondent, typically have too many congressional districts in their circulation area to devote much space to each representative's activities. Their Washington correspondent concentrates on the state's senators.

Who "Covers" the House Members. When members of Congress get local coverage, most often the source of these stories is their Washington offices. Any benefit that a senator or representative has helped the district obtain will get favorable coverage back home. Thus economic-development grants are routinely announced through the office of the district member of Congress rather than by the administrative agency.

Larger papers usually use these press releases, though they more frequently rewrite them. Smaller papers may print them verbatim. This news is supplemented with hard news stories written by local reporters when the legislator visits the district.

Congressional staffs spend a major portion of their time churning out favorable publicity for home consumption. They draw upon the considerable resources available to them, including staff media experts, House and Senate recording studios, and the franking privilege, which permits free mass mailings. Individual members of Congress are thereby well protected from unfavorable publicity back home, so thoroughly dominating what is said about themselves that other politicians are envious. This control is one clue as to why local opinion, especially of House members, is overwhelmingly favorable.

National Coverage of Congress

The prestige press and the wire services are the major sources of national news about Congress. Such news is filtered from the prestige newspapers to the television networks, and from wire-service reports to the regional newspapers.

Congressional leaders complain that in the national media the Congress is more often abused than properly appreciated. Robinson and Appel found some supporting evidence: although most congressional stories they examined were neutral, the rest were all negative. The public seldom sees a positive image of Congress, they concluded.[11]

Emphasizing the Negative. Senator William Proxmire (D-Wisconsin) told reporter David Broder, "In more than thirty years and in literally tens of thousands of conversations back in my state, with people of every political persuasion, I have yet to hear one kind word, one whisper of praise, one word of sympathy for the Congress as a whole."

Robinson reports that members of Congress overwhelmingly feel that negative coverage in the prestige press and network television has increased since 1960. The legislators, he says, distinguish between two types of congressional reporters. "Members tend to define the nationals as 'hostile' and the locals as 'gentlemanly.' "[12] When General Westmoreland sued *Time*, liberal Democrat and then speaker of the House Thomas (Tip) O'Neill said it more succinctly; "Capitol Hill," he remarked, "is cheering for Westmoreland."

Robinson speculates that reporters' cynicism about government may be the result of Vietnam and Watergate, or the new breed of college educated reporters who cover Congress. National reporters may be more aggressive, we suggest, also because competition has become more intense among the prestige press and among the television networks.

Sometimes news commentators make negative comments just to add color to routine stories, but this treatment also reflects an attitude. David Brinkley inserted this anti-Congress spin to a routine story: "The Supreme Court has given Congress thirty days to straighten out the problem. It is widely believed in Washington that it would take Congress thirty days to make instant coffee."[13]

LARRY WRIGHT
Courtesy Detroit News

© The Detroit News, 1983 by permission of the Detroit News

Negative Activity. Whether intentionally or not, the Founders designed the national role of Congress to be a negative one. And journalists find it useful to present Congress as a body reacting to presidential initiatives. This approach stresses dissent, conflict, and obstruction, and journalists stress it by playing "fight promoter." Reporters in need of a story seek out a member of the president's party, hoping for a quotation critical of the president. If none can be found, opposition leaders or members who themselves are considering a run for president are often ready with a cutting comment.

A major source of negative stories is the congressional committee. Television reporters are inclined to concentrate on "committee action of one sort or another — committee reports, committee votes, and above all, committee hearings."[14] Committees often undertake such investigative activity in reaction to proposals by the president or his appointees, as they did in the Iran–Contra hearings. Even when the investigation is aimed at private parties, the committee report may imply that the president should have done something about the subject, especially when House or Senate are not controlled by the president's party.

Television also highlights conflict by concentrating on congressional power centers. These are the leaders who can be shown calling the president on the telephone or trooping into his office to inform him of congressional sentiment. Often their message is that his proposals face opposition. And they are the members who can obstruct, causing presidents to bargain with them to achieve the administration's program goals.

In turn, the president and his staff radiate negative stories about

Congress. Members of the administration will characterize Congress as do-nothing or irresponsible.

Susan Miller observes that national congressional news also focuses on scandal or official misconduct.[15] The FBI "Abscam" case on bribery resulted in jail terms for several representatives and a senator. The evidence included films, made to order for television — videotapes of lawmakers boasting about their influence to a phony Arab oil magnate.

Congressional Celebrities Get National Coverage

But the positive side of national coverage is that network television has turned some members of Congress into celebrities. Television exposes these members to national audiences in ways not possible when print media dominated Congressional coverage. Viewers are led to accept their celebrity status by the other media celebrities, the television anchors, who question them and listen attentively to their answers.

Who Then Are the Celebrities? Television journalists grant celebrity status to those they believe have political influence. To qualify, generally members of Congress must demonstrate that they can influence the president's policies. The status is almost automatic for the majority-party leaders. The names and faces of Speakers Tip O'Neill and James Wright and Senate Majority Leaders Robert Dole and Robert Byrd became familiar to television viewers and newspaper readers during the Reagan years. Journalists accorded them celebrity status because the president was forced to consult with them frequently.

Stardom also rewards those who can demonstrate negative political power by attempting to block a president. Mavericks such as Senators Wayne Morse and Ernest Gruening, who opposed the Gulf of Tonkin Resolution and who from that time on protested against Vietnam War involvement, made news. One of the few Washington memorials to a legislator is the Robert Taft carillon, which every fifteen minutes chimes out the time across the Capitol lawns. Senator Taft, a conservative Republican from Ohio, led fight after fight against proposals by Presidents Roosevelt and Truman, and on occasion, against his own party's president, Dwight Eisenhower.

Investigator-Celebrities. Edward Jay Epstein observed that television increasingly emphasizes the investigative activities of Congress and deemphasizes its role in lawmaking. Lawmakers admired by their colleagues for legislative skills may go unnoticed.[16]

Fellow legislators regard some of these investigators as guilty of grandstanding, described by Donald Matthews as "behavior calculated to get your name in the headlines without legislative accomplishment."[17]

Celebrity status comes easy for congressional investigators, especially if they put on an investigative sideshow that embarrasses the president. Senator Joseph McCarthy became an instant celebrity by charging that Communist party members had infiltrated the State Department and the U.S. Army under President Eisenhower.

During the Truman presidency, Richard Nixon came to national attention by heading an investigation aimed at one of Democrat Franklin Roosevelt's aides at Yalta — Alger Hiss. Ironically, Senator Sam Ervin of North Carolina, Representative Peter Rodino of New Jersey, and others achieved celebrity as members of the committee investigating Richard Nixon and the Watergate break-in.

But sometimes it is the witness rather than the members of Congress who steals the spotlight, as Lt. Col. Oliver North demonstrated.

Candidate-Celebrities. Journalists also treat as a celebrity any member of Congress who announces a run for president. Journalists treat this act as a direct challenge to the incumbent. Such candidates are readily available for quick interviews or Sunday-morning talk shows. Most governors who seek the presidency find it more difficult to reach national celebrity, if only because they are too far from media centers.

Stereotype-Celebrities. Some legislators increase their exposure as national celebrities because they fit a national stereotype. They look as if central casting had sent them over to the television studio. This photogenic quality does not itself bring celebrity status, but it enhances any attention attracted for other reasons.

Senator Robert Taft looked the crusty conservative, proud to be known as a watchdog of the Treasury. Senator Sam Ervin during the Watergate hearings appeared the simple, honest, cracker-barrel lawyer from backwoods North Carolina. In part he was just that. But his witticisms and expressive eyebrows made many forget that he had graduated from Harvard University Law School.

Representative William Gray of Philadelphia fits a familiar liberal stereotype: the intelligent and knowledgeable black from a deprived background, who, given a chance, would perform effectively. Senator William Proxmire of Wisconsin gains media attention whenever he gives his "golden fleece award" to someone he feels has wasted government funds. But he also fits the conservative image of the wine-and-cheese liberal, a person who jogs to work, experiments with hair transplants, and has had Rockefeller connections. And Speaker Tip O'Neill perhaps got added media attention because he so perfectly fit the picture many viewers thought an organization Boston Irish politician should look like.

Do Authorities Become Celebrities? Who does not receive celebrity attention, at least on television? The answer often turns out to be those who shape major legislation. Newspaper reports make us familiar with the names of their laws, such as Gramm-Rudman-Hollings, the budget-balancing act. But the legislators themselves somehow stay in the shadows. They could walk down the main street of Peoria without drawing attention, something such familiar figures as Edward Kennedy or Tip O'Neill could not do.

The in-depth analyses of print journalists give more attention to the statements and actions of authorities, those expert on a subject. But they spotlight their opinions rather than their personalities. House members are most likely to receive national media attention by becoming authorities; only the Speaker can anticipate celebrity status unrelated to specialized knowledge.

MEMBERS OF CONGRESS USE JOURNALISTS

Senators and representatives with static ambitions look mainly for media coverage in their own state or district. Those with progressive career ambitions must also worry about gaining favorable coverage in the constituency they hope to represent.

Career Ambitions and Media Coverage

A news reporter asked a researcher, who had just spent six months observing the U.S. Senate, what she considered her most significant observation. It was the discovery that most senators have hearing problems. "No matter what anyone says, they interpret it to mean they are being encouraged to run for president."[18]

Senators do have to consider many factors before they give in to ambition: their age, their record, and whether they will be up for reelection to the Senate in the presidential year. Researchers have found that major predictors indicating who might run are absence of national electoral liabilities and willingness to take political risks. Most senators adopt static ambitions and stress media coverage in their home states.[19]

Almost all House members also have static ambition and generally spend energy on district coverage. A few decide to risk all in a try for a Senate seat, if the opportunity presents itself. And fewer still, such as Democrat Richard Gephardt of Missouri and Republican Jack Kemp of New York, have made a try for the presidency.

Senators can expect to be in the national spotlight from time to time. And because they represent states (rather than vaguely defined house districts), national coverage can add luster to reputations back home. They hope the coverage will present them as leaders influencing national policy, especially if they are also portrayed as defenders of their state's interest on the national stage.

A senator's greatest competitor for news coverage is usually the other senator representing the state. Donald Matthews wrote that "each senator watches the publicity of his colleague very closely indeed, and many a feud has been touched off by the fact that one senator seemed to be getting better publicity than the other. Sometimes full-scale 'publicity battles' will break out."[20]

The Importance of the Press Secretary

Members of Congress soon learn they will get little coverage in district newspapers or radio and television unless they provide a steady supply of stories. They know such stories enhance reelection possibilities because they build favorable name recognition. A primary goal also is the symbolic image showing the "concerned" legislator working on behalf of constituents. Only "casework" — servicing individual constituent requests — helps reelection chances as much.

Even the members of Congress who own newspapers or television stations or who have themselves been journalists need help to do an adequate job in media relations. Writing in the late 1950s on government–press relations, Douglass Cater observed that the highest-paid congressional staff member is likely to be the person who handles press relations.[21] The same is true today except that more staff are involved. Today each U.S. senator has an average of sixty-eight staff members; representatives about half that many.

The press secretary and some aides are likely to be former journalists who give advice on press relations and make sure that routine public-relations details are handled properly. Other journalists somewhat patronizingly call them "flacks," feeling superior because they claim not to have not sold out to get a job "peddling" a legislator.

Some members of Congress prefer to assign media responsibilities to their entire staff rather than to a press secretary because a press secretary may know media techniques but very little about the subject of the news story. Rather than have just a few persons on the alert for potential news stories, staff with specialized duties are taught to spot potential stories, write the news releases, and get them distributed properly. Press relations, they say, are so important that they must be everyone's responsibility.

The media staff are keenly aware that their bosses need publicity. They also sense daily the intense competition for newspaper space or television and radio time back in the district. Hence, they are always on the alert for the angle that will give them an advantage over the competition.

Preparing Press Releases. The most valuable media function that the staff performs is to produce that steady stream of press releases for district consumption — three or more each week for a representative is routine. Photos may also be provided. The staff works out schedules to meet the deadlines for district weeklies and dailies, making certain that even small weeklies get their share of newsworthy stories. They must also see that the legislator's press releases are being printed. The press secretary may send exclusives to one media source in order to encourage more favorable coverage in another.

Many congressional offices prepare and send a weekly "special report" about Washington activities. The smaller dailies and most weeklies in the district faithfully reprint them in full. Supplementing this handout may be telegrams or phone messages when a federal facility has been won for the district or the legislator does something else relevant to the constituency.

Press secretaries, especially those working for senators, pride themselves on having an occasional story published in the national media. They get their release into the congressional press rooms early in the morning, hoping it will become one of a reporter's news stories for the day. At least they can hope to get it on a wire-service regional report.

The secretaries sometimes compete intensely among themselves. It was known that President Nixon was about to veto a natural-gas bill. The secretary for Senator Clifford Case (R-New Jersey) waited patiently in the Senate press gallery for confirmation of the veto to come over the teletype. When it came he immediately passed out a press release giving the senator's reaction. Another senator's press aide came hurrying in with his boss's press release, but discovered he was one minute too late and so missed the opportunity for extensive coverage.

Electronic News Releases. The staff prepares short "beepers" for radio and film clips that can be inserted into news broadcasts. Many also offer a weekly recorded report. The Capitol switchboard assists by transferring the recording to several stations at once. On video clips the staff member may sit with back to the camera asking the legislator questions as a reporter would. Viewers may not sense the difference. Congress has studios that prepare these electronic offerings "at cost," markedly less than a commercial studio would charge.

Creating Media Events. Especially useful are press secretaries who can sense what may make an attention-getting story with symbolic value, one showing that the legislator cares. An aide for Connecticut Senator Lowell Weicker read a news story about a constituent who had shipped her dog by air and found it dead on arrival. The staff member called the Department of Transportation and major airlines to find out how many pets arrived thus. As a result, the department issued new regulations, and the senator was shown introducing a bill regulating the transport of pets. The payoff was registered in letters from animal lovers in Connecticut and possibly votes in the next election.[22]

An uninspired but still useful media event is the symbolic appearance before a district audience, such as addressing local farmers about debt problems. But the stories can be more imaginative. A press secretary for some budget-cutting Republicans arranged a photo opportunity with the senators huddled over the president's budget document, pencil in hand. The photo was unusual because all the pencils had erasers at both ends, signifying that these senators would not add items; they could only delete. The photo got national coverage.

Contacts with Reporters. The press secretary also arranges for the legislator to meet with reporters, both nationally and locally. For an issue that is really important, the press secretary may entice reporters to a press conference or an interview.

Some aides regularly visit the Capitol press room to chat with reporters, making contacts that may lead to a news story or television interview. The secretary will also fill in television or radio reporters before live interviews by briefly giving facts and figures that the boss has stated on the issue. It is likely that the legislator will then be asked questions to which these facts are the answers.

Other Activities. Many press secretaries produce a newsletter that is mailed to constituents. The skilful ones bring together media coverage with these more personal and direct messages. Sometimes questionnaires to be returned by constituents are used for further media publicity.

Reading the local newspapers is another staff chore. The staff prepare summaries of state or district news events, perhaps enabling the legislator to champion a local issue before its worth is generally recognized. The legislator will also appear knowledgeable when visiting the district. Usually, though, members avoid taking sides on strictly local or state issues.

Legislators Act on Their Own Behalf

Press secretaries can be helpful, but they are only aides; successful politicians must also help themselves. Washington provides the stage settings for such media entrepreneurship, particularly for those desiring national media attention. It is up to the legislator to exploit the possibilities.

David Weaver and G. Cleveland Withoit studied twenty years of AP coverage of senators to determine how they got into the news. They examined such factors as size of the legislator's staff, seniority, size of state, and committee and leadership positions. They concluded that the best predictor for media coverage was how much the senator did — the quantity of the individual's activities.[23]

Law Making. A legislator can make news, at least in the home district, just by introducing a bill that could improve conditions for the homefolks. Lou Cannon writes that of the 20,458 bills introduced by members of the House in the 92nd Congress, 7,999 had identical wording, differing only in minor details. Many legislators wanted to get credit back in the district for an idea that seemed good, even if it was someone else's.[24]

But the path for converting a bill into a law is a rocky one, drawing publicity that few legislators genuinely earn. Getting one's name on a major law is an event that the legislator can point to as evidence of being on the job, especially if the law can be shown to benefit the home district. But it is doubtful that those back in the district fully appreciate how difficult it is to achieve this demonstration.

Capitol Interviews. Near the Senate chamber is a lobby where, on his rare visits to the Senate, the president waits. But mostly journalists use the room to interview senators. When senators on the floor hear that a reporter wishes to speak to them, very few refuse to respond, especially if the reporter represents a newspaper or a regional wire service from the home state. The House equivalent is the Speaker's lobby.

Most in demand are legislators who can be counted on for a colorful or controversial quote (notable quotables). But reporters also turn to authorities on specific topics for background information. When the CIA briefed members of the Senate Intelligence and Energy committees about the 1987 Soviet nuclear-plant disaster at Chernobyl, members of both parties granted press interviews, revealing part of the information that was supplied to them.

Favored Sources. Reporters usually choose a few legislators as their preferred sources, persons who are readily accessible and who give reliable information, leaks, and tips about developing stories. These sources may or may not share the journalist's political orientation. Occasionally one can identify the sources resorted to by national columnists, especially the muckraker journalists, simply by the kind treatment such sources get in their copy.

The legislator may supply background information about issues and personalities, those who oppose and favor a bill, which pressure groups are involved, what amendments may be offered, or what the vote is likely to be. The information does not necessarily go in only one direction: the legislators may also learn something they had not known.

Open Hostility. On rare occasions, a journalist and a legislator clash. Delmar Dunn writes of an often-quoted legendary exchange. At the end of the antagonistic interview the member of Congress asks sarcastically, "Well, is everything you are writing today the truth?" The reporter replies, "Yes, everything not enclosed in quotation marks!"[25]

Members of Congress have been so outraged by stories that they have attacked reporters by name on the floor. Douglass Cater reports that the experience doubly hurts the reporter, partly because it suggests to other legislators that the journalist cannot be trusted.

More often than not, however, the relationships are cooperative, perhaps too much so. As in contention with the president, open conflict is apt to produce little gain for either side. The journalist wants this story and more in the future, and the legislator wants the publicity; they avoid deep and long clashes. And unlike presidents, legislators know that reporters need not be beholden to any legislators because often they can find alternate sources.

If most legislators make themselves available to reporters in Washington, access is doubly easy back in the district. Rarely is either journalist or legislator faced with an adversary.

Making News in Floor Debate. It may appear that a legislator can easily gain journalistic attention with a speech on the floor of the House or Senate. But they have rarely done so, even in the print media, which cover Congress in greater detail. The speeches are apt to be trivial. Though the House rules limit debate to five minutes, the Senate permits unlimited debate. Senators thus have the opportunity to make major policy statements, some of which occasionally make headlines.

Journalists consider a statement newsworthy when a leader identified with a cause announces a switch in position, as some senators did during the Vietnam War or the Nixon impeachment hearings. But usually, columnist Mary McGrory observes, "In the Senate, debate often means one member standing in an empty chamber, being heard only by a bored presiding officer who is signing his mail or autographing pictures of himself."[26]

The Effect of C-SPAN. But broadcast of congressional debates on C-SPAN has brought change. The speech may not make national news but the legislator's staff can turn brief statements on the floor of Congress into "sound bites" packaged for news broadcasts back in the district. They can also be used in campaign television spots.

Reporters noticed that after C-SPAN started, members made more brief speeches and offered more amendments in regular debate. Each day, the House also sets aside an hour for one-minute speeches, made to order for district clips.

And in January 1984, shortly after such cable broadcast began, a dozen Republicans discovered the "special-orders" procedure for making speeches at the end of the day. This period could be useful, especially becuase other members of Congress were not there to respond. They especially criticized the Democratic Speaker, Tip O'Neill. By May, he had had enough, and ordered that the television cameras show the empty seats in the chamber and that a statement be shown on the screen informing viewers that the House had completed its legislative business for the day. The sound bites were now somewhat less useful for local news broadcasts or campaign ads.

Legislators making speeches also became more aware of their image, and began wearing more colorful clothing and makeup. Observers even noticed an increase in blow-dried hair and agonized attempts to deepen speaking voices. Some members introduced eye-catching "visuals." Shortly after C-SPAN began broadcasting, Bud Shuster (R-Pennsylvania) opened House debate on a lame-duck session holding a stuffed Donald Duck. "We think Donald Democrat, this poor little lame duck, is symbolic of what is happening here," he said, holding his stuffed animal up for the cameras.

Some observers anticipate that C-SPAN coverage will less significantly affect Senate floor debate. Reporter Hodding Carter of PBS observed that "Major figures in the Senate are already blow-drying their hair.

They live in a television world right now, rushing out to talk to the cameras right after a vote.... There are only a handful of senators left who treat the Senate as a place for extended debate."[27]

Committee Hearings. Some standing committees have their own press secretaries to ensure full publicity. The House has more than 150 sub-committees, the Senate, 90, but each of these is small. Their members may hold hearings in Washington or out of town. A member alone may hold a hearing in his or her home district, if the chair approves. With a suitable topic and careful planning, a legislator can generate a good deal of favorable publicity.

The chair of a hearing opens proceedings with a statement, an opportunity to make news. Staff members take care of details such as lining up newsworthy witnesses, and they prepare a white paper on the topic that is passed out to reporters as the hearing begins. It sets the theme. Most hearings last only a day or two, but some create enough newsworthy stories to last weeks.

Televised hearings can backfire. Senator Joseph McCarthy conducted probes that made him a major political figure. But the television hearings also in time aroused critics among journalists and fellow politicians, and helped impel his eventual (televised) downfall. Other legislators distrusted his influence based on television skills alone. Such senators, they feel, have not paid their dues to the legislative body; they have not gained status legitimately through congressional seniority, which upholds legislative traditions, or made a solid contribution to the making of legislation.[28]

But the unexpected can happen. A witness may steal the spotlight from the legislators as Lt. Col. Oliver North did in the Iran–Contra hearings of 1987. The witness all expected to be the victim ended up lecturing Congress for inconsistency in supporting the Contras in Nicaragua while many Americans applauded him.

The Watergate hearings turned out better for Congress — they produced a cast of House and Senate celebrities. Most legislators experienced little negative fallout, but they also found that celebrity status faded rather quickly. Even less attention-getting hearings such as those on starvation in America or Conrail can produce valuable publicity, but only for the moment and only with segments of the population.[29]

The Presidential Aspirants. Presidential aspirants have to look for every opportunity to gain media attention: becoming a national celebrity is not easy. They often pay a price in unpopularity with fellow legislators by looking like grandstanders or publicity hounds, too blatantly seeking media attention.

Such could have been the fate of John F. Kennedy. But with the help of Theodore Sorenson, Kennedy wrote *Profiles in Courage*, describing the heroism of seven former senators. Some critics said the book was meant to flatter his Senate colleagues and gain their good will. At the same time, they pointed out, he was seeking ways to "escape" the Senate and become president.

Those aspiring to be president often seek assignments to the Armed Services and Foreign Relations committees for the aura of foreign-policy expertise that connection brings. Others arrange task forces abroad, especially if they involve interviews with foreign leaders.[30] They frequently schedule news conferences, a technique that has some risks because the legislator cannot always control the outcome. Even if the conference is carefully planned, the legislator fully primed, and a news release available, some reporter may ask an off-the-wall question that elicits an unexpected answer. And, just as in presidential press conferences, the surprise upstages everything else that the legislator hoped would be printed and broadcast.

Even before television, Richard Nixon made a national reputation in the "pumpkin" papers hearings, in which Whitaker Chambers accused Alger Hiss of being a communist. It started Nixon on the road that ended with the presidency. Senator Estes Kefauver revealed the potential in televised hearings in 1951 with the Senate's Special Committee to Investigate Organized Crime in Interstate Commerce. At that time only sixty-two major markets had television stations and most of the sets were in barrooms. The extent of citizen reaction astonished politicians, making Kefauver a national celebrity and a heroic one. He became a major contender for the Democratic presidential nomination in 1952 and vice-presidential nominee in 1956.

A favorite tactic for gaining media attention is reacting to a presidential initiative. Presidential contenders try to send out symbolic messages to potential supporters, who most often know little about them. Democratic Senator Joseph Biden of Delaware drew national media attention in his campaign against confirming William Rehnquist as Chief Justice. A legislator can use a presidential initiative to disarm his own potential opponents. A Democrat commenting on a Republican president's budget proposal may try to get across the message, "I'm the kind of fellow who is liberal on social issues but conservative on financial matters." Liberal Republicans may attempt to reassure their party's conservative wing by stressing their concern for preserving American family values.

All these activities are helpful to potential candidates. But the legislators know they are gaining national attention when they are invited to appear regularly on one of the Sunday talk shows or on the extended news show of PBS, *The MacNeil/Lehrer Report.* These have select audiences, including many of the opinion-making elite — nationally and locally.

Talk shows can be a strong influence in debates on national issues. In 1965 CBS broadcast a ninety-minute program in which legislative "hawks" and "doves" on the Vietnam War defended their positions and discussed whether bombing of North Vietnam should be resumed. It was followed by an interview with Senator William Fulbright (D-Arkansas), chair of the Senate Foreign Relations Committee. He confessed that he had erred in sponsoring the Gulf of Tonkin resolution, the basis for United States involvement in Vietnam. Members of the CBS news operation, such as William Small and Fred Friendly, later wrote that they considered these programs a major contribution by television to the resolution of a national issue.[31]

Such participation also made some of these politicians national celebrities, a position that in turn leads to other television appearances on mass audience shows such as *Today* or *Good Morning, America.*

Les Aspin Seeks National Attention. Some members of Congress seek national attention in the media almost exclusively for personal satisfaction. One of the more successful, Representative Les Aspin (D-Wisconsin) recognized that few of his constituents read stories about him in the national prestige press. His main payoff from that coverage, he said, came from realizing his influence on debates over important national issues.

Aspin described how he compiled a file of news stories in the prestige press that ran from "Aspin Reveals 35-Year-Old Retirees" to "Aspin Says Soviets Covering up on Anthrax."[32]

First, he says, the member of Congress who is not a celebrity will get coverage only with an information story, something not known before, or by presenting a new viewpoint on a previously reported story. Such stories require time to dig out information and a plan. Thus, as good editors do, Aspin sought to anticipate the events that might make news: the story that will be in the news two weeks from now. His membership on the House Armed Services Committee gave him a sense of where a story on the military might be heading.

If the story has general appeal, he says, the wire services can best distribute it to a national audience. The story that got Aspin his greatest response revealed that the Army was using beagle puppies to test poison gas. In another case he found that the Navy, in a test of the Phalanx antiship missile that was supposed to be simulated, in fact sank the

U.S.S. *Hollister*. His press release said, "With missiles like these, who needs enemies?"

But more often Aspin aimed his stories at those he called the aficionados, decision makers who are part of the national policy debate. They follow closely events reported in the prestige press.

Aspin worked up a detailed strategy, almost making a game of it. The staff person specializing in the topic prepared the press release. Aspin then called up reporters with the same specialty and told them the story was coming. After they got the release, he phoned them again and gave them a little more information. He said, "if you know a particular reporter has a certain interest in one aspect, you try to hold a little of that back. Give the reporters a little of the thing you know they are interested in — little twists for them to put in, down in about the third or fourth paragraph."

Aspin planned his stories for Monday because that was a slow news day. He sent the releases out on Thursday with a "do not release until Monday" notice. He says that reporters, like everyone else, do not like to work on weekends. They would get his release on Friday morning, use it as their Monday story, and go away for the weekend.

But media attention did not protect Aspin from wrathful fellow Democrats who objected to his support for the antiballistic missile and the Nicaraguan Contras. He was almost removed as chair of the House Armed Services committee. Some may even have resented the attention he got in the media, dismissing him as a grandstander.

CONGRESSIONAL ELECTION CAMPAIGNS

Members of Congress are so avid in seeking publicity because of the one climactic event that most will soon face — an election. For incumbents with static ambitions, the effort pays off: 90 percent of House and 80 percent of Senate incumbents who seek reelection succeed. Even more survive primary challenges.

Media Based Challenges

Incumbents from marginal house districts and senators know that they may be vulnerable. Challengers may exploit the opportunity to unseat them with a well-planned media campaign. Gary Jacobson found that of twenty-one House incumbents defeated in 1972, two-thirds were defeated by challengers who spent more on television and radio ads than they did.[33] Paul Dawson and James Zinser estimated that television and radio campaigns in Senate races made winners of marginal losers in a majority of cases.[34]

Also more vulnerable perhaps are legislators from districts with newspapers that have their own Washington correspondents. A Nader study found that 95 percent of the first-time House members elected in 1972 came from districts in which television or newspapers had their own Washington source. (Of course, other characteristics, such as district competitiveness, also help explain this pattern.)[35]

When the campaign officially begins, free broadcast coverage for incumbents — taped messages to the folks back home — ends. Congress normally adjourns and so the opportunity to use official business to gain media attention disappears. The incumbent faced with a major challenge must now depend on campaign ads and stories to mobilize support.

Using the Media in Campaigns

Jacobson found that the correlation between use of broadcast advertising and voter support quadrupled between 1956 and 1970, and continued to edge up in 1972.[36] Robinson, Goldenberg, and Traugott each estimated, in more recent studies, that congressional incumbents and challengers spend well over half their campaign budgets on mass media advertising, especially broadcast advertising.[37]

Cost Effectiveness in House Campaigns. For both politician and journalist, media coverage is relevant only when the media circulation area and the political district are congruent. Metropolitan newspapers and television have too many house districts within their circulation and viewing areas to devote much free coverage to these races. They will settle for a few "rundown" reports of area congressional races, and occasional reports on contests that have unusual aspects.

Similarly, House candidates conclude that employing paid media in metropolitan outlets is generally wasteful. They put their money in more narrowly focused advertising, such as billboards, yard signs, and community newspapers. Occasionally though, in intensely competitive races, House candidates will buy expensive television or radio ads just to demonstrate that they are serious candidates.

Electronic and print journalists in middle-sized cities, though, give the two or three congressional races in their circulation area continuing coverage, especially if the outcome is in doubt. And candidates in geographically large districts with several small media markets use some television coverage even for relatively low-budget campaigns. But they rely most heavily on smaller city dailies and weeklies and local radio. Radio ads can more easily be targeted to selected audiences — such as those who listen to country music, middle-of-the-road music, and "music of your life."

Cost Effectiveness in Senate Races. Challengers in Senate races have a better chance to get free media coverage and a cost-effective advertising campaign than do challengers in most House races.[38]

Journalists consider these as major races and so give continuing coverage. Even in large media markets such as St. Louis that are near a state border, many of their readers and viewers live in the area the winning candidate will represent. Senate candidates strive to get free print coverage of campaign events and may place some newspaper ads, but the lion's share of their advertising budget goes to television.

The Incumbent Advantage

News stories about incumbents that appear between campaigns give them a head start in the name recognition that challengers have to achieve before they have any chance to succeed. House members especially can receive overwhelmingly favorable coverage, since so many of the stories were prepared by their own staffs.

The incumbent advantage generally continues through most campaigns. Arthur Miller found that incumbents received twice as much campaign coverage as challengers and that most of it was positive.[39] Especially in newspaper coverage of House races, the incumbent almost always got preference, though the advantage varied from district to district.[40] Moreover, newspaper endorsements usually went to House incumbents rather than to challengers.

The Challenger's Problems. Challengers have little chance of achieving name recognition in a short time or creating a favorable image unless they can publicize themselves through the paid media. They must depend on the paid media because free media coverage is usually concentrated in the last weeks of the campaign. Tidmarch, Hyman, and Sorkin found in a study of metropolitan papers that 40 percent of the last month's campaign stories were printed in the last eight days of the campaign.[41]

Journalists and citizens alike think challengers' efforts are futile unless they can raise the funds for a visible campaign in the paid media. Challengers, of course, find it more difficult to raise funds than do incumbents. In districts that coincide with media circulation areas, though, challengers are found to be more successful.[42] And every dollar an unknown challenger spends on advertising, especially in the less visible primary challenges,[43] brings greater payoffs than the same amount spent by the incumbent.[44]

Senate races offer most hope for challengers, even though free media coverage favors the senatorial incumbent. Relative unknowns have managed to make the Senate races competitive partly because they almost always get some free coverage in both newspapers and television, which they can supplement with their paid media ads.[45] Even if they already are fairly well known, House challengers have less chance against incumbents because of the difficulties in putting on a paid media campaign and gaining free coverage.[46]

Elements of a Successful Campaign

For both incumbents and challengers in media-dominated races, being able to come across well on television is obviously crucial. The goal is to create a favorable image.

Whom do challengers try to reach? Edie Goldenberg and Michael Traugott found that a challenger's news stories and ads are especially effective in swaying the less educated and those who have been politically inattentive.[47] An attractive candidate on television can win their support. Media campaigns are less effective among those who regularly read political news stories, including the publicity sent out by incumbents between elections.

Editorial endorsements are especially helpful to challengers because they add legitimacy, as if recognizing a qualified person who has a reasonable chance of winning. Goldenberg and Traugott found that even voters supporting the incumbent tended to view more favorably news-paper-endorsed challengers.[48]

Using Issues. Issues or ideological positions can be two-edged, because they can alienate as well as generate support. Usually, incumbents prefer to stress image and deemphasize issues, but challengers, being underdogs, sometimes use issues to attract attention. Still a favorite "issue" is the incumbent's integrity.

Senate challengers in a Texas primary discovered that the incumbent's literature claimed he supported formation of Department of Education, and yet he had voted the other way. Rather than having the challenger make his integrity a campaign issue, though, they "planted" the story with reporters and allowed them to publicize the charge. They reasoned that campaign ads or even speeches are less likely to be believed than is a news report. The incumbent was defeated.[49]

A Closing Note

Richard Fenno maintains that, as media dependency increases, especially in Senate contests, candidates will have to focus more frequently on policy issues.[50] Several students have found that voters in recent Senate elections are more interested in what candidates believe.[51]

Yet many students question whether issues are really discussed in most congressional campaigns. Examining Senate campaign ads, Richard Joslyn found that 77 percent contained vague references or none at all to a candidate's actual position on issues.[52] Television media consultants also generally encourage "good-guy" image campaigns with issues "fuzzed": "Yes I understand that farm debt is an important problem. I intend to take some action on it after I'm elected." Specifics are left dangling lest someone be alienated by suggested solutions.

Jon Hale found in a Texas Senate race that the candidates did sometimes discuss issues in their speeches and ads, but only if they believed it would help win the election. Hale contends that journalists should force candidates to take stands.[53]

But politicians have career goals and so too do journalists: one seeks getting elected, the other, gaining readers and viewers. Neither sees the primary task as educating the voters. Studying how four dailies covered the 1984 Texas campaign, Hale found, as Patterson and McClure had in an earlier study, that journalists stressed the hoopla and the horse-race aspects of campaigns.[54]

He found that even though almost two-thirds of the news reports included some issue references, most commonly these mentions were being analyzed as tactical moves that candidates employed to gain advantage. The issues themselves remained unanalyzed. And militating against in-depth coverage was the fact that journalists regarded issue positions as stale news, once a candidate had mentioned them in one campaign speech.

We are left with the earlier conclusion by Patterson and McClure — citizens find out more about a candidate's stands from the televised ads than from the television news coverage. Though journalists find that many readers and viewers think issue discussions boring, still, the candidate may find it useful to discuss issues in depth for specialized audiences. For the mass citizenry, information on issues is only an occasional democratic by-product. (See Chapter 1.)

NOTES

1. Elmer E. Cornwell, Jr., "Presidential News: The Expanding Public Image," *Journalism Quarterly* 36 (Summer 1959): 275–283. Cornwell analyzed news content in *The New York Times* and *Providence Journal* from 1885 to 1957 and found that presidential news increased markedly and steadily. A study following the same techniques found a continuation of this trend for the period 1959 to 1974. See Alan P. Balutis, "Congress, the President and the Press," *Journalism Quarterly* 53 (Autumn 1976): 509–515.

2. Thomas Curtis, "The Executive Dominates the News," *Congressional Quarterly* (Jan. 30, 1968), pp. 1483–1484.

3. Lynda Lee Kaid and Joe Foote, "How Network Television Coverage of the President and Congress Compared," *Journalism Quarterly* 62 (Spring 1985): 59–65.

4. Michael J. Robinson, "A Twentieth-Century Medium in a Nineteenth-Century Legislature: The Effects of Television on the American Congress." In *Congress in Change, Evolution and Reform*, ed. Norman Orstein (New York: Praeger, 1975).

5. Nelson Polsby, *Congress and the Presidency*, 2nd ed. (Englewood Cliffs, N.J.: Prentice-Hall, 1971), pp. 67–70.

6. Stephen Hess, *The Washington Reporters* (Washington D.C.: Brookings Institution, 1981), pp. 101–102.

7. Hess, *The Washington Reporters*, p. 49.

8. Michael J. Robinson and Maura E. Clancey, "'King of the Hill': When It Comes to News, Congress Turns to the *Washington Post*," *Washington Journalism Review* (July/August 1983): 46–49.

9. Sharon Geltner, "Matching Set: Brian Lamb and Cable's C-SPAN," *Washington Journalism Review*: 29–33.

10. Cited in Ben H. Bagdikian, "Congress and the Media: Partners in Propaganda," *Columbia Journalism Review* (January/February 1974).

11. Michael J. Robinson and Kevin R. Appel, "Network News Coverage of Congress," *Political Science Quarterly* 94 (Fall 1979): 407–418.

12. Michael J. Robinson, "Three Faces of Congressional Media." In Thomas E. Mann and Norman J. Ornstein, eds. *The New Congress* (Washington, D.C.: The American Enterprise Institute, 1981), pp. 55–96, at p. 77.

13. Michael J. Robinson and Kevin R. Appel, "Network News Coverage of Congress," *Political Science Quarterly* 94 (Fall 1979): 412–414.

14. Robinson and Appel, "Network News Coverage of Congress," pp. 407–418.

15. Susan Miller, "News Coverage of Congress: The Search for the Ultimate Spokesman," *Journalism Quarterly* 54 (Autumn 1977): 459–465.

16. Edward Jay Epstein, *News from Nowhere* (New York: Random House, 1973), pp. 250–252. See also Robinson and Appel, "Network News Coverage of Congress," p. 417.

17. Donald Matthews, *U.S. Senators and Their World* (Chapel Hill: University of North Carolina Press, 1960), p. 217.

18. Dick West, "Researcher Uncovers Peculiar Habits and Character Traits

Inside Jungle of the U.S. Senate," United Press International syndicated column, May 24, 1981.

19. Robert L. Peabody, Norman J. Ornstein, and David W. Rohde, "The United States Senate as a Presidential Incubator: Many Are Called but Few Are Chosen," *Political Science Quarterly* 91 (Summer 1976): 237–258; and Paul R. Abramson, John H. Aldrich, and David W. Rohde, "Progressive Ambition Among United States Senators: 1972–1988," *Journal of Politics* 47 (February 1987): 3–35.

20. Matthews, *U.S. Senators and Their World,* p. 216.

21. Douglass Cater, *The Fourth Branch of Government* (New York: Random House, 1959), p. 47.

22. Delmar Dunn, "Symbiosis: Congress and the Press." In ed. Robert O. Blanchard, *Congress and the News Media* (New York: Hastings House, 1974), pp. 240–249.

23. David Weaver and G. Cleveland Withoit, "News Media Coverage of U.S. Senators in Four Congresses, 1953–1974," *Journalism Monographs* No. 67 (April 1980).

24. Lou Cannon, *Reporting: An Inside View* (Sacramento: California Journal Press, 1977), p. 182.

25. Delmar Dunn, "Symbiosis: Congress and the Press." In Robert O. Blanchard, *Congress and the News Media* (New York: Hastings House, 1974), p. 244.

26. Mary McGrory, "Senate on Television Would Be a Bore," syndicated column, Sept. 26, 1985.

27. Arthur Unger, "Hodding Carter III Talks About Television's Role in Government," *Christian Science Monitor,* May 5, 1986, 36–37.

28. Michael J. Robinson, "A Twentieth-Century Medium in a Nineteenth-Century Legislature," p. 243.

29. For a discussion on the strategy of setting up a hearing see Brett Fromson, "Inside a Senate Hearing: How Reform Got Derailed," *Washington Monthly* (December 1981): 14–23. See also Susan H. Miller, "Congressional Committee Hearings and the Media: Rules of the Game," *Journalism Quarterly* 55 (Winter 1978): 657–663.

30. Peabody, Ornstein, and Rohde, "The United States Senate as a Presidential Incubator," pp. 237–258.

31. Fred Friendly and William Small, *To Kill a Messenger: Television News and the Real World* (New York: Hastings House, 1970).

32. Katherine Winton Evans, "The News Maker: A Capitol Hill Pro Reveals His Secrets," *Washington Journalism Review* (June 1981): 28–33.

33. Gary Jacobson, "The Effect of Campaign Spending in Congressional Elections, *American Political Science Review* 72 (June 1978): 489.

34. Paul Dawson and James Zinser, "Broadcast Expenditures and Electoral Outcomes in the 1970 Congressional Elections," *Public Opinion Quarterly* (Fall 1971): 398–402.

35. Ben H. Bagdikian, "Congress and the Media: Partners in Propaganda," *Columbia Journalism Review* (January/February 1974).

36. Gary Jacobson, "The Impact of Broadcast Campaigning on Electoral Outcomes," *Journal of Politics* 37 (1975): 781.

37. Michael J. Robinson, "Three Faces of Congressional Media." In Thomas E. Mann and Norman Ornstein, eds., *The New Congress* (Washington, D.C.: American Enterprise Institute, 1981), p. 70, and Edie Goldenberg and Michael Traugott, *Campaigning for Congress* (Washington, D.C.: Congressional Quarterly Press, 1984).

38. Lyn Ragsdale, "Incumbent Popularity, Challenger Invisibility, and Congressional Voters," *Legislative Studies Quarterly* (May 1981): 201–218; and Barbara Hinckley, *Congressional Elections* (Washington, D.C.: Congressional Quarterly Press, 1981).

39. Arthur Miller, "The Institutional Focus of Political Distrust." Paper presented at the meeting of the American Political Science Association, Washington D.C., September 1979, p. 39. See also Robinson, "Three Faces of Congressional Media," pp. 80–82.

40. Peter Clarke and Susan Evans, *Covering Campaigns* (Stanford: Stanford University Press, 1983); Edie Goldenberg and Michael Traugott, *Campaigning for Congress* (Washington, D.C.: Congressional Quarterly Press, 1984), and Charles Tidmarch and Brad Karp, "The Missing Beat: Press Coverage of Congressional Elections in Eight Metropolitan Areas," *Congress and the Presidency* 100 (Spring 1983): 47–61.

41. Charles M. Tidmarch, Lisa J. Hyman, and Jill E. Sorkin, "Scribes, Touts, and Pamphleteers: Press Coverage of the 1982 Election Campaigns in Twelve Metropolitan Newspapers." Paper delivered at the annual meeting of the Midwest Political Science Association, Chicago, April 17–20, 1985.

42. James E. Campbell, John R. Alford, and Keith Henry, "Television Markets and Congressional Elections," *Policy Studies Journal*, 13 (September 1984): 665–678.

43. Gary C. Jacobson, "The Effects of Campaign Spending in Congressional Elections," *American Political Science Review* 72 (June 1978): 469–491. See also, by the same author, *The Politics of Congressional Elections*, (Boston: Little, Brown, 1983.)

44. John Wanat, "Political Broadcast Advertising and Primary Election Voting," *Journal of Broadcasting* 18 (Fall 1974): 413–422.

45. See for example the analysis of the 1984 Nebraska Senate race in Jan P. Vermeer and Joseph R. Mouer, "A Senate Incumbent and Challenger in Newspaper Headlines: A Preliminary Exploration." Paper delivered at the the meeting of the Midwest Political Science Association, Chicago, April 1985.

46. Edie Goldenberg and Michael Traugott, *Campaigning for Congress* (Washington, D.C.: Congressional Quarterly Press, 1984).

47. Edie N. Goldenberg and Michael W. Traugott, "The Impact of News Coverage in Senate Campaigns." Paper delivered at the the meeting of the American Political Science Association, New Orleans, September 1985, p. 8.

48. Goldenberg and Traugott, "Impact of News Coverage in Senate Campaigns," p. 9.

49. Ken Vest and Richard Paul, "A Tale of Two Press Secretaries," *Washington Journalism Review* (October 1984): 18–20.
50. Richard F. Fenno, Jr., *The U.S. Senate: A Bicameral Perspective* (Washington, D.C.: American Enterprise Institute, 1981), p. 18.
51. Alan Abramowitz, "A Comparison of Voting for U.S. Senator and Representative in 1978," *American Political Science Review* 74 (1980): 633–640; Barbara Hinckley, "House Reelections and Senate Defeats: The Role of the Challenger," *British Journal of Political Science* 10 (1980): 441–460; and Eric Uslaner, "Ain't Misbehavin': The Logic of Defensive Issue Voting Strategies in Congressional Elections," *American Politics Quarterly* 9 (1981): 3–22.
52. Richard Joslyn, "The Content of Political Spot Ads," *Journalism Quarterly* 57 (1980): 92–98.
53. Jon F. Hale, "A Lot or a Lot of Nothing? Press Coverage of Issues in the 1984 Texas Senate Race." Paper presented at the meeting of the Midwest Political Science Association, Chicago, April 1985.
54. Thomas Patterson and Robert D. McClure, *The Unseeing Eye* (New York: Putnam, 1976).

8

☆ ———————————————————————————— ☆

Bureaucrats,
Judges,
and Journalists

In the preface to his *People and Power in Political Washington*, Stewart Alsop wrote, "When this book was about half finished, I was driving west from Capitol Hill on Constitution Avenue in a taxi . . . . I was passing the National Gallery on my left, and I noticed on my right an imposing building in vaguely classic style, flanked by two muscular rearing horses. What was it? I peered out of the taxi, and made out a sign over a doorway: Federal Trade Commission. I'd never set foot in the building, and I had only a very vague notion of what the Federal Trade Commission was supposed to do."[1]

Alsop had spent more than twenty-five years as a journalist in Washington, D.C. He wrote a syndicated newspaper column and a weekly political endpiece for *Newsweek*. But he confessed that his book would be no comprehensive *Inside Washington*. It would cover "only the Washington that political journalists inhabit and the people they write about."

Alsop's confession illustrates a trait that sets bureaucrats and judges apart from elected officials — much of what they do goes unreported. What gets reported are those aspects of administration that affect the president; in the eyes of journalists the president is also the sun around which these other entities revolve.

CHAPTER OVERVIEW

In this chapter we review how bureaucrats and judges interact with journalists and how journalists address the problems they face in reporting on the actions of the bureaucratic agencies and the courts. We begin with the people who manage the bureacracy, examining first the setting that makes covering them more difficult than reporting on Congress or the presidency. We see how stories from the bureaucracy are reported. And we consider how the Supreme Court, more than any other political agency in government, buffers itself from journalistic surveillance and criticism.

HOW BUREAUCRATS DEAL WITH JOURNALISTS

The thirteen major departments in the federal bureaucracy are represented in the president's Cabinet: State, Defense, Justice, Health and Welfare, Education, Agriculture, Commerce, Labor, and others. The president appoints their heads, called secretaries, whom the Senate then confirms or rejects. These and their major aides are the bureaucracy's political appointees.

Within each department are many subunits with special assignments and responsibilities. Career bureaucrats staff and head these agencies. These administrators get their positions through civil service or other

personnel programs such as those run by the armed forces or the foreign service.

But not all the agencies are part of the departmental structure. The most important of these are the independent regulatory agencies — independent because they generate rules for the industries they regulate and, over these, exercise semijudicial functions. The Federal Trade Commission, the Federal Communications Commission, and the Securities and Exchange Commission are examples.

Problems in Covering the Bureaucracy

Journalists face difficulty in digging out stories about the bureaucracy. Size gives protection from scrutiny. One need only walk around Washington or drive past the Pentagon in Arlington, Virginia to be impressed by the bulk of administrative agencies. And, of course, what you see is not all of it: much of the federal bureaucracy is scattered throughout the country. Covering every major agency and their programs requires massive human effort. Much that is covered is just what bureaucrats want reported.

Second, the subjects bureaucrats often deal with are complex, even to specialists. How well does a generalist reporter understand how rail freight rates are set or how synthetic fuels are developed?

Moreover, bureaucratic working life at the lower levels is usually routine and seldom newsworthy. Only when a catastrophe appears, as when the space shuttle Challenger blew up in 1986 or farmers went bankrupt one after another in the mid-1980s, do journalists try to penetrate the internal administration of the government agencies responsible for the programs.

How Bureaucrats and Journalists Interact

Because of the complexities encountered in covering bureaucracy, the administrator is more likely to seek out the journalist than the other way around.

Political appointees want publicity for their policy initiatives. They are likely to cooperate in backgrounder interviews if they think they can get a favorable hearing. Or they may use journalists to float a trial balloon, or gain support for a program they are launching. In time, of course, some become soured with reporters, feeling journalists only seek out facts damaging to the administration. They may then intentionally misdirect the reporter or devise a cover-up strategy.

Professional career bureaucrats hope that news coverage will bring more resources to the agency and thereby enhance their careers as the agency grows. They want the information they provide to broaden acceptance of the programs they administer, ease enforcement, communicate with other bureaucrats and politicians in the policy sphere, and help gauge public reactions and timing for new programs. They hope for favorable publicity or at least to get the agency's side of the story reported. And above all they seek citizens' support that will be translated into increased budget appropriations.

Lower-level bureaucrats such as district Medicare officials trying to administer an established policy sometimes share this interest. But they are more likely to regard media attention as "trouble." Most of the time they are correct.

Thus, bureaucrats, like other politicians, also play a tricky game of cat and mouse with journalists. Their techniques vary as do their career goals.

The Public Information Officer. Information released about an agency's programs is supposed to be controlled by the public information officer. Federal agencies require clearance with them of all texts, public statements, or speeches that professional career bureaucrats make. Such bureaucrats usually must have special permission to talk to reporters. Often an agency's policy requires a public information officer to be present at such an interview, and perhaps report on the discussion. Sanctions for unauthorized leaking of information can be severe: transfer, reduction in pay, forced resignation or retirement, and the silent treatment or shunning.

Dan Nimmo concluded that these information officers had three ways of defining their responsibilities.[2] Some say they pass along to reporters only information that superiors give them for release. Others see as their responsibility informing or educating the public. The constituency may need to know about new regulations or services available to them from the agency, or why the agency's mission is so important to them.

The third type of information officer is the promoter, a public relations partisan for the agency, who sees the job as advancing the agency's goals and well-being. Favorable news is given prominence, in fact is even dug out for the reporters; less favorable news is buried if possible. Most reporters as well as many elected politicians regard these "agency flacks" as promoters, and are somewhat skeptical, even contemptuous of their efforts.

The News Release. The usual way in which journalists are informed about agency programs is the news release, sometimes provided as part of a press conference managed by the public information officer, a way of stressing the issue's importance. Commonly these get-togethers feature a political appointee. Journalists may also be encouraged to interview knowledgeable career bureaucrats, especially those in middle management, most of them not identified by name in the stories.

Bureaucrats criticize generalist reporters because the journalists sometimes do not understand the subtleties or technical aspects of the agency program, especially when they condense or attempt to rewrite agency news releases. Journalists in turn are likely to accuse the agencies of bureaucratic gobbledygook. They are most likely to accept at face value bureaucratic releases on technical issues relating to natural science, health, or the environment, and view handouts in other areas as not based on scientific evidence.

REPORTING BUREAUCRATIC NEWS

The public is frequently told that bureaucrats set much of important national policy. Yet studies of media coverage consistently show that bureaucratic activities, except in a few major agencies, are a secondary source for news. Journalists first of all are less interested in the technical aspects of a program, important as they may be. They are interested in a program's political implications. But these implications usually mean that the policy involves controversy. The best controversy, from the journalist's viewpoint, is that involving the president and his administration. Second, political implications may mean a change in policy that significantly affects a segment of their readers or viewers.

Covering Political Stories

All Cabinet officials are a potential source of political news, for their proposals may involve controversy. They regard themselves as major policy innovators — that, after all, is why the president chose them. Any political appointee who makes controversial proposals, as President Reagan's Secretary of the Interior James Watts did on environmental matters, will get extensive coverage.[3]

Much of the other political news about bureacratic programs is filtered first through Congress. To reporters covering regional stories, an announcement that the Environmental Protection Agency Superfund will finance cleanups in their region is political news, generally learned from congressional staff when a member of Congress announces it.

Reporters of the prestige press and other major media also turn to congressional staff for leads on stories with political implications.

Congressional staff may be very knowledgable about an agency's problems and sensitive to the political aspects of a story. They are also part of the Capitol gossip network and may have an outlook independent of the agency's goals or objectives. The journalists can then follow up the story with representatives or senators and in the agencies themselves.

Bureaucratic Beats

The wire services and some major newspapers cover such agencies as State and Defense as part of their regular beats. Agencies routinely reported include those providing news of conflicts in international relations. Also covered are those through which the administration deals with the economic health of the nation or segments thereof, a major element in political campaigns. Most other agencies get coverage only when they are involved in a major breaking story with political implications.

Topical Beats

Recently, some editors have begun to wonder if dividing the bureaucracy into beats is the best way to get at major bureaucratic stories. The subject that makes a good news story sometimes cuts across several agencies and into Congress and the president's office. Understanding these interagency relationships may require a reporter with special background.

Then too, a reporter assigned to the same beat for years may be co-opted, becoming friendly with an agency source and finally an advocate for the agency. This closeness may happen partly because of familiarity and sympathy with the agency's programs but may also ensure faster access to more stories.

Changes from the beat pattern were first made in covering international affairs. One reporter at the State Department, another at the Pentagon, and a different one covering the House Foreign Affairs and Senate Foreign Relations committees got only parts of the story. It became evident that a beat could be defined by subject as well as by institution. Having a few reporters assigned to a "diplomacy" beat combining State, Pentagon, and the others seemed to make sense. Such reporters in time become knowledgeable specialists pursuing stories with international aspects, such as foreign-trade policy, with Commerce, Agriculture, and perhaps Transportation, as well as Congress and the president.

Even within a department such as Defense, specialists in weapons technology or disarmament are needed to understand what goes on.

Other specialized fields now include the environment, energy, the economy, and consumer affairs. When an editor considers an issue of special worth, the Washington Bureau may begin to experiment with assigning a more specialized reporter to that subject as a beat.

This approach is still in transition. Most reporting of the bureaucracy is still handled as institutional beats — the reporter goes down to Foggy Bottom to find out what is happening in State or to Justice to pick up the latest FBI handout. Perhaps such routine checking will always be needed.

Investigative Reporting

Investigative reporters also pursue stories with a political slant. Generally the story is about a presidential initiative, though it may also cover problems that should be on the political agenda, the street people, for one.

The Freedom of Information Act. The popular name for the act providing investigative journalists with at least one anticoverup tool is Freedom of Information — if the document requested is in the executive branch. But as we saw earlier, the freedom includes hurdles.

Reporters must know what to look and ask for. If the request is not as specific as "the director's expense account for June 1983," it will face delay. And, journalists know, a story delayed can well be a story denied. Refusal to produce the document because it is in one of the excluded categories can be overturned only by a lengthy appeal. During the Reagan years, the media firm was charged reproduction costs if the bureaucrat did not agree with journalists that the document requested was relevant to a current news story. As we have seen, Congress reversed this policy. The government may also hand over censored documents with crucial parts blacked out.[4]

Bureaucratic Leakers. Although leaks are a major source of news for investigative reporters, often the information leaked is only partial: leakers above all want to be sure that their leaking cannot readily be traced. Woodward and Bernstein describe how such information can be used. You act as if you know more than you do and sometimes secure further information. Or you make shrewd guesses and then ask bureaucrats to confirm or deny.

Journalists sometimes also pressure leaks by accusing bureaucrats of a coverup. They also use genteel blackmail, threatening to publish what they have in order to get more accurate information. A few are said to collect damaging information on individuals that they later use to encourage cooperation.

INFORMATION LESS FREQUENTLY REPORTED

Some subjects go unreported because they have little direct influence on presidential policy making, no matter how they may affect the quality of the average citizen's life. These subjects most frequently include the way in which government programs are actually administered at the individual citizen's level, internal politics of bureaucratic agencies, and subjects that journalists find difficult and boring.

Routine Administration — How Good Is It?

Information is often difficult to gather about the routine aspects of administration. Reporters themselves acknowledge that the reporting on routine agency responsibilities is inadequate.

Tom Wicker of *The New York Times* points out that prison conditions get attention only when prisoners riot, a major escape occurs, or a parolee or work-release prisoner murders someone. Otherwise journalists seemingly assume that nothing's happening even though, Wicker writes, homosexuality, drugs, and other crime may be epidemic inside the prison. Inmates may be honing new criminal techniques while taxpayers pay $12,000 a year or more per prisoner for a system that satisfies no one.[5]

Consider another example of that which does not get reported. Often, with a great deal of fanfare, a cabinet officer just, as we saw, like presidents do, announces a new program to attack a commonly recognized problem. Journalists focus on these announcements and the politician is praised for innovation. But seldom do journalists go back six months later to report how the new program is working. Unless a disaster occurs almost no one examines if the program is effective.

Edward R. Murrow and Fred Friendly, in their *See It Now* reports, pioneered the television-documentary of how government policies affected individuals. Occasionally such reports are also made in the print media. But these are relatively rare because of time and other resources required for such reporting. To dig out the facts a reporter may have to spend months on the story — the network managers of their day criticized Murrow and Friendly because gathering their reports cost so much.[6]

Politics of Bureaucracy

Journalists seldom take notice of the political infighting among top-level political and career bureaucrats. Generally such stories are reported only when the controversy touches the president, as in Reagan's emphasis on defense over welfare.

But competition among agencies is continuous. Edward Epstein says journalists err in viewing the bureaucracy as a monolithic institution. "This blind spot, endemic to journalists, proceeds from an unwillingness to see the complexity of bureaucratic in-fighting and of politics within the government itself . . . . If governmental activity is viewed as the product of diverse and competing agencies, all with different bases of power and interests, journalism becomes a much more difficult affair."[7]

Competition for Resources. Bureaucratic infighting occurs because resources are limited. The federal budget is never large enough to fund all worthwhile programs. And top-level career bureaucrats can easily explain how much more important their agencies' activities are than are programs of other agencies.

John Kingdon describes the lengths to which agencies go to get the publicity to expand programs. He calls one technique "bureaucratic buccaneering" — a publicity method that career administrators used to achieve rapid expansion in the National Institutes of Health. To persuade Congress to increase funds, they presented testimony by supposedly impartial outside sources to journalists and legislators on nongovernment paper so that it would not have the distinctive government watermark. When their letter arrived, "nobody on the Hill would be able to hold it up to the light and see that there was an NIH connection."[8]

Competition for Status. Professional bureaucrats move up the career ladder as their agency resources increase; the head of a larger agency is more important and holds higher rank than the head of a small one. Such an agency requires more upper-level administrators to supervise its larger staff. And agency heads who are able to advance the programs of an agency by skilful public relations are likely to advance more rapidly than others.

Competition for Power. A very few career bureaucrats desire publicity for themselves. Media relations and boldness have enabled them to build an agency into their private power preserve. The most successful public entrepreneurs were J. Edgar Hoover of the FBI, Hyman Rickover of the Navy nuclear-powered submarine program, and Robert Moses, whose special province was public works in New York state.[9]

The entrepreneur role is difficult for career bureaucrats, for they risk one of their major sources of power, which Eugene Lewis calls the "apolitical shield" — the idea that the bureaucrat is an anonymous and neutral public servant, merely carrying out policies set by elected officials. Lewis suggests that the bureaucrat must appear free of "partisanship, greed, self-interest, and personal aggrandizement."

Public controversy in the media destroys that image. The entrepreneurs mentioned above were politically skilful enough to make it appear that controversy occurred precisely because they were apolitical. Their critics were portrayed to reporters as "politicians" who wanted to play politics with the FBI, or the Navy's nuclear submarine program, or New York's park system.

Bureaucratic Politics and Leaks. Journalists such as Jack Anderson make it appear that all anonymous sources in the bureaucracy are whistleblowers. Outrage at corruption or inefficiency, as we saw, does occasionally motivate the anonymous source. Patriotism too may make such whistleblowers speak out.[10]

But most bureaucratic leakers have more political or personal motives, relating to competition among agencies and individuals. Such motivations are seldom reported or speculated on.

The most common political reason for a leak is the intent to control policy. It may be an attempt to sabotage a presidential initiative by mobilizing opposition before the president gets the enterprise off the ground or thinks it through carefully. Bureaucrats may leak to find allies in other agencies or to activate client groups by letting them know steps that are being considered, especially when career bureaucrats feel a political appointee is undermining professional standards or goals. Leaks from Interior or the Environmental Protection Agency against Reagan's political appointees were one of the methods used to alert fellow professionals and sympathetic members in Congress and get them to protest.

The bureaucratic leaker may try to change the public's picture of reality by providing new information. When leakers suggested that funds for the Nicaraguan Contras were being diverted to private individuals, they were attempting to color gray the public image of the group that President Reagan had been calling freedom fighters. Some design leaks to direct information to the White House and thus change the president's views. They leak information to journalists to bypass politically appointed agency heads or officials who surround the president.

Leaks can be used to build up one's own status or to discredit a bureaucratic rival. A subtle career motivation is to demonstrate who is in charge or who speaks for the president. A leak from the State Department may reveal that a political appointee other than the secretary devised the program that the president favors.

Some leaks, as we saw, are official, designed to aid administration policy making. Sometimes, the leak is a trial balloon to determine in advance the reactions to a change in policy. Or leaks may be orchestrated to build support for a policy already decided upon. When a leaker in the Pentagon indicates that Russian missile strength is greater than supposed, the leak may be meant to justify proposals for a defense buildup.

Leaks will also be used to protect or increase an agency's resources. Some have speculated that leaks from the FBI about CIA employees who conducted the Watergate break-in were designed to discredit the CIA and encourage Congress to leave domestic surveillance completely in the "capable" hands of the FBI.

Leaks can gain allies for future battles. Among the most useful of allies may be the reporter who was supplied the information. President Kennedy regularly provided such information to Ben Bradlee for *Newsweek's* "Periscope" page — items suggesting events that might occur in the future. Leakers may also use leaking to advance a career, gain revenge, or discredit a rival in their own agency.

Reporters rarely speculate about any of these motivations, perhaps because they feel that to question a leaker's motives is to destroy a useful source. But their editors perhaps should ask reporters more frequently about the motives driving these anonymous sources in the bureaucracy.

The Boredom Factor

When Tom Wicker joined *The New York Times* Washington bureau in 1960, he was assigned to cover the regulatory agencies. "This assignment," he wrote, "evoked snickers from old hands in the bureau because for years almost all new *Times* reporters in Washington were told that they would cover 'the regulatory agencies.'" He says, however, that none ever did, at least not for long. Wicker himself soon got a transfer to the political beat on Capitol Hill.[11]

Stephen Hess found these agencies rated as low-prestige beats, a judgment he reached by observing the average age of those covering different beats. The regulatory agencies served as a kind of hazing or initiation practice, a beat for the newly hired, at the bottom.[12]

As a beat, the regulatory agencies present, in extreme form, many of the problems that make reporting bureaucratic news so difficult.

Wicker describes why. It was "too diverse in subject matter and procedures and personnel to make a coherent 'beat,' merely because these commissions all regulate something. Beyond that, however important these agencies may be, their work is slow, mostly arcane, and only rarely productive of quick, easily understood news — let alone front-page headlines." Seldom does one come up with a dramatic story.

In other words, covering these important agencies is not what most reporters had in mind when they chose to become journalists. Learning what is going on practically requires that the reporter specialize in the field. And much of the information is gained by studying and teasing information out of dry documents as rigid deadlines close in. Reporters favor stories that can be gathered by word of mouth, generally by starting with a piece of information and adding to it from different sources. The interviews that reporters do get within the bureaucracy are often circumscribed by the public information officer, who is sitting in.

Still, big news is made in these agencies. The FCC relaxes the requirements on television advertising, the Interstate Commerce Commission changes freight rates in ways that affect what consumers pay for products, the Federal Drug Administration relaxes testing time required for an AIDS medicine — these stories carry a good deal more weight than the news that President Reagan eats jellybellies. Wicker and most journalists agree that what the bureaucracy does is important, but they would rather someone else covered these activities.

THE MEDIA AND THE SUPREME COURT

In Chapter 1 we wrote that most politicians are not so naive as to believe that journalists serve only as conveyor belts for their political pronouncements. But unlikely as it seems, U.S. Supreme Court justices have employed such a model for more than 150 years with considerable success. And journalists, until recently, have not vigorously objected.

Perhaps, even if reporters had fought back, the justices would not have changed the rules of the game. Why? Because the Court and the justices have depended less on journalists to further their careers than have other politicians. They have life tenure and few have progressive political ambitions. Of course, the relationship between justices and journalists may change as the increasingly politicized Court becomes involved in controversy and finds it needs greater public support for its decisions.

And so the Supreme Court justices have managed to shield themselves from public opinion in a manner that other politicians envy. The judges still control much of the information reported about themselves and their work.

Yet the justices want it both ways — they stonewall journalists but still want them to get out accurate and detailed reports about the justices' decisions. Their almost universal complaint, as in our quotation from remarks by Justice William O. Douglas in Chapter 1, is that journalists usually garble the justices' decisions.

Justice Thomas Clark blamed the public's misunderstanding of the first school-prayer case squarely on media distortions. Justice Wiley Rutledge wrote, in *Pennekamp v. Florida,* "There is perhaps no area of news more inaccurately reported factually, on the whole, though with some notable exceptions, than legal news."[13]

In this section we examine the justification for such complaints, which some journalists might call mere petulance.

The Setting

The Supreme Court has nine justices, whom the president appoints and the Senate confirms. They serve for life and can be removed only by impeachment. Although no Supreme Court justice ever has been impeached, for fifteen years Justice William O. Douglas was periodically threatened with impeachment, once by Congressman Gerald Ford.

Some still argue that the writers of the Constitution never intended the Court to have the power of judicial review — the right to declare acts of Congress, the president, or state governments unconstitutional. Few, however, question the Court's right to exercise that power today. About 5,000 cases are appealed to the Court each year but it accepts only about 150 for rehearing. Lawyers on each side generally have a half hour of oral argument to supplement their written briefs. The court issues written opinions for about 100 of these cases.

The Court meets from October to June or mid-July, the justices hearing arguments the first four days of each week and on Friday discussing the cases in secret conference. Upon reaching a tentative decision, the chief justice, if he is with the majority, assigns a justice to write the opinion. In other instances, the senior justice in the majority assigns the writing. Other justices may write concurring or dissenting opinions if they wish. During the summer recess justices consider notes that clerks have made about appeals for the next year's session.

How the Court Informs the Public. Justices announce their decisions by reading opinions in open court. The proceeding is planned to ensure that decorum in the court remains undisturbed. The wire-service reporters and major members of the prestige press have seats before the bench. A few others have seats on the side, but most gather in a basement room.

Court aides, upstairs and in the basement, provide journalists with a copy of the opinion only when the justice who wrote it begins reading. The wire-service desks have tubes with which those in the Court can send messages to reporters in the basement, if they wish.

The justices are proud of saying that "The Court speaks once, and then is silent." They rarely discuss specific cases before or after decisions are announced or reveal how they reached a decision. Even after justices retire and write their memoirs, secrecy is the rule. Many even destroy their papers, including draft versions of opinions later revised.

The Supreme Court as Policy Maker

During the 1920s Chief Justice Howard Taft designed the marble palace in which the court meets. A sign inside the door in gilt letters orders "Silence." Inside the pillared, draped courtroom sit the black-robed justices. Behind are the justices' offices, with armed guards stationed to screen visitors.

Taft wanted to emphasize the majesty or "mystique" of the court — one journalist described the intent as overawing the peasants who come tiptoeing in to gaze in wonder and speak in hushed whispers.[14] The atmosphere also appears to awe journalists.

The mystique was designed to emphasize that the justices are above partisan politics. And until social realists and political scientists began analyzing the court's decisions, the public appeared to accept the mechanical theory of judicial review: that the justices place a statute next to the Constitution and with their highly trained legal minds readily detect whether the statute is constitutional.

Legal scholars now generally recognize that political bargaining permeates the judicial process of deciding on the constitutionality of statutes.[15] Alpheus T. Mason points out that, "From John Jay [the first chief justice] to Warren Burger, the Court has consisted largely of politicians, appointed by politicians, confirmed by politicians, and empowered to decide controversial public issues."[16]

Nevertheless, most judicial scholars conclude that the justices generally are persons of above-average abilities, compared, Mason says, to "run-of-the-mill legislators and presidents."

Politics and the Supreme Court. Appointments to the Court are made for political reasons. Earl Warren became chief justice not for his judicial talents but because he ran for president in 1952. At the Republican convention he was persuaded to throw his support to Eisenhower, and in return was promised the first vacancy on the Supreme Court. It turned out to be the job of chief justice. Eisenhower wanted to pass Warren over until the next vacancy, but Warren insisted that a promise was a promise. Eisenhower appointed him chief justice and the Senate confirmed him.[17]

The justices' own political convictions rather than legal precedent or the Constitution's wording alone — their sense of what is right and fair — enter into their decisions. Scholars can predict very accurately each justice's decisions on new cases with mathematical scaling techniques based on the justice's past decisions. The situation justices enjoy encourages them to express their political prejudices. They are shielded from most outside pressures. Having reached the pinnacle of their political careers, they no longer strongly need journalists' services to advance ambitions that are now static.

In reaching decisions, they politick and bargain with each other just as other politicians do to find a compromise wording that will marshal a majority opinion. Justices may shift sides if the opinion writer concedes points or includes specific wording. Judging from the Woodward and Armstrong account in *The Brethren*, the conflict within the conference room may become bitter, sometimes bordering on childishness.

The justices are politicians enough to recognize that the Court needs support from public opinion if their decisions are to stand. The compromises the justices reach are generally within the bounds of what the public will accept, and so help to keep the Constitution and the laws in harmony with present realities. Mason says the Court helps the nation peacefully resolve conflict, in a sense institutionalizing revolution, or at least legitimizing change.[18]

Other politicians recognize that the court functions as a political body. The justices' opinions inevitably become associated with the partisan politics of presidents and Congress. Republican Eisenhower later called the Warren appointment "the biggest damned fool mistake I ever made." And Warren, as if to emphasize how far his opinions pleased Democrats rather than his former colleagues in the Republican party, resigned from the Court when Lyndon Johnson was still president, before President-elect Richard Nixon could take office and fill the vacancy.[19] And in the waning years of the Reagan presidency, several octogenarian justices seemed determined to reject retirement at full pay and thus deny Reagan the opportunity to fill their vacant chairs.

Finally, most students of government recognize that such Court decisions as those on civil rights, abortion, and criminal procedure often are more influential than many acts coming out of Congress or the executive branch.

If the justices' decisions are so political, why do journalists treat them as different from elected politicians?

Reporting the Court's Decisions

An experienced court reporter argues that the court deserves the kind of reporting it gets because it does so little to assist journalists in reporting on their activities. He says it has "the most primitive arrangement in the entire communications industry for access to an important source of news material and distribution of the information generated by that source."[20]

The Court's Journalists. Reporting the Supreme Court has all the features that most journalists try to avoid. Reporters sit in a basement room waiting to be presented a complicated legal document that they quickly have to puzzle out for themselves. They cannot interview the major sources of the story to ask them what they meant by a convoluted statement.

Meanwhile they know that newspaper editors do not regard most judicial decisions as very important or very newsworthy. They regularly cut the reporter's copy unless the case involves freedom of the press. An ambitious reporter, already making a name in bylines, is likely to consider assignment to the Court a dead end. One study found that the average reporter stayed only two and a half years.[21] After some years of reporting the Court for television, Fred Graham left to become an anchor for a Tennessee television station.

One reporter who covered the court for twenty-two years said of his fellow journalists there: "I know of no beat where reporters are lazier and do less to penetrate the process they're supposed to cover than legal reporting."[22]

The justices discourage investigative reporters. Irreverence is frowned upon, respectful passivity is encouraged. Other reporters say the Supreme Court reporters are overly cautious, too deferential, and understate the events they report, lest they be accused of hyping the story.[23]

Item: The court provides reporters with a limited number of copies of opinions. The regulars get their copy but if there is a shortage, the others must share what is left; complaints are not acknowledged.

Item: The court previously announced decisions on Mondays, sometimes in batches of twenty or more. Then it decided to spread release of its opinions throughout the week. Reporters asked the press officer why the change was made. He said he would ask. He later told them he could not give out that information. (It appears the justices did not want to appear to acquiesce to a journalist's suggestion that the decisions be spaced.) Journalists did not report the "no-comment" response.[24]

Problems in Covering the Court. Although the court has a press officer, the office seems unable to so influence arrangements as to benefit journalists. Reporters do not even know which decisions the court will announce; they know in advance only the number of decisions, not the specific ones that will be announced in that week.

Second, reporters do not get advance copies of opinions; they get the majority opinion in page proof only when the justice begins reading it upstairs. Until recently, these proofs had no summary headnotes such as are prepared later for the lawyers who regularly use the *U.S. Reports.* The journalists also receive the concurring opinions and dissents as they are read.

Third, the order in which justices read opinions is set by their seniority, not by the importance of the decision. The most important opinion of the day may be read after deadline time for some journalists.

Fourth, the opinions may be very long, laden with legal argument and citations. Including concurrences and dissents, they have run as long as a 250-page novel. (The *Miranda* decision had 37,000 words.) One court reporter remarked that "Decision day is like taking an open book exam in constitutional law."[25]

How the Public Learns About Decisions. Most Americans learn about a Supreme Court decision from what gets reported by the wire services — AP, UPI, and the Dow Jones service of the *Wall Street Journal.* On rare occasions television and radio flash these reports in special bulletins; more often they save them for "news breaks" or the next news report.

Wire-service reporters sort out from the cases reported those they consider significant. They then send a short statement on their content over the wire. Each wants to be first with the news. Estimates say wire-service subscribers have this news, often fairly accurate considering the constraints under which wire reporters work, within five minutes after the justice begins reading. Canned follow-up summaries — stories prepared in advance with separate leads for the possible outcomes — come later.

The national office and local wire-service bureaus edit this copy to fit their clienteles. The story is often condensed or rewritten because of the flood of other news or to emphasize a regional angle. Local papers or radio and television may fill out the story by collecting immediate reactions from local politicians or individuals who have a special interest in the decision. These people may have only the sketchiest idea about the Court's decision and the reasoning that formed it.

Commonly now, the wire services and syndicated columnists prepare end-of-session analyses and in other articles analyze the justices' political complexion. The appointment of a new justice brings detailed news stories.

Besides the wire services, the *Washington Post, Washington Times, New York Times, Wall Street Journal,* and television networks have full-time reporters at the Court. The print-media reports are the fullest. The *Post* and *The New York Times* deadlines give their reporters time to study the opinions before they write their stories. Their Washington bureaus also can easily solicit reactions from the chairs of the House and Senate Judiciary committees and from other notables.

Reporters from regional newspapers in other parts of the nation or special-interest publications are usually part-timers, having other beats to cover as well. They appear when a decision in their specialized interest seems imminent. On such subjects their reporting may be especially knowledgable and thorough.

How Much Information Does the Public Get? David Erickson found that *The New York Times* reported on roughly 80 percent of the decisions during a term. It alone prints the full text of decisions, but only for landmark cases. Two Midwest papers carried stories on slightly more than 25 percent of that term's decisions. Most of these regional papers gave only highlights from the top decision of the day. One listed an additional 25 percent of the cases in a wire-service weekly roundup. Erickson concluded that none of the coverage was adequate, but that quantity and quality of reporting were related — the greater the quantity the better the quality.[26]

Doris Graber, studying Chicago newspapers and local and national television news, found that judicial coverage, including news from the local courts, amounted to 3 to 5 percent.[27]

Chester Newland and David L. Grey each studied news reports on specific decisions and came to similar conclusions. They suggest that pressure on journalists for speed and brevity collide with the Supreme Court's insistence on secrecy and ritual. Newland wrote that news reports "virtually ignored what the Supreme Court had said, and generally even what it had decided, and reported instead national, state, and local reactions and conjecture."[28]

Improved Reporting of Decisions. Some of the regulars attempt to learn more about the cases under consideration by doing research. Some also listen to the lawyers' Court presentations and may interview them before a decision is announced. Full-time Court reporters sometimes attend lectures by justices at conferences or law schools, hoping to get a clue to their thinking. The information collected goes into a file on each case.

The Association of American Law Schools, supported by the American Bar Association, now provides, for a fee, the publication *Preview*, with background information on major cases. With this resource reporters can cut back on some work in maintaining their own files on the 150 or so cases being considered.

The difficulty is that reporters do not always have time to consult their files before deadlines because they do not know in advance which cases are being decided. Those with deadline pressure try to guess, but only in the final weeks of the term can they be relatively sure which cases may be up for decision soon.

Some reporters, to better understand the decisions, undertake legal training. In 1955, Justice Felix Frankfurter told James Reston of *The New York Times* that such education would be a good idea. Critics, though, say that the extra knowledge negatively affects reporting because the news stories such journalist-lawyers write are too theoretical and often defend the Court rather than report the decisions.

Trends in Court Coverage

Reluctantly and gradually, the Court has adjusted to make reporting of its decisions marginally easier. Proofs of opinions were first distributed to reporters in the late 1920s. Until then, reporters had to report relying on their understanding from the opinion reading, waiting until the last sentences to find out how the case was decided. In 1935, press aides began handing out the proofs as the justice began reading the opinion rather than after he finished. In 1961 the Court changed the reporting time from noon to 10 A.M., perhaps for the justices' convenience, although it also helped journalists meet their deadlines. And "Decision Monday" was abandoned in 1965 so that decisions would not pile up on one day.

Even though "judicial activism" has thrust the Court into some of the most politically emotional issues of our time, the Court has not altered other procedures that would assist journalists. Thus far they have refused to provide news releases or background briefings, and rarely permit interviews on general matters about the Court. To do otherwise, justices maintain, could color their written opinions and destroy the dignity and independence of the body.

The Court rejected the suggestion by the Association of American Law Schools to have a legal scholar on hand at decision time to answer journalists' questions. The consultant's remarks, the Court feared, might

"How was I?"

© Washington Star, 1981 by permission of Universal Press Syndicate

be given official standing. It also rejected a proposal to give journalists advance opinions even if they agreed to stay in a locked room to study them. And most emphatically it rejected the idea that it permit televising justices giving opinions. Chief Justice Burger called television cameras in the courtroom "the most destructive thing in the world. Show business and judicial business," he said, "just won't mix."[29]

Television, its proponents argued, would encourage the justices to write opinions and justify them in language that a lay audience could comprehend. Students point out that in some controversial cases, chief justices have assigned writing of the opinion to justices who communicate readily.

Slits in the Scarlet Curtain

The steps the Court has officially taken to change its traditional procedures and make news reporting easier are only part of the picture. Informal changes have also been occurring.

Investigative Reporting. In the late 1970s, for the first time a team of investigative reporters attempted to cover the Court by encouraging leaks of information that theretofore had been secret. Robert Woodward and Scott Armstrong interviewed more than 170 former law clerks, several justices, and two dozen other Court employees. In *The Brethren* they presented the "inside story" of the conference deliberations for major cases in the first seven years of Chief Justice Warren Burger's tenure, from 1970 through 1976.[30]

Woodward and Armstrong seemed shocked to discover political conflict among the justices. They imply that when justices disagree, those not taking the position the authors preferred were giving in to base motives. Yet, Justice Brennan had observed, "It's unfortunate that people don't understand that this Court has to address and decide issues which always have two, and sometimes many more than two, legitimate and reasonable answers."[31]

But a major fault is that Woodward and Armstrong became prisoner to their sources. Law clerks, their major leakers, are always the "good guys," frequently reported as urging wavering justices to take the "right" path. The authors write of the decision on abortion: "The language remained Blackmun's; the more rigorous analysis was the work of the clerk," a statement many scholars would question.[32] The justice who receives least criticism in this book is Justice Brennan, another source. His private notes on the Nixon tapes case are the basis for a seventy-five-page section.

The authors begin with a theme to which they hoped to relate the information they dug out. They seem to have expected to find another Watergate, with President Nixon's appointee as chief justice busily undermining constitutional government. They had to settle for portraying Chief Justice Burger as indecisive, bumbling, and somehow underhanded for wanting to influence the other justices. The liberal justices thus are the good guys. Justices Douglas and Marshall are criticized just briefly when they run afoul of their law clerks.

Despite these weaknesses in emphasis, the work *The Brethren* is a major advance in covering the Court's deliberations. More than one reviewer has suggested that the Court has every right to preserve secrecy in its deliberations while a case is being decided. But at some later time, ours being a democratic system, the justices should be willing to make all information available. To make the Court accountable to citizens, justices, like other political leaders, should be willing to justify their actions beyond the Court setting. The justices' rejoinder might be, Why should we? Our decisions stand as written and, to those who will take the time to study them, are self-explanatory."

Other Leaks. During the 1970s, *Time,* public radio, and ABC television reporters all reported leaks revealing the Court's projected action in specific cases.[33]

In June 1986, the court did not report its expected decision on the Gramm-Rudman-Hollings budget-balancing law. The justices were thought to have delayed because they were angered by ABC's Tim O'Brien, who had reported when the Court would announce its decision and that the vote would be 7 to 2 against upholding one provision of the law. Seemingly, the Court was determined to prove him wrong, at least on when the case would be announced. He was correct in other respects. O'Brien had accurately reported court actions in advance on several other occasions. Following one such report, a Supreme Court printer was transferred.

Less than a month after this leak, *The Washington Post* correctly reported a case in which a Georgia law against sodomy was upheld. Justice Powell had switched sides during the last weeks of consideration, they said, changing a 5–4 majority against the state law into a 5–4 majority upholding its constitutionality.

New Pressures on the Court. Because they work in Washington, justices get most of their news through the prestige press, which has generally approved editorially of the Warren Court's opinions. But the justices have become less insulated and much more aware of opinions formed by television and the wire services' reports to the nation's other media outlets.

At one time only the "John Birchers" were disturbed enough to show disapproval by posting "Impeach Earl Warren" signs along secondary roads. Now other citizens outside Washington have begun to pressure the Court. The decisions on school prayer and abortion inundated the Court with letters — 5,000 in the prayer case of 1962 and 45,000 in the 1972 abortion case; 75 percent of them were critical.

The abortion decision aroused continuing demonstrations aimed at the justices, some opposed to the decision, others upset because the number of justices favoring the decision declined from 7–2 in 1971 to 5–4 in 1986. Justice Blackmun received death threats and was picketed at speeches in law schools. Abortion clinics were bombed and in a most bizarre incident, a bullet was fired into Blackmun's apartment, perhaps by a group calling itself "The Army of God." The FBI investigated, but no arrests were made.

Groups now regularly urge members to vote for and against presidential candidates, keeping in mind that their likely court appointments will be felt for many years. The Christian Right and civil-rights and civil-liberties groups especially have been aware of this influence. The Court's decisions have been a campaign issue in every election in the past generation. Richard Nixon campaigned against the Warren Court in 1968;

women's groups in 1980, exacted from Ronald Reagan the promise that his first Supreme Court appointment would be a woman, as it was.

And Senate confirmation of justices has raised questions beyond legal competence or financial honesty. Two of President Nixon's appointees were rejected because of doubts about their stands on racial issues. Rehnquist's appointment as Chief Justice resulted in close scrutiny of his previously stated political opinions and acts.   The successful campaign against confirmation of Judge Robert Bork, a Reagan nominee, perhaps more than any other confirmation process, highlighted the political role of the Supreme Court.

The Judges Break Their Silence. Some justices, at least obliquely and perhaps recognizing their involvment in political issues, in a few instances have justifed their political positions and even discussed types of cases in interviews. Justice Brennan told reporters he thinks some day the Court will abolish the death penalty altogether.[34] And Justice Rehnquist meanwhile told college audiences that he expected the Court to overturn the abortion decision some day.[35] Justices Stevens, Blackmun, and Brennan all publicly warned against a "rightward shift" of the Court as the result of Reagan appointees.[36]

Four justices have appeared on television. The clearest case of justifying a specific decision was made by Justice Blackmun in an hour-long PBS interview. In 1982, on the tenth anniversary of the abortion opinion that he wrote, he complained of being called "butcher of Dachau, murderer, Pontius Pilate, King Herod, you name it." He pointed out that he had not made that decision alone; six other justices had joined him in the opinion.[37]

And for the Future?

The Supreme Court has always been deeply involved in the political process; because it has the power of judicial review, it can hardly avoid the responsibility. Since the Warren Court announced the school de-segregation decision in 1954, the Court has been activist, willing to overturn previously settled decisions. It is likely to remain so. Richard Posner, conservative federal appeals judge and former University of Chicago Law School teacher, argues that if liberal justices favor activism and conservatives always favor following precedent, soon all decisions will be liberal. He concludes that conservatives must also become activist.[38]

As Court decisions continue to make political news, some reaching further than many acts of Congress, justices should expect demands that they be more publicly accountable. Journalists, in turn, are likely to treat the Court more as they do other political entities. The Court should expect journalists to make more demands that it change its traditions and rituals, just as its decisions have changed traditional ways of doing things for other segments of society. Indeed, the justices themselves may find a slowly increasing need to use the media to explain and comment on their actions.

David Grey comments, "It seems somewhat inconsistent for the Supreme Court to talk about First Amendment rights such as freedom of the press as an essential part of democratic dialogue and yet discourage efforts at improved public insights into the Court itself and the workings of the law."[39]

A Closing Note

This chapter has a common theme. We have dealt with media coverage with which journalists themselves are unhappy. They recognize that important policy decisions are being made that are not adequately reported.

Reporting about the bureaucracy needs to follow a more analytical and documentary style; not tied exclusively to news events. This was the kind of reporting that Edward R. Murrow assumed would dominate television, rather than the more episodic evening news. For the Supreme Court, most reporters would say that the need is for less secrecy and ritual in the Court's procedures. To achieve that openness, they would favor more aggressive journalism.

NOTES

1. Stewart Alsop, *The Center: People and Power in Political Washington*, (New York: Harper & Row, 1968), p. vii.
2. Dan D. Nimmo, *Newsgathering in Washington: A Study in Political Communication* (New York: Atherton, 1964), pp. 45–47.
3. John Kingdon found that in the Departments of Health and Transportation, political appointees set most of the agencies political agendas. Career bureaucrats commonly spent their time suggesting alternative ways in which to achieve the program goals of political appointees. John Kingdon, *Agendas, Alternatives, and Public Policies* (Boston: Little, Brown, 1984), pp. 32–37.
4. Steve Weinberg, "Trashing the FOIA," *Columbia Journalism Review* 23 (January/February 1985): 21–28.
5. Tom Wicker, *On Press* (New York: Viking, 1978), pp. 176–179.
6. A. M. Sperber, *Murrow: His Life and Times* (New York: Freundlich Books, 1986), pp. 351–413.
7. Edward Jay Epstein, *Between Fact and Fiction: The Problem of Journalism* (New York: Vintage Books, 1975), p. 32.
8. Kingdon, *Agendas, Alternatives, and Public Policies*, p. 37.

9. Eugene Lewis, *Public Entrepreneurship: Toward a Theory of Bureaucratic Political Power* (Bloomington: Indiana University Press, 1980).

10. Leon V. Sigal, *Reporters and Officials: The Organization and Politics of Newsmaking* (Lexington, Mass.: D. C. Heath, 1973), pp. 131–150.

11. Wicker, *On Press*, pp. 43–44, 177–180.

12. Stephen Hess, *The Washington Reporters* (Washington, D.C.: Brookings Institution, 1981), p. 49.

13. A study of state judges in two states revealed that their basic criticism too of journalists was inaccuracy and incomplete reporting. Robert E. Drechsel, "Judges' Perceptions of Fair Trial — Free Press Issue" *Journalism Quarterly* 62 (Summer 1985): 388–390.

14. Alsop, *The Center*, pp. 316–317.

15. Harold Spaeth, *Supreme Court Policy Making* (San Francisco: W. H. Freeman, 1979).

16. Alpheus Thomas Mason, "Eavesdropping on Justice: A Review Essay," *Political Science Quarterly* 95 (Summer 1980), p. 296.

17. Alsop, *The Center*, p. 321.

18. Mason, "Eavesdropping on Justice," p. 301.

19. Bob Woodward and Scott Armstrong, *The Brethren: Inside the Supreme Court* (New York: Simon & Schuster, 1979), p. 10.

20. John P. MacKenzie, "The Supreme Court and the Press," In Kenneth S. DeVol, ed., *Mass Media and the Supreme Court: The Legacy of the Warren Years*, 2nd ed. (New York: Hastings House, 1976), p. 355.

21. Larry Berkson, *The Supreme Court and Its Publics* (Lexington, Mass.: Lexington Books, 1978), p. 58.

22. The quote is from Lyle Denniston, former Court reporter for the *Washington Star*, in David Shaw, "Legal Issues: Press Still Falls Short," *Los Angeles Times* (Nov. 11, 1980), and David Shaw, "Media Coverage of the Courts: Improving But Still Not Adequate," *Judicature* 65 (June-July 1981): 18–24.

23. David L. Grey, *The Supreme Court and the News Media* (Evanston: Northwestern University Press, 1968), p. 54.

24. Grey, *Supreme Court and News Media*, p. 55.

25. Grey, *Supreme Court and News Media*, p. 44. From an interview with Dana Bullen of the *Washington Evening Star.*

26. David Erickson, "Newspaper Coverage of the Supreme Court: A Case Study," *Journalism Quarterly* 54 (Autumn 1977): 605–607.

27. Doris A. Graber, *Mass Media and American Politics* (Washington, D.C.: Congressional Quarterly Press, 1980), pp. 66–67. See also Ethan Katsh, "The Supreme Court Beat: How Television Covers the U.S. Supreme Court," *Judicature* 67 (June-July 1983): 6–12.

28. Chester A. Newland, "Press Coverage of the United States Supreme Court," *Western Political Quarterly* 17 (March 1964): 15–36. Quotation from p. 27. and Grey, *Supreme Court News Media* pp. 83–120.

29. Forty states allow some form of televised court procedures but the Supreme Court forbids recordings and photographs of the Court in session. Associated Press report, Nov. 27, 1984.

30. Woodward and Armstrong, *The Brethren.*
31. Interview with Justice Brennan by Glen Elsasser, "Senate Groups Cram for Rehnquist Quiz," *Chicago Tribune* (July 27, 1986), p. 5.
32. Woodward and Armstrong, *The Brethren*, p. 229.
33. Woodward and Armstrong, *The Brethren*, pp. 237–238, and William Rivers, *The Other Government: Power and the Washington Media* (New York: Universe Books, 1982), p. 88.
34. Kathryn Kahler, "High Court Brennan Is Confident Death Penalty on Way Out," Newhouse News Service, July 19, 1986.
35. Woodward and Armstrong, *The Brethren*, p. 414.
36. John A. Jenkins, "A Candid Talk with Justice Blackmun," *New York Times Magazine*, Feb. 20, 1983; and Stuart Taylor, Jr., "Justice Stevens Is Sharply Critical of Supreme Court Convervatives," *The New York Times*, Aug. 5, 1984, p. 1.
37. Associated Press News Story, "Ton of Letters Ripped Court's Abortion Ruling," Dec. 6, 1982.
38. Gordon Crovitz in a book review of Richard A. Posner, *The Federal Courts* (Cambridge: Harvard University Press, 1985); *Milwaukee Journal,* March 15, 1985.
39. Grey, *Supreme Court and News Media*, p. 140.

9

American Journalists and World Events

In the last battle of the War of 1812, General Andrew Jackson defeated the British in the Battle of New Orleans, a week after the United States and Britain had signed a peace treaty. That news had not yet reached the Louisiana battlefield. In fact, slow communications was a reason for our being at war with England. The British navy had blockaded American ports, but lifted the blockade two days before Congress, by a narrow majority, declared war. The news did not reach the capital until much later.

Marshall McLuhan, the communications analyst, observed that technology had changed this disastrous isolation and made the world a global village. The world became smaller when the transatlantic telephone cable was laid in 1858. The wireless, radio, and finally television, videotape, and satellite transmission have since made it possible to transmit news from almost anywhere within minutes.

In 1983 Americans sitting in their living rooms could watch agents of Philippine President Ferdinand Marcos murder his political rival, Benigno S. Aquino, as he stepped off a plane. Three years later, they could follow play by play as Aquino's widow, Corazon, drove Marcos from power in that small nation half a world away.

But not all events are so readily reported, for politics determines what is communicated, and some of the information that might be reported is suppressed. News that the citizens of the global village see or read about is skewed toward events in nations that permit independent journalists and give them free movement.

CHAPTER OVERVIEW

We begin by viewing the global village of communications in which multinational relations are played out. We review the approaches differing government systems take in trying to control political information. We consider the quantity and quality of foreign coverage for American audiences, and the problems American foreign correspondents face. We discuss how politicians attempt to manipulate foreign events to their own advantage and that of their nations. And we conclude by reviewing how professional standards of journalists relate to national problems in international relations.

Extended media coverage of the war in Vietnam had a major effect on the outcome of the war. Revolting color closeups of dead and wounded beamed "live" from the battlefield, executions recorded live, pictures of naked children fleeing napalm attacks, all directly affected the national will to continue that war. The reaction led, ultimately, to this last humiliating moment in United States withdrawal, from atop the United States embassy in Saigon. A major event, it was revealed, could be greatly altered by journalists on television and in print.

THE SETTING: THE GLOBAL VILLAGE OF COMMUNICATIONS

In Chapter 1 we saw that journalists, independent of the government, report news of political events that citizens can use to criticize their governors. These reports make it legitimate for citizens to oppose government actions in democracies such as France, Britain, and the United States. Though journalists do not have access to all the news in any of these nations, enough news is reported to allow citizens to question their leaders' actions.

Democratic politicians sometimes complain that such coverage puts them at a disadvantage. Ze'ev Chafets, director of the Israeli Government Press Office under Prime Minister Menachem Begin, stated that "The Syrians were able to massacre, say 10,000 civilians, or 8,000 — we don't know exactly how many, but many thousands — in private . . . . They don't let journalists go there at all." But in Israel, he argued, almost every action involving its Arab population, even minor clashes with police, is reported internationally. Chafets called the failure to emphasize the absence of news from inside Syria, "acquiescence in the ground rules of thugs."[1]

Reporting from Nondemocratic Nations

Authoritarian governments can never completely dominate all elements in the society: a church, unions, universities, and even journalists remain somewhat independent. The government suppresses journalists when it can, but more often it plays a cat-and-mouse game of intimidation. In totalitarian nations, the government controls what is reported by making all organizations a part of the government system, including the media; it controls internal communications.

Authoritarian Intimidation. Authoritarian governments bully and harass editors who display independence of the ruling party. The question of how much journalists can report is always a little unclear. In Guatemala, newspapers are published with blank spaces or spaces filled with pictures of old-time movie stars such as Ava Gardner — stories the censor cut. But citizens are free to speculate about what was cut.

Editors in such nations lead a precarious existence, never being sure how free they are. Governments from time to time make an example of selected journalists to intimidate the rest, declaring them subversive, disloyal, or traitorous. They may be arrested or subjected to intensive questioning. Some have their presses smashed by mobs and their news-papers shut down, and some have been assassinated.

South Africa illustrates the off-again, on-again pattern of repression. In October 1977, the government shut down the leading black newspaper and arrested its editor. A few months later the government freed the editor and permitted the paper to reopen, assuming that the editor had gotten the message. As things heated up in 1986, reporters were at first barred from reporting disturbances in the black townships. Then they were warned that the government would enforce the emergency media restrictions — prohibitions against reporting "subversive statements," which included support for sanctions against South Africa. Reporters were allowed back into black townships, but were forbidden to take pictures. Then as violence increased, reporters were barred from Soweto Township. In 1987 a tight lid was clamped on all reporting, but news of clashes between police and blacks still reached the international media, though in less vivid detail.

Totalitarian Suppression. The totalitarian media are a part of the governmental apparatus and often are as important in advancing national policy as is the bureaucracy or the army. The government decides which facts will be reported, when they will be made known, and how they will be interpreted.

Important events are not reported as they occur, but only after the official line has been decided upon. During that lag, citizens may be prepared for the news that is coming. Then the government media report the facts that fit the official interpretation.

Several days passed before the Soviet government reported details about the Chernobyl nuclear power-plant disaster, and then only after protests from nations downwind. These early reports emphasized the reassuring news that loss of life was minimal and that the situation was under control. Much later, fuller details were released. In another disaster, the Soviet Union waited six days to report that they had shot down a Korean airliner. During the period of waiting, pieces appeared in the official media about spy planes. The official explanation then claimed that the airliner was on a spy mission.

Totalitarian censorship is effective. The Soviet Union does not inform the world about its war in Afghanistan. And little news came out about what was happening when the Khmer Rouge took over Cambodia. And news that is unreported remains mostly invisible. One study found that the television networks devoted only twenty minutes of news time to the genocide occurring in Cambodia between 1975 and 1979.[2] Flora

Lewis of *The New York Times* wrote, "The world tends to forget what it doesn't see and hear in living color and shrieks."[3]

What of *Glasnost*?　In 1986, the new Soviet leader, Mikhail Gorbachev, announced a policy of greater openness *(Glasnost)* — his way of getting a stagnant Communist economy off dead center by inviting internal criticism. The Communist Chinese had already begun a similar experiment, but had pulled back when students desiring greater freedom rioted in 1987. And the Soviet Union under the 1960s leader Nikita Khrushchev had had "an interval of freedom," crushed within a brief period and Khrushchev removed from office by others in the Soviet leadership.

A major beneficiary of *Glasnost* has been the journalist. The Chernobyl disaster was later analyzed in detail, as also was the Soviet policy of interning critics of the system in mental institutions. Even the leader himself was subjected to criticism as reporters and editors steadily pushed the boundaries of what might be written and broadcast.[4]

But experts disagreed on the answers to two crucial questions: Was *Glasnost* only a facade to fool the Western world into believing that communist systems could become democratic? Would *Glasnost* become a permanent policy or would it prove to be a brief period of liberalization — an experiment deemed too risky for the rulers to be continued?

As we write, Soviet journalists and politicians as well face the same problems that characterize authoritarian societies — how far is "too far"? Can Afghanistan be discussed and criticized? Will the Soviet leaders set limits by the familiar techniques of harassment and intimidation?

Keeping News Out

Complete isolation from the global village of news is becoming harder to achieve. The Voice of America beams news in twenty-one languages and estimates that 28 million Soviet citizens listen regularly, despite government jamming. Another 18 million Soviet citizens listen to Radio Liberty, and 15 million more to the BBC (British Broadcasting Corporation). In news-hungry Cuba, current copies of newsmagazines are smuggled in — a copy of *U.S. News and World Report* sold for $208 on the black market. And Radio Marti and television programs from Miami have large audiences.

Pressure created by news that seeps in, however, is more devastating to authoritarian than to totalitarian governments. Such officials find that information from outside can affect their nation's internal politics, even toppling a leader, as in Haiti, Iran, South Korea, and the Philippines. The possibility suggests why many third-world authoritarian nations joined the Soviet Union in 1980 in trying to set up a "New World Information Order." Under the auspices of UNESCO, it would have required licensing of reporters and ensured that only "responsible" news reporting occurred.

JOURNALISTS WHO COVER FOREIGN EVENTS

The foreign correspondent's career has been thought romantic since the turn of the century, when Richard Harding Davis swashbuckled his way across the world and came home to write and lecture about his adventures.

But placing a journalist in a foreign post is expensive, estimated to be between $100,000 and $200,000 a year, which includes travel, personal expenses, and cable charges for each correspondent. *U.S. News and World Report* spends close to $250,000 annually to keep a reporter in Tokyo. The average newspaper or television station cannot afford a corps of foreign correspondents. Only six United States newspapers had correspondents in Moscow in 1968; today the number is about fifteen.

Who Regularly Gathers the Foreign News?

Four "Western" agencies have permanent correspondents stationed around the world: the Associated Press, United Press International, Reuters of Britain, and Agence France Presse. About 300 Soviet journalists gather news for Tass. A relatively new organization, the Inter Press Service, gathers stories about development in third-world nations. It is associated with UNESCO and grew out of third-world dissatisfaction with Western media coverage.[5]

Only a few newspapers and magazines have extensive field personnel: *The New York Times*, The Washington Post-Los Angeles Times Service, *The Chicago Tribune*, and *Time*. And these regulars are spread thinly. Journalist Theodore White wrote that in the 1950s he was stationed in Paris for a press service with a beat that included all of Europe. Many correspondents are stationed in Nairobi, Kenya because of its relatively free atmosphere. M. L. Stein reports that some of these have a beat covering all of East Africa, and some, he says, are assigned the whole continent.[6]

Most American newspapers and even the television networks follow the same procedures they use in covering national news, depending on the wire services and the prestige press for on-the-spot reports. Occasionally some of the larger regional papers "parachute in" a correspondent to a hot spot for a few weeks. And so the number of foreign correspondents varies with the events to be covered. In 1932, 465 full-time American journalists were assigned to posts abroad, an estimated 350 are employed today. But in 1945, 2,700 correspondents were covering World War II, and in 1963, 1,200 to 1,400 were in Vietnam. When the war in El Salvador was a major story, it attracted 792 correspondents.

Other Sources of Foreign News

Part-time journalists sometimes augment the regulars. These stringers are journalists who happen to be near a trouble spot such as the Cameroons when a story breaks. They may also be people with a contract to file stories regularly or on request. They may receive some regular form of compensation, but the paycheck is usually based on column inches filed or printed. Some may after a period of trial be recruited for a permanent position.

The White House press corps also supplements those stationed abroad, for it follows the president when he travels. And from their Washington locations the departments of State, Defense, and Treasury are primary conveyors of political news from abroad. Other federal agencies provide foreign news within their areas of specialization, as Commerce and Agriculture do on international trade.

Analysis of the news that is reported reflects how important these other sources are, most obviously in television reports; visuals or lack of them give away the source. James F. Larson found that the evening television news anchor read 42 percent of the international stories without visual footage. Most of these items came from wire services or perhaps stringers. Another 26 percent of the stories were foreign news from domestic sources; the president, members of Congress, or someone at the Pentagon or Department of State provided the details. Only 32 percent of the foreign reports had footage shot abroad.[7]

Hazards Foreign Correspondents Face

A foreign correspondent's job includes many minor discomforts. Camera crews may lug equipment long distances and in wartime conditions, often over rough terrain. Language difficulties and unfamiliar cultures make getting accurate information and giving balanced analysis difficult. Africa has more than 800 languages and India almost as many dialects. Good translators are a rarity. Add to these hazards physical discomfort, illness, loneliness, and weariness. One American correspondent stationed in Nairobi summed it up: "After a two- or three-week trip to Chad or Ethiopia, I'm just too damn exhausted to do any work here."[8]

News that they report is often locally controversial, so that they can expect groups to pressure their media superiors. Americans for a Safe Israel prepared a film titled "NBC in Lebanon: A Story of Media Misrepresentation." With NBC film clips, they attempted to demonstrate that NBC coverage of the Israeli invasion of Lebanon was slanted against Israel.[9] But the major problem American correspondents face is local attempts to prevent full reporting.

Censorship and Harassment. Few democracies are as easy to cover as our own government. The Italian reporter for the magazine *L'Europeo* calls our capital a "fairyland," because officials generally return phone calls. "In Italy," he says, "if you phone someone he won't reply. If you write, he will ask your party, which newspaper, and then he'll say it is too risky to speak."[10] Costa Rica and Japan license journalists.

Editors of major publications in Israel, a nation that feels constantly under siege, regularly meet with army and senior government ministers to review stories. By unwritten agreement the editors submit to a form of self-censorship. During the invasion of Lebanon, however, some editors printed news the army wanted suppressed. But reporters charge that the editors' committee still kills stories.[11]

President Jose Napoleon Duarte of El Salvador told *Newsweek*, "I am losing the war not on the battlefield but in the pages of *The Washington Post* and *The New York Times*." During the last week of his election campaign, stickers appeared on the windshields of foreign journalists' cars, saying, "Journalists! Betray Your Own Country, Not Ours!"[12]

Soviet Harassment. In 1961 the Soviet Union stopped censoring news that foreign journalists report to the outside world. But they make it extremely difficult to gather information except from official sources. Western reporters have their offices in a guarded compound from which Russian citizens are shooed away. They may not travel beyond a twenty-five-mile radius of the Kremlin without permission, which takes about a week to get. The Soviets do not publish a phone book, a tool that would provide access to government officials.

Harold Piper, Moscow bureau chief for the *Baltimore Sun*, writes, "Parallel to the bureaucratic restrictions is a constant undercurrent of intimidation and harassment. Aside from having the trim stripped off my car several times while it was parked next to the police post outside my house, nothing nasty ever happened to me until this summer. [The government television network sued him and Craig Whitney of *The New York Times* for libel.] I know reporters who had their tires deflated, who were anonymously roughed up, whose wives were taken for long scary rides by taxi drivers."[13]

Lars-Erik Nelson wrote that "tough and inquiring correspondents" face "a variety of accusations, petty harassments, and cheap slanders. Generally it's just an abusive article in *Pravda* or *Izvestia* . . . . They'll steal your car for a couple of days, tell the U.S. Embassy you're an adulterer, or broadcast television pictures of you when you have drunk one vodka toast too many at some banquet to peace and friendship."[14]

Physical Danger. Ernie Pyle was only one of many journalists killed covering World War II. But smaller wars also bring casualties. An old story goes that when a revolution occurs, 200,000 people are trying to get out of the country and twelve are trying to get in — all American journalists. Nineteen journalists were killed in 1983 and twenty-one in 1984.

Anne Geyer, once a foreign correspondent, says that many nations view journalists as hostile, rather than neutral.[15] The Ayatollah Ruhollah Khomeini of Iran expressed that feeling: "The pen in the hands of the foreign press is a pen in the hands of the enemy, something that is worse than the bayonet to the fate of mankind."[16]

Joanne Omang, *Washington Post* reporter in El Salvador, adds, "In many Latin American countries, even where the press is free, journalists have usually been paid employees of either governments or their opponents. Their articles are openly slanted toward one side or the other. The idea of a balanced view is more than foreign. It is anti-patriotic."[17]

During the Falklands War, Argentinians kidnapped American and Norwegian correspondents, harassed them, and threatened to kill them for reporting unfavorable news. In 1987, ABC-TV correspondent Charles Glass was chained to a cot 62 days in Lebanon before escaping. Shiite extremists have held AP reporter Terry Anderson for almost three years. In El Salvador, four Dutch journalists following rebel forces were killed. On February 13, 1985, during the Israeli invasion of Lebanon, Israeli soldiers fired three shots at an NBC camera crew. A week later, Israeli tank shells killed two CBS employees in the village of Kfar Melki. Other journalists nearby were convinced that the tank crew intentionally aimed at the CBS car.[18]

Expulsion — the Ultimate Professional Penalty. Stories filed from Ghana and Tanzania became fewer after 1965, only partly because crises

U.S. JOURNALIST WANDERS INTO SOVIET NEWS SPACE

© William Day, by permission of William Day and the Detroit Free Press

were less frequent than during an earlier period. The authors of a study concluded that there was "a tendency for the Western press to report crisis events only when journalists judge that they are important enough to risk possible expulsion."[19]

In 1984, twenty-two journalists were expelled from various nations. Those ejected from the Soviet Union over the years include reporters for the *Washington Post,* Associated Press, *New York Times, Los Angeles Times, Time, Newsweek,* ABC News, and CBS News. And in 1986, *U.S. News and World Report* correspondent Nicholas Daniloff was arrested and accused of spying. Most Western observers believed Daniloff was entrapped to provide the Soviets with an excuse for expelling him and to provide a person to trade for a Soviet United Nations employee arrested in the United States for spying.

How Correspondents Get Stories

Correspondents covering a crisis such as civil war in El Salvador are frequently stonewalled and walled off. Officals consider them a nuisance or a menace as they try to confirm army casualties, number of displaced persons, or damage to buildings. Press conferences are few and the information dispensed there unreliable. Journalists are often frightened and uncertain where to go for accurate news. The government regards interviews with persons on the antigovernment side as propaganda for the rebels. Print journalists accuse television journalists of taking the "easy" option of going after exciting battlefield visuals rather then hard political news.[20]

Elsewhere public officials and their public pronouncements are a major source for routine stories. Many nations provide official news through prepared releases or closely supervised tours. Verifying these government reports is a constant problem. Low-ranking officials are forbidden to meet with foreign reporters and what major leaders say in interviews, as one may anticipate from American experience, is not always accurate.

Sometimes local journalists who cannot publish a story themselves because of censorship provide the story to foreigners. As in America, government officials also leak stories, but in many nations such dissemination is dangerous to the official as well as to the reporter.

Stories that local newspapers print, especially if they are mouthpieces for government, are another source of news, but they often require sophisticated interpretation. American reporters in Moscow read the eight pages of *Pravda* carefully for clues to changes in policy, and they speculate about information that may be excluded. They look for hidden hints. In some Latin nations, American reporters have found stories that purport to be about France, but they find the writer is really describing events in his own nation.

Reporters also attend ritualistic functions to determine who is present as army or school children march by. They watch local television to see which national leaders appear — absences may signal illness or falling from favor. And the journalists talk to each other, but not always in local bars as the stereotype suggests.

Some news is gathered in an even more roundabout way from United States or other diplomatic personnel assigned to the nation. William Claiborne of *The Washington Post* describes how the Soviet war in Afghanistan is covered: "At noon every Tuesday, a half dozen or more foreign correspondents, based in Islamabad, Pakistan's capital, gather in a windowless room on the ground floor of a Western embassy building for a briefing on the progress of the war in Afghanistan. [An unidentified official] who frequently stumbles over the pronunciation of the names of unfamiliar towns, begins reading from a long teletyped cable from his country's mission in Kabul . . . . Attribution is strictly limited to 'Western Diplomatic sources.'" Questions are not allowed.[21]

AMERICAN REPORTS OF FOREIGN EVENTS

Conventional wisdom says that Americans have little interest in foreign affairs, that news editors tell them more than they want to know. The facts, though, are more complicated. Publications and broadcast outlets serve different publics, and so treat international events differently. Editors provide as much foreign news as they believe will attract readers or viewers — and readers' tastes vary.

Coverage in Depth

The early history of foreign reporting gives us a clue as to which citizens desire foreign news in depth — in 1500 the Swedish government was the first to require its foreign emissaries to report back accurate information. In our own time government agencies such as the Department of State, Congress, and the military still want detailed reports.

Add to these the citizens labeled by political scientist Gabriel Almond "attentive publics," persons who are intensely interested in international news even though they have no official responsibility. Some are involved in peace and antinuclear groups. Others have personal interests in an area, such as Jewish and Arab Americans in the Mideast, blacks in South Africa, and Irish Americans in the Northern Ireland struggles.

In 1688, Lloyds Coffee House in London began systematically collecting commercial information. At the same time, the five brothers of the House of Rothschild, living in five European capitals, built a banking empire by pooling economic information. Persons involved in commerce still want to know in detail about economic decisions being made abroad and how the dollar stands with the pound or the yen.

Detailed Reporting. Those who desire detailed information have two types of sources. Specialized magazines and journals provide overview stories and analyses of trends. The prestige print press — *New York Times, Washington Post, Christian Science Monitor,* and *Wall Street Journal* — provide some in-depth information with analyses of trends.

These papers generally have larger editions, but they are far from comprehensive in their foreign coverage. S. M. Mazharul Haque found in a 1979 study that *The New York Times* devoted 13 percent of its news hole to international stories, *The Washington Post,* 10 percent, and the *Christian Science Monitor,* 21 percent.[22]

Regional newspapers, especially the smaller ones, do not see their mission as providing extensive coverage of international events. They save most of their news hole for national and local news.

Crisis Coverage

Television is the source of foreign news for most Americans, and it devotes much of its small news hole to international affairs. James F. Larson examined a random sample of 1,000 broadcasts between 1972 and 1981 and found that on an average night seven of the seventeen stories reported (41 percent) were on international topics.[23]

But such news is necessarily brief and attention grabbing. Television thus has become the chosen medium for "crisis junkies," a phrase that probably describes most of us. Television news, radio, and major news magazines thrive on a diet of unfolding minidramas from foreign lands. Each holds center stage for a few days or perhaps a week. Then some other foreign event pushes it aside and attention is drawn from the Mideast to the Philippines to Korea and then on to some other international trouble spot. In a study of *Time* and *Newsweek* it was found that 70 percent of the international coverage was of this episodic type.[24]

Content and Quality of Foreign Reports

Sociologist Herbert Gans examined coverage in both print and electronic media to determine the kind of foreign stories reported in the United States. His list heavily emphasizes political stories, especially crisis events, the kinds of stories that journalists define as political news: drama, conflict, human interest.

Major Topics Covered. Gans found that American editors favored these types of stories; (1) American activities in foreign nations, including visits by presidents and hostage stories; (2) events that directly affect Americans, such as arms-control negotiations and summits; (3) Communist-menace stories; (4) European royalty and changes in leaders of nations; (5) dramatic political conflicts such as wars or revolutions; (6) catastrophic events such as mass drownings, earthquakes, airplane, bus, and train wrecks, or devastating storms; and (7) the excesses of dictators.[25]

Quality of Reporting. The accuracy of reports from authoritarian and totalitarian nations is sometimes questionable because of restrictions on and intimidation of foreign correspondents. High standards of accuracy also may not be met when media organizations "parachute in" reporters to cover hot spots as they occur, rather than depend on permanent correspondents. The temporary reporters lack established contacts for sources. Walter Laquer of the Georgetown Center of Strategic and International Studies states that this limitation and censorship have reduced and will reduce even more in the future the amount of foreign news that Americans receive.[26]

Coverage of international events suffers from some of the same defects as coverage of domestic politics. Foreign officials describe American reporters as arrogant, irresponsible, and sensation-mongering. Two Soviet journalists, in a later assessment of the Chernobyl nuclear disaster coverage, mentioned an American headline that screamed out "2,000 deaths!" The Soviet journalists deplored the hyping and sensationalism designed to gain readers and viewers.[27]

Foreign news is often presented as entertainment rather than for enlightenment. Reporters seek out crises that can provide a continuing visual story for television — frequent newsbreaks and updates that run through several days. Each reporter wants a scoop, to be first with news of what happened and to receive plaudits from journalistic superiors and colleagues. And each knows that human-interest reports get broadcast and printed. Hijackings or assassinations can be reported to provide as much drama and suspense as a television chase movie. Hodding Carter, PBS media critic, believes that a major defect in such coverage is a "dearth of perspective and continuity." Foreign news, he suggests, is presented in disjointed segments. Readers and viewers lack the background information to put news in context. Each day's events are presented as if they had no connection to events of yesterday and the day before. Headlines tell the sensational- aspect until the stories have been fully milked, and then that nation and event disappear from public view.[28]

Third-World Coverage. When the third-world nations proposed the UNESCO New World Information Order, they argued that much of the news coverage they received was superficial and negative. Foreign journalists, they said, never reported "the good news." They claimed that the coverage concentrated on disasters and of news of the "economically affluent, politically powerful, and those culturally similar to the U.S." The important third-world events, such as successful development projects, were extensively ignored.[29]

Several studies made during the 1970s supported this criticism, particularly in journals filled with overview articles. [30] But conditions changed. In the 1980s, Harque found that 65 percent of the international news in the three dailies he examined was about third-world nations.[31] And David Weaver and G. Cleveland Wilhoit reported that 60 percent of foreign stories were about third-world nations. But they concluded that journalistic fascination with crisis events, not pro- or anti-third-world bias, accounted for the kind of coverage to which these nations were objecting.[32]

dearth-
inadequate

Much foreign news, particularly in television and the news magazines, is concentrated on negative events. So too is much American domestic news: it attracts readers and viewers, providing entertainment, not enlightenment.

A more telling criticism might expose ethnocentrism, the failure to see events from a foreign perspective. Walter Laquer calls it "mirror imaging — explaining political events and personalities abroad in terms of symbols familiar to American readers." He says that we attempt to put our own labels — liberal and conservative, hawk and dove — on such diverse foreign leaders as Iran's Khomeini or Libya's Khadafi.[33]

POLITICIANS INFLUENCE FOREIGN NEWS REPORTING

International reporting becomes important to American and foreign politicians for two related reasons: it can help their domestic political careers, and they can use it as a weapon in international diplomacy.

Foreign Events and Presidential Campaigns

A publicized trip abroad to meet foreign leaders generally signals that the politician is running for president. Richard Nixon scored a news triumph when as vice president he met with Soviet leader Nikita Khrushchev in a finger shaking confrontation in a Russian kitchen, widely reported in the United States.

A successful player in this game was Democratic presidential aspirant Jesse Jackson, who presented his headline-grabbing trips as humanitarian efforts. In 1983 he secured the release of Navy flier Lt. Robert Goodman, downed over Syria. A trip to Cuba to meet Castro gained release for members of separated families. At the 1985 summit, he met privately with Russia's Gorbachev and on the next morning's talk shows said that he had argued for disarmament and pressed for the release of more Soviet Jews. [34]

One of the presidential debates in 1984 was set aside to discuss foreign issues, an indication of their weight in campaigns. Challengers have tried to use foreign events to attack incumbent presidents. In 1972, George McGovern attempted to make Nixon's Vietnam policy a major campaign issue. Yet C. Richard Hofstetter and Robert H. Trice found that television reports of foreign affairs gave President Nixon a clear advantage over his opponent. [35]

Almost every presidential election has several foreign-policy issues that become part of the campaign debate. Hofstetter and Trice also found, however, that in 1972, although Vietnam and the Arab–Israeli conflict were major stories, fewer than one-third of the "campaign" stories involved foreign news.[36] Only dramatic events, such as the Iranian hostage crisis in 1980, have the potential to influence the election. Trade negotiations, disarmament, the strength of the dollar in foreign markets, even administration policy in Central America may be thought too complex to deal with.

American Presidents at the Summit

Attempting to influence public opinion at home and abroad is almost daily a part of presidential governing. Among the more subdued efforts of this sort was newly elected President Reagan's announcing that the foreign press corps in Washington, which numbers more than 400, could draw lots to ask a question at his second press conference. But here we single out more important efforts: summit negotiations as instances of presidential diplomacy, and attempts to influence domestic and world opinion through the media.

Managing the Logistics. Reporters concluded that the Carter administration made news of meetings with foreign leaders difficult to cover because of inadequate planning. The bitterest chapter that Jody Powell, President Carter's press secretary, wrote about his White House experience is not about Iran but about a major Carter triumph — the Camp David Accords. A Marine drill team performed at Camp David amid already strained media relations. Powell writes, "The crowning blow came with the playing of the National Anthem. While Egyptians and Israelis stood silently, the press corps, with few exceptions, refused to stand. I could not believe my eyes. American journalists . . . expressing their pique about logistic arrangements through disrespect of the flag."[37]

President Reagan's first summits too were media failures, but mainly because of his inept performance. At his first conference in Ottawa, Lou Cannon writes that the president told old welfare jokes to bewildered leaders of other nations. On the return trip he was "exhausted and defensive" and "so incoherent that two reporters who interviewed him turned to aides for an interpretation." The next summit at Versailles, Cannon writes, showed little improvement: the president fell asleep while meeting with the Pope.[38]

When the press corps is abroad, Barbara Matusow writes, it is in a somewhat isolated and controlled setting, giving the president a major advantage if he and his aides are smart enough to use it. The Reagan team recognized the opportunity they were missing in influencing opinion. Matusow describes how the 1984 London Conference was managed, she and other journalists ruefully felt, in a "masterful way."[39]

The Reaganite preplanning in 1984 was careful and thorough. Michael Deaver and his staff and selected journalists flew to Europe several times. They inspected each site that the president would visit. They considered logistics for journalists, security, and phone lines. One such trip gave Deaver the idea of the president's visiting his ancestral home in Ireland. Also included was a visit to the Normandy beaches on the fortieth anniversary of D-Day.

On his return Deaver and the senior Reagan aides began work on a communication plan — what the president should say at each stop and how to have him say it. Next, Deaver arranged to have each major American official who would be at the summit appear on talk shows and also give separate background briefings to selected journalists. Meanwhile, the president met with reporters from the six nations whose leaders would attend.

At the summit itself, the team provided journalists with a steady flow of news events. They had concluded that if journalists do not have content to write about, they begin to concentrate on form — the stumbles the president makes.

The press secretary gave morning and afternoon briefings. Smaller forums were held for representatives from larger news organizations. Interviews with participants, other than the president, were provided for reporters from *The New York Times* and *The Washington Post*. Deputy press secretaries were available to answer questions from any reporters. The press secretary's office provided a stream of press releases, biographies of other nations' leaders, and verbatim transcripts of statements.

The press aides elaborated events to create additional stories. They stressed that they regarded certain presidential statements as especially important to ensure that journalists would report them. Journalists then added to their stories that the presidential office considered what the president said especially important. The president, addressing the Irish Parliament, offered a proposal he had made previously; it was given a new twist so that reporters would have a new peg. Andy Glass, Washington bureau chief of Cox newspapers said, "Everything is structured to make it easier to do things [their] way."

A second aspect of control involved detailed attention to the personal and professional needs of the press corps. News releases were timed

© Chicago Tribune, by permission of Tribune Media Services

to meet deadlines. The reporters were given enough time for work, sleep, and an occasional night off. Phones, facilities, and food were given high priority. Free coffee was provided. Hotel arrangements were carefully checked. Information was provided on such practical matters as the value of the American dollar in the nations visited.

Finally, as at home, the president was unavailable for interviewing; reporters complained they seldom got close enough to ask him questions. Instead, television was given numerous photo opportunities. Reporters criticized some as sterile and meaningless, including the visit to the Irish homestead at Ballyporeen. But they dutifully photographed the president for the evening news.

Reporters' objections to being manipulated were generally unnoticed. Sam Donaldson of ABC summarized the experience as "more rigidly set down than a Hollywood picture . . . . We become the equivalent of Hollywood directors, script writers, and cameramen. We even distribute their pictures for them." The similarity to a carefully scripted movie production occurred to others as well, including, one assumes, the president and his aides.[40]

Foreign Leaders Influence American Opinion

America is so intent on what other nationals think of us that we sometimes forget that foreign rulers see influencing American opinion as a major priority.

The Soft Sell. Andreas Papandreou, a socialist with anti-American leanings, became prime minister of Greece in 1981. One of his first acts was to hire the New York public-relations firm of Fentom Communications, Inc., at $6,000 month. He wanted them to stimulate news stories about Greece that would convince the American public that socialist governments are not all bad. [40]

He was not alone. Canada hired former White House aide Michael Deaver. South Africa has a major public-relations effort directed at the American public. Among others hiring public-relations firms are Saudi Arabia, Turkey, Haiti, and Venezuela. Some nations, including even Iran, have run full-page ads in the prestige press to tell their story to American opinion leaders. [42]

Foreign diplomats meet regularly with American journalists. The national embassies distribute news releases and arrange television appearances when their nation is in the news. Most invite American journalists to their parties. Some journalists refuse to attend, but others consider these gatherings opportunities to make new contacts if not gather news stories. [43] Journalists consider West ·Germany, Egypt, Japan, India, and Great Britain the most skilled in press relations.

Increasingly, foreign nations have public-relations firms prepare visuals for television or magazines. Japan had a video report released eight days before Prime Minister Yasuhiro Nakasone visited the White House in 1985. It showed American fruit finding its way to Japanese markets. American ambassador Mike Mansfield was shown saying that Japan's markets had more American goods than many Americans thought. Stations may use segments in their news reports; others air the entire piece without indicating its source. [44]

Occasionally, foreign representatives to the United States take a somewhat harder line. In November 1982, Israeli ambassador Moshe Arens told America's newspaper editors that his assistants had done a four-month study of newspaper coverage of the war in Lebanon. He gave out ratings for the monitored papers, ranging from −53 for *The Washington Post* to +56 for *The Atlanta Constitution.* Shortly afterward, former Israeli defense minister Ariel Sharon filed a $270,000 libel suit against Time Inc., claiming inaccurate reports on his actions in the

Lebanese war. The figure was relatively small because Sharon wanted the corporation to admit fault, not to compensate him monetarily.[45]

The Soviets Become Media Conscious. General Secretary Gorbachev has come to appreciate how much style matters in influencing world opinion. The Gorbachevs' first visits to Western Europe were a calculated media triumph. His goal was to destroy stereotypes about the closed, gray Russian system.

He arrived almost nattily dressed, his wife Raisa wearing Christian Dior creations. In London, she passed up a tour of Karl Marx's house to see the crown jewels. In France she visited an impressionist art exhibition and fashion shows at the Pierre Cardin and Yves Saint Laurent salons. A journalist of the left-wing journal *Liberation* said, "The days of the big, round women, bewigged in sauerkraut fashion . . . who walked a few paces behind their husbands . . . are really finished."

The general secretary was interviewed on French television, and the program appeared uncensored on the same night on state-run Soviet television — a unique event. Soviet citizens saw their leader being grilled about the treatment of dissident Andrei Sakharov. The next day he held a forty-minute news conference for foreign journalists. He lost his temper only once, when Dan Rather asked about Soviet treatment of Jews. He unveiled a new arms-control proposal. And, like a campaigning candidate, he waved at French crowds and visited a Peugeot auto plant, climbed behind the wheel of a metallic-gray luxury version of the Peugeot 309, and joked with workers on the line that he was going to drive the car back to Moscow.[46]

Have Journalists Replaced Diplomats? Some observers argue that the media are used as a diplomatic channel in ways that have made traditional diplomacy obsolete. Patricia A. Karl writes, "The media are increasingly part of the process (if not the entire process) in the communications between governments and publics about international politics."[47]

We take a somewhat less sweeping view. Nevertheless, one may find numerous illustrations of politicians using journalists to send messages to — more often, past — each other. Secretary of State Henry Kissinger got his first hint that Chinese leader Mao Tse-tung would welcome relations with the United States from a magazine article rather than through diplomatic channels. Edgar Snow, well-known reporter on Chinese affairs, wrote of being specially invited to the Gate of Heavenly Peace. He felt that Chinese leaders, by their behavior toward him, were signaling their interest in a Sino-American rapprochement. Snow wrote in *Life* magazine that Mao would be happy to talk with President Richard Nixon "either as a tourist or as president." The invitation was recognized and accepted.[48]

The most frustrating incident for the United States in such media diplomacy was that surrounding the hostage crisis in Iran. Iranian officials refused to meet with American diplomats. Instead they stated their demands to reporters; one was that the United States investigate the crimes of the Shah, former Iranian ruler. The Carter administration had no clear information about the student militants who had taken over the United States embassy or whom they could negotiate with to end the crisis.

MEDIA AND AMERICAN FOREIGN POLICY

In Chapter 1, we described the customary relationship between politicians and journalists as one of competition and guarded cooperation, characterized by some skepticism on both sides. We suggest that the Vietnam experience altered the relationship in respect to foreign-policy initiatives.

Foreign-policy reporting includes an issue not found in domestic reporting: the national interest.

Politicians in time came to understand that the professional career considerations of journalists might take precedence over friendship or ideological preferences; journalists would report even stories that injured politicians they liked or admired.

But some asked, should professional career requirements take precedence over patriotism?

Journalists and politicians today differ over the kinds of events that should be reported "in the national interest." Journalists frequently claim that American officials seek to keep secret matters that the public should know about. In response, Politicians claim that media publish information without considering national security. Today, neither group appears to trust the other to act responsibly. But it was not always so.

American Reporters and the CIA

In 1953, Joseph Alsop, a major columnist, traveled to the Philippines at the request of the CIA. He was one of more than 400 journalists who carried out secret assignments between World War II and the end of the Vietnam War.[49]

Some journalists were asked only to share their notebooks and where possible to gather information useful to our government. But some went further, identifying citizens abroad who might be recruited for the CIA information network — that is, as spies.

Publishers also cooperated. The *Louisville Courier Journal* placed a CIA agent on its payroll for a year so that he could then pass as a practicing journalist. Between 1950 and 1966, ten CIA employees were provided cover as employees of *The New York Times*. Most of America's major electronic and print media assisted the CIA in one way or another.

The Vietnam War and journalists' distrust of American official policy strained these relationships. The arrangements themselves became public knowledge with revelations in the Senate Intelligence Committee investigation, chaired by Senator Frank Church of Idaho, a leading critic of the Vietnam War.

Following publication of the Church Committee report, much of the cooperation ended. Between 1973 and 1976, CIA Director William Colby began scaling down contacts with journalists. Operatives employed by media firms were told to become freelancers. Some were placed on foreign publications that the CIA funded. Payments to all but a few journalists ended.

Colby's successor, George Bush, announced in 1976 that "Effective immediately, the CIA will not enter into any paid or contractual relationship with any full-time or part-time news correspondent accredited by any U.S. news service, newspaper, periodical, radio or television network or station."

But left unanswered was the question of what journalists owed to their nation's government. In 1987, fellow journalists criticized ABC correspondent Barbara Walters because she transmitted secret messages from an Iran arms dealer, Manucher Ghorbanifar, to President Reagan. She had interviewed Ghorbanifar with Saudi Arabian Adnan Khashoggi on the *20-20* program, and after the program Ghorbanifar asked her to take the message to the president.

Walters said she "felt terrible" being an intermediary but thought the information needed to be relayed.

Legacy of the Vietnam Experience

American foreign relations as reported today is still colored by influences begun by journalistic coverage of the Vietnam War and by the alleged extensive official deceptions at that time.

Journalists trust official foreign-policy actions less, but many also have felt justified in casting aside former restraints. Increasingly intense competition for ratings and circulation added to this impulse toward changed attitudes.

Vietnam correspondent David Halberstam contends that critical television coverage of Vietnam was justified. The networks gave administration leaders ample opportunity to gain American support. The news coverage did not lose the war, Halberstam claims, rather the administration failed to make its case. Perhaps without that television coverage the war might have ground out another 50,000 deaths before we recognized that our situation was hopeless.[50]

Yet many military officers firmly believe that the Vietnam War was lost only because war's horrors were displayed on the television evening news. They say that reporting beamed at only one side of the conflict would have lost the American Revolutionary War for the colonists and won the Civil War for the South. Some appeared to believe that the television coverage increased casualties. The military's memories of Vietnam made it easier for them to deceive reporters and keep them from the scene in 1983 when United States troops invaded Grenada.

In this atmosphere, officials are evasive about even minor details, threatening legal reprisals for imagined transgressions, and reporters single-mindedly search for "smoking guns" within American government. Pulitzer prizes are not won, observed Morton Kondracke, executive editor of *New Republic,* for exposing KGB activities. Rather, prizes go to those who expose the duplicity of a president, the United States military, or the CIA. [51]

Reporting Military Stories. One year after Grenada, the Navy held a two-day conference at the Navy War College in Newport, Rhode Island. Journalists and military personnel were invited to air complaints and suggest how to improve relations. None would be attributed. The comments suggest the prevailing air of distrust.

A journalist who had learned that naval vessels were being completed below cost and ahead of schedule complained that the Navy took two months to give him facts or the name of an official he might interview. The Navy's instinctive reaction, he suggested, was to suppress the news — to keep everything secret from journalists, even when the story was favorable to the military.

Next, a Marine Lieutenant Colonel told how his squad had successfully infiltrated Syrian lines and set up an artillery spotting post in the Lebanese hills. A television journalist reported the story on the evening news, including the location of the post. The marines made it back safely, but the advantage was lost. The officer said that the event left him with a "knot in the stomach" when dealing with the press.[52]

After journalists protested about being excluded from Grenada and the Department of Defense agreed to set up a pool for the next military action, another incident reinforced mutual distrust. Though journalists were sworn to secrecy, in the April 1985 pool alert, even before the task force left for what turned out to be a training exercise in Honduras, a bureau chief at Mutual Radio, which supplied one of the pool members, informed the other radio networks' bureau chiefs that the pool was alerted. The story of a coming military action quickly spread through Washington. The DOD suggested that the test proved journalists could not be trusted and their decision in Grenada had been the correct one. [53]

In rebuttal, journalists could point out that the Reagan administration, before the truck-bomb disaster, had been unwilling to admit the marines' precarious position in Lebanon, preferring a defiant posture despite news reports of danger. Many journalists might also ask if the American public would have learned from their government of right-wing death squads and the murder of American nuns in El Salvador, or human-rights violations by the Contras in Nicaragua. *Newsweek* editors could point out too that journalists have not always behaved irresponsibly: their staff knew that six United States diplomats were hiding in the Canadian embassy in Iran during the hostage crisis but did not publish the story.

Early in 1986, CIA director William Casey recommended that the Justice Department prosecute NBC-TV under a 1950 law that previously had been used only against spies and traitors. A network story about United States submarines that eavesdrop inside Soviet harbors, he charged, had illegally disclosed classified information.[54] Later in that year *The Washington Post* reported that the Air Force had fifty Stealth fighters in operation. Letters to the editor asked why the paper was printing information that would only be "aiding and abetting the enemy."[55]

Reporting about Hostages and Terrorists. Officials claim that television news inflames emotions during hostage crises. Television presents the event as a horrifying entertainment, much as the yellow press once reported coal-mine disasters. In the sixty hours during which the 1985 TWA hijacking lasted, ABC, CBS, and NBC each made about forty special reports.[56]

The television industry is also accused of magnifying the significance of these events. With 43,000 traffic deaths each year, critics argue, why concentrate so much coverage on the hijacking of TWA Flight 847 in Beirut in which only one person lost his life?

It is also claimed that television coverage makes dealing with kidnappers more difficult. One observer called the routine television coverage of some hostage's wife or mother pleading on television for the president to give in to hijackers' demands "the pornography of grief." More serious charges are that excessive coverage gives terrorists a platform, glorifies them, and invites further terrorist acts.[57]

But hostage Kurt Carlson claims that the Iranians planned to kill the hostages. "The media," he says, "focused on all 39 of us, keeping us from being broken up into different groups, and put pressure on the governments involved to negotiate our release." [58] Martha Graham, chair of *The Washington Post*, argues that every time terrorists appear on television, they lose more support around the world.[59]

Lieutenant General William Odom, director of the National Security Agency, in 1986 addressed a Davidson College audience on the battle against terrorism. "The biggest problem we face now, he claimed, "is leaks. Leaks cost us large amounts of money and policy opportunities. The leaks over the Berlin disco affair [where American military personnel lost their lives from a planted bomb] and the intelligence associated with it probably will mean that we will be unable to prevent the deaths of Americans in other terrorist incidents."[60]

In May 1986, NBC broadcast an exclusive interview with Mohammad Abul Abbas, the terrorist who planned the hijacking of the ocean liner *Achille Lauro* in the previous October. The United States government had indicted Abbas for the hijacking and murder of one of the passengers and offered $250,000 for information leading to his arrest. Then NBC got the interview by promising not to reveal where Abbas was hiding. Charles Oakley, head of the State Department's counter-terrorism unit, accused the network of ". . . becoming his [Abbas's] accomplices in order to give him publicity."[61]

Also in 1986, the Reagan administration was found to have inaugurated a "disinformation campaign," with planted stories in American and other newspapers suggesting that an invasion of Libya was imminent. Its purpose was to discourage terrorist activity, but journalists said that it would cause the truth of future government pronouncements to be suspect.

In 1977, Hanafi Muslim terrorists, occupying the B'nai B'rith building in Washington, D.C., were interviewed on radio talk shows. As the police were negotiating a resolution, a talk-show reporter asked a terrorist, "How can you believe the police?" And during the TWA hijacking in 1985, a network reporter announced that a "Delta Force" was being sent to Algiers to free the hostages. The terrorists then disregarded their previous deadline and took off for Beirut two hours early, fearing the Boeing 747 would be disabled on the ground in Algiers.

A Closing Note

Lloyd Cutler, White House counsel under President Carter, suggests that television coverage of international events causes policy making to become even more irrational than does sensationalism. Television's almost instantaneous and dramatically graphic journalism, he says, influences both the timing and content of foreign policy making.

He argues that television forces the president's hand, creating "a political need" for a prompt presidential response — something for the evening news broadcast. If the president delays, the administration is portrayed as weak, divided, or indecisive, and opponents begin attacking to gain political advantage. If the president decides on a disagreeable choice, a negative reaction is broadcast. Television reporting therefore retards creation of a national consensus behind the president in time of crisis.

Cutler's comments reflect the Carter experience during the Iranian hostage crisis. Television news programs daily announced a count of days over the many months that the American hostages were held in Iran — Cutler called it the "TV doomsday clock." This suspense was like the Chinese water torture to President Jimmy Carter, perhaps encouraging him to approve the ill-conceived attempt to rescue the hostages.[62]

The problems caused by international television spectacles are exacerbated when warfare rages between government officials and journalists, when each distrusts and attempts to frustrate the other. The competitive pressures that encourage sensational reporting are magnified. Evidence suggests that since 1959 television coverage has overemphasized the significance of terrorist actions, has given a single interpretation that becomes widely accepted, and is inaccurate even when focusing solely on terrorist acts against American citizens.[63]

The adversary relationship also encourages the tendency of officials toward secrecy and deception of the public. Neither side hesitates to manipulate the other in the name of a cause that they consider a higher good. That appears to have been the justification Lt. Col. Oliver North gave for attempting to deceive Congress and the American public while he took actions that he admitted were illegal. The amount and accuracy of information declines. And the prospects for rational foreign-policy making look dim indeed.

NOTES

1. Tom Hundley, "Ze'ev Chafets, Israeli Journalist, Criticizes U.S. Mideast Coverage," *Detroit Free Press*, Dec. 2, 1984, p. 1.
2. Morton Kondracke, "Is the Press Responsible for a Weak Foreign Policy?" *Detroit Free Press*, May 24, 1984.
3. Flora Lewis, "Afghanistan: Long Live the Resistance," *New York Times Service*, June 6, 1986.
4. Ellen Mickiewicz, "Soviet Viewers Are Seeing More, Including News of the U.S.," *New York Times Magazine*, Feb. 22, 1987, p. 29. For a contrary view, see Angus Roxburgh, *Pravda: Inside the Soviet News Machine* (New York: Braziller, 1987).
5. C. Anthony Giffard, "The Inter Press Service: New Information for a New Order," *Journalism Quarterly*, 62 (Spring 1985): 17–24.
6. M. S. Stein, "UNESCO Debate Muted in Nairobi," *The Quill* (January 1982): 10–11.
7. James F. Larson, *Television's Window on the World* (Norwood, N.J.: Ablex, 1984).
8. M. L. Stein, "UNESCO Debate Muted", p. 20.
9. Edward Walsh, "NBC's Mideast Conflict," *Washington Journalism Review* (October 1983): 22–23.
10. Joseph Atkins, Jacqueline Duke, Joy B. Fukumoto, Wayne Kondro, Alhaji G. V. Kromah, and John Perrotta, "Welcome Strangers: The Foreign Press Corps in Washington," *The Quill* (May 1981): 30–32.
11. Moshe Negbi, *Paper Tiger*
12. Joanne Omang, "How the Fourth Estate Invaded the Third World," *Washington Journalism Review* (June 1982): 46.
13. Harold Piper, "Slander in Moscow," *Washington Journalism Review* (September/October 1978): 56.
14. Lars-Erik Nelson, "Soviets: We Don't Negotiate with Kidnappers, Do We?" *New York Daily News Service*, Sept. 4, 1986.
15. Georgie Anne Geyer, "News Correspondents Do Vital Work," Universal Press Syndicate, Feb. 23, 1986.
16. *The Washington Post*, Dec. 20, 1979.
17. Omang, "How Fourth Estate Invaded...," p. 47.
18. Alexander Cockburn, "Israel's War Against Foreign Journalists," *Wall Street Journal*, April 11, 1985, p. 27.
19. William A. Hachten and Brian Bell, "Bad News or No News? Covering Africa, 1965–1982," *Journalism Quarterly* (Autumn 1985): 626–630.
20. See Omang, "How Fourth Estate Invaded...," for a vivid description of what covering the war in El Salvador was like.
21. Quoted in Richard Reeves, "Can Reporters Rely on 'Official News?'" Universal Press Service, May 23, 1985.
22. S. M. Maszharule Hague, "Is U.S. Coverage of News in the Third World Imbalanced?" *Journalism Quarterly* 60 (Autumn 1983): 521–524.
23. James F. Larson, *Television's Window on the World* (Norwood, N.J.: Ablex, 1984), p. 36.

24. Robert L. Bledsoe, Roger Handberg, William S. Maddox, David R. Lenox, and Dennis A. Long, "Foreign Affairs Coverage in Elite and Mass Periodicals," *Journalism Quarterly* 59 (Autumn 1982): 473.
25. Herbert J. Gans, *Deciding What's News: A Study of CBS Evening News, NBC Nightly News,* Newsweek *and* Time (New York: Pantheon, 1979), pp. 30–36.
26. Walter Laquer, "Foreign News Coverage: From Bad to Worse," *Washington Journalism Review* (June 1983): 32–35.
27. Victoria Irwin, "U.S., Soviet Journalists Scrutinize Each Other's Coverage of Chernobyl," *Christian Science Monitor,* May 5, 1986.
28. Hodding Carter, "Ask Them Yourself," *Family Weekly,* May 3, 1981.
29. Andrew K. Semmel, "Foreign News in Four U.S. Elite Dailies: Some Comparisons," *Journalism Quarterly* 53 (Winter 1976): 736.
30. Semmel, "Foreign News," and Bledsoe et al., "Foreign Affairs."
31. Hague, "U.S. Coverage of News": 523.
32. David H. Weaver and C. Cleveland Wilholt, "Foreign News Coverage in Two U.S. Wire Services," *Journal of Communication* (Summer 1981): 55–63 and, by the same authors, "Foreign News Coverage in Two U.S. Wire Services: An Update," *Journal of Communication* (Spring 1983): 132–148.
33. Laquer, "Foreign News Coverage": 33.
34. Jack W. Germond and Jules Witcover, "Jackson: Foreign Free-Lance," Tribune Media Services, Nov. 22, 1985.
35. C. Richard Hofstetter and Robert H. Trice, "Television News, Foreign Policy, and Presidential Campaigns: The Case of 1972," *Georgia Political Science Association Journal* 8 (Spring 1980): 93–119.
36. Hofstetter and Trice, "Television News."
37. Jody Powell, *The Other Side of the Story* (New York: Morrow, 1984), Chapter 4, "Camp David Eve," pp. 71–87. See especially pp. 72–75.
38. Lou Cannon, "On the Summit State, Reagan Was Masterful," *Washington Post Service,* May 13, 1986.
39. Barbara Matusow, "Abroad: The White House Writes the Lead," *Washington Journalism Review* (Sept. 1984): 43–46.
40. Matusow, "Abroad."
41. James Buie, Maura Casey, Gregory Enns, Vanadana Mathur, and Mark Williams, "Foreign Governments Are Playing Our Press," *Washington Journalism Review* (October 1983): 21–24.
42. Buie et al., "Foreign Governments . . . ."
43. Susan Wallers, "The Seduction of Hildy Johnson," *Washington Journalism Review* (April 1980): 26–29.
44. Jeanne Saddler, "Public Relations Firms Offer 'News' to TV, Electronic Releases Contain Subtle Commercials for Clients," *Wall Street Journal* April 2, 1985, p. 6.
45. Buie et al., "Foreign Governments . . . ."
46. Kitty McKinsey, "Gorbachev Wows 'em on French Visit," *Detroit Free Press,* Oct. 6, 1985, pp. 1, 16A.
47. Patricia A. Karl, "Media Diplomacy." In Gerald Benjamin, ed., *The Com-*

munications Revolution in Politics (New York: Academy of Political Science, 1982) pp. 143–152.

48. John Maxwell Hamilton, "Ten Years After Death, Edgar Snow's Shadow Still in the Picture," *The Quill* (January 1982): 17.

49. Carl Bernstein, "The CIA and the Media," *Rolling Stone* Oct. 20, 1977; Richard H. Leonard, *Point-Counterpoint* (Chicago: Scott, Foresman, 1983); and Stansfield Turner, *Secrecy and Democracy* (Boston: Houghton Mifflin, 1985).

50. David Halberstam, *The Powers That Be* (New York: Alfred A. Knopf, 1979) pp. 708–718.

51. Kondracke, "Is the Press Responsible for a Weak Foreign Policy?"

52. Brad Knickerbocker, "Journalists, Warriors Trade Salvos on How Media Cover Wars," *Christian Science Monitor,* Nov. 28, 1984, pp. 1, 40.

53. Associated Press story, "Pentagon Press 'Pool' Springs Leak," April 23, 1985.

54. Associated Press story, "NBC Violated Secrecy Law in New Leak, Casey Charges," May 20, 1986.

55. Letter to the editor, *The Washington Post,* Aug. 30, 1986.

56. Brian Donlon and Ben Brown, "How News Crews Respond to a Hijacking," *USA Today,* June 17, 1985, p. 3D.

57. "TV News Under the Gun," *Newsweek,* April 13, 1981, pp. 104–107, and "Does TV Help or Hurt? Journalists Are Accused of Giving Terror a Platform," *Newsweek,* July 1, 1985, pp. 32–37.

58. *Chicago Tribune Magazine,* June 29, 1986, p. 3.

59. Associated Press story, "Coverage of U.S. Hostages Defended," Feb. 3, 1980.

60. *Detroit Free Press,* Aug. 9, 1986, p. 7B

61. "A Question of Ethics," *Maclean's* (May 19, 1986), p. 25.

62. Lloyd N. Cutler, "Foreign Policy on Deadline," *Foreign Policy* 56 (Fall 1984): 113–128.

63. Michael X. Delli Carpina and Bruce A. Williams, "Television and Terrorism: Patterns of Presentation and Occurrence, 1959 to 1980," *Western Political Quarterly* 40 (March 1987): 45–64.

APPENDIX

Reporting on State and Local Politicians

REPORTING ON STATE POLITICIANS

Throughout, we have recalled how media coverage has focused more and more on national politics. And we have followed that pattern as well.

In learning about relationships between politician and journalist, through, both students and faculty may experience as we did that necessarily the speakers we can invite to our classrooms are generally state and local politicians and journalists. We have therefore included brief observations on how state and local reporting of what politicians do differs from from national reporting.

Career Ambitions

Politicians with progressive career ambitions hope state government will prove to be just a way station on the road to Congress. Governors eye the Senate, some the president's cabinet, the vice presidency, or even the presidency. Whether they say so or not many regard state government as the minor leagues, a perception that reaches both journalists and citizens.

Such politicians may not hesitate to bypass the capitol reporters and try for national coverage. In Michigan, the governor's press secretary offered a major story to *The New York Times,* which agreed to print it if they had an exclusive. The governor's office agreed. More commonly, governors and other politicians attempt to build state support, perhaps for a later run for the Senate, releasing stories to fit the state's major metropolitan paper deadlines or to television stations around the state.

Many journalists similarly have progressive rather than static ambitions: a career at the state level is not always satisfying, for the pay may not be high and the hours are irregular. Television journalists seem to be perpetually moving on. As more reporters work for chain newspapers, they expect to be considered when opportunities open up within the parent organization. Those whose careers do not take them to the national stage often find other state or local outlets for their talents, such as public-relations jobs with government or private corporations.

How State Government Differs

States as diverse as New York and California, the Dakotas and Mississippi, Hawaii and Alaska share characteristics that distinguish them from national government. All share the trait of low visibility, for states are in the blurry middle between national and local governments. Citizens are often not sure what functions the state bureaucrats perform in the federal system — mainly routine administration, many seem to conclude.

And so citizens regularly report in opinion polls that they are least interested in state government and politics, an opinion reinforced by national communication and transportation patterns. Old distinctions blur as people move across the nation in pursuit of school or job, feeling less attached to a state or town than their parents did.[1]

Editors, gatekeepers for the media, are thus likely to crowd out news of what state politicians do in favor of other political stories.

The State's Part-Time Politicians

An enduring but gradually receding image of state government depicts it as run by amateurs, unlike the bureaucracies in most cities or the nation. But some state governments have become highly professional. In one of the few extended studies of how reporters cover state government, David Morgan describes in detail how Governor Nelson Rockefeller manipulated New York state journalists in a way that Presidents Roosevelt, Kennedy, or Reagan might have admired, using some of the same techniques they found so successful.[2]

The image problem of state government appears to grow out of state legislators' behavior. Even the most professional of these bodies has mostly members who live elsewhere, commute great distances to the capital, and are absent for long weekends, a situation found in no other governmental unit. And a dwindling number of states still limit their legislative sessions, some meeting as little as two months a year.

Part-time legislators have less time to fully grasp their increasingly complicated state units. They live away from home for short periods in a strange, possibly small city filled with lobbyists and other temptations; some get into trouble. Legislators commonly complain that journalists are only interested in reporting scandal and corruption. Perhaps those are the stories most easily reported.

Fred Fico compared coverage of Indiana's limited session with that of Michigan's year round state legislature. He found that in Indiana's part-time legislature too much happened in too short a period for reporters to fill in major details. They used fewer sources in stories, interviewed legislators less frequently, and gave attention to fewer topics than reporters covering the full-time legislature.[3]

The power of the press camera to relay disturbing images can re-shape local and national policies. Television and newspaper accounts of police dogs lunging at blacks during the May 1963 civil rights demonstrations in Birmingham, Alabama, created a national sensation. News pictures such as this became the grist for congressional debate and contributed directly to breaking the logjam on the civil rights bill of 1964.

Staffing of Capitol Press Bureaus

Covering a statehouse well is a challenging assignment. States have active governors, extensive bureaucracies, and more of them are moving to full-time legislatures. All provide a flow of news stories. In California, even the state supreme court issues press releases. In Michigan, a journalist estimated that in a year 13,000 releases are dropped off at the capitol press room, an average of fifty each working day. He figured that legislators issue 40 percent of these stories, the governor's office 30 percent, and state agencies 30 percent.[4]

But because readers lack interest, most state press bureaus are understaffed. Television staffs are particularly light, because filmed coverage requires special equipment and personnel and quick transfer of signals from the capital city. Roughly twenty reporters of all types work full-time at the Michigan capitol. In Albany, New York, in 1978 when Morgan did his study, twenty-four were on duty. In 1973, Illinois had fewer than a dozen.

Statehouse bureaus are often poorly staffed as well. Editors assign their younger and less experienced reporters, using the statehouse as a training ground. Frequently the only political reporting experience such journalists have is covering the city-hall beat, and many arrive with little knowledge of state government. Some are out-of-state journalism-school graduates. As these journalists develop skills, editors transfer them to jobs seen as more prestigious. But generally at the capitol one also finds those who Tom Littlewood of the Chicago *Sun-Times*, in one of the first descriptions of statehouse reporting, described as "cynical oldtimers."[5]

During legislative sessions, some editors add temporary reporters to the statehouse assignment. But these are likely to be reporters who do not know their way around the capitol and have few sources to turn to for stories.

These statehouse journalists have little time for investigative reporting or even for thumbing through all the press releases. Delmer Dunn described the procedure in Wisconsin as developing a few reliable private sources, and for the rest of the stories gathering news from traditional places: governor's press conferences, meetings, and skimming the releases.[6]

The wire-service reporters spend a large part of their time reviewing, condensing, and rewriting press releases. In many states, wire copy goes out every half hour.

Extent of State Government Coverage. The capitol press corps includes one or more reporters from the capital city's newspaper. They serve a "company town," where the company is state government. Such papers are likely to provide the most detailed coverage because they know their readers are state politicians and bureaucrats; some, such as the *Sacramento Bee,* are outstanding.

The reporters representing newspapers, and sometimes television, in the state's largest cities generally favor brief items, but also are likely to feature a columnist who provides analysis. Reporters representing a chain of papers within the state are likely to follow similar procedures.

Most other papers and radio and television stations in the state get their news from the wire-service reporters. They also use their local legislators as a major source, contacting them whenever a breaking story affects the community. And local newspapers, radio, and television will generally present their legislators' releases and tapes.

State government presents special problems for television stations because a steady flow of visuals is so costly. Sometimes stations share televised reports from the capitol, most frequently for a predictable event such as a governor's state-of-the-state speech. But most state news is from the wire services and is presented with the "talking head" of the local newscaster. Over her or his shoulder is a box showing a picture of the state capitol with words such as "state budget hearings" across its face.

Most favored are stories of staged media events or stories that can be anticipated, such as the secretary of state announcing that 85 percent of the polling places in the next election will be barrier-free to accommodate the handicapped.

In a number of states, public television stations join in broadcasting discussion programs on state politics, some of them of high quality. Studies consistently suggest that those who get their news of state government from newspapers are better informed, though television is a major source of such news for most citizens.[7]

REPORTING ON LOCAL POLITICIANS

Though local governments vary from the largest metropolis, New York, to small communities served only by weekly newspapers or none at all, we will examine only the extremes, for their news characteristics and the kinds of reporting of local activities that they receive. Unlike state governments, almost all have journalists who report major activities, at least the events that arouse some controversy.

Large Urban Centers

In the largest cities, the form of government is similar to that of the nation: the mayor is the equivalent of the president, the council is the legislative body, and local trial courts and a mammoth bureaucracy make up the rest. Like the state and nation, they also have partisan elections, and their mayors are active political and administrative leaders, not figureheads. In some cities, they still control many patronage appointments.

Big-city mayors are major newsmakers, known throughout their states and often beyond. They set the local agenda by the programs they sponsor. Their idiosyncrasies are as well known as their names and faces. Some like Mayor Koch of New York and Feinstein of San Francisco, as well as those of Washington and Chicago, become national figures. Local television and print reporters frequently ask them to comment on events that affect the city's citizens. Mayor Edwin Koch of New York City holds as many as three press conferences a day.

News coverage in the biggest cities is similar to that of the national government. Local television covers the major political stories involving conflict. Television news concentrates on the central city and pays attention to outlying communities only for a particularly newsworthy event. Secondary items may be somewhat haphazardly selected. One analysis of the day's local evening news on three metropolitan stations found that eighty different items had been reported. But only twelve had been reported on all three newscasts.[8]

The city's newspaper or newspapers provide in-depth analysis and editorial comment. But many of them are being pushed to become regional or even statewide papers, so that they do not identify wholly with the city. In some, the mayor runs against the local media, especially when they feature urban murders or muggings. Mayor Coleman Young of Detroit echoed a common theme when he accused the Detroit dailies of "trashing the city for the entertainment of readers in the suburbs."

Occasionally journalists turn to investigative reporting, generally using a scandal within the city's administration. They may from time to time run an in-depth story on how some service such as the police department is being administered.

Even in large urban centers with active political parties, media coverage can make a difference in elections. A study of a partisan election in Columbus, Ohio, linked such reports to knowledge of local affairs, and knowledge, in turn, of how respondents voted.[9] A study of a mayoral race in Chicago argued that the media influenced the outcome by presenting facts about the incumbent as her critics saw her, and facts about the challenger, as his friends saw him.[10]

The Smaller City

The characteristic that distinguishes middle-sized and smaller cities from larger ones is the absence of national political parties. Two-thirds of American city governments, including many suburbs, are nonpartisan. Many of these cities have reform governments — the council-manager system. The administrative leader is a professional bureaucrat, usually recruited from outside the community. Managers become adroit in influencing what the council considers and how it decides. In all but the largest cities, politicians are part-time amateurs. Few have ambitions to move to any office higher than that of figurehead mayor.

Before television, and still in most middle-sized or smaller cities today, a monopoly newspaper may dominate civic activities and greatly influence city politics; it need not worry about a strong mayor backed by fellow partisans, setting the civic agenda. Such a newspaper, even a weekly, builds public confidence in its leadership by setting itself up as defender of community interests and creator of a local consensus, a tactic commonly described as "boosterism."

Such a paper can stand as an independent arbiter of local political and civic affairs, a kind of guide and conscience for the community. Because its constituency is the whole city, it takes a broad view. Civic leaders, such as the Chamber of Commerce or social agencies, seek its support. Business leaders and politicians find that newspaper support is often crucial to sell a project. And in elections its endorsements can make or break politicians on the way up and destroy support for a city manager.

Television is handicapped in such a role because its broadcasts cover so many local governments. It must squeeze its local news into the twenty-two or so minutes that also include sports and weather. The anchors are often temporary and somewhat inexperienced. They move on to larger market areas, advancing in their career, or are fired because of declining ratings. Print journalists may also move to other jobs, but the changes are less obvious to the reader.

Extent of Local Reporting. Print journalists criticize local television news shows for their "happy-talk" chitchat between the "news readers," and their "fuzz and wuz" (police at accident scenes) sensational coverage of fires and auto accidents to catch viewers' attention. Nevertheless their strength is that people are more likely to believe what they see than what they read. At least one study found that citizens perceived local television news to be a more credible, truthful, and important source of local news than the local newspaper.[11]

In many smaller cities, print journalists need not report all stories just because they fear their competition will do so. Their competition is radio and television, both of which usually report only major political stories. Perhaps the major disadvantage these local reporters face is that many in the community know their editor personally. Complaints are more easily transmitted in casual daily contacts than in the metropolis.

Newspaper journalists can filter the news according to their standards of newsworthiness. A study of a Bloomington, Indiana newspaper revealed that only 59 percent of items in a year's worth of council minutes were reported. The researchers designated some items as major by counting the words devoted to them in council minutes. Only a third of these were reported, most of them economic topics such as finances, building construction, economic investment, and industrial development. When shown the study results, the Bloomington reporter who covered council meetings said he consciously "boiled down" education, animal protection, honors and awards, and historical documents and awards. These, he said, were not controversial and therefore not newsworthy.[12]

In one widely used textbook on urban politics the authors argue that coverage is often shallow because it is unprofitable for the print media and because news space is too limited. Resources invested in more intensive coverage will not increase circulation by much. Still, for the most part, local citizens do not demand more local news. Newspaper attention to local civic affairs even now occurs more often because editors think readers ought to be informed about governments close to home, than as a response to citizens' demands. Citizens, editors say, are getting more local news than many desire.[13]

JOHN DARLING By Armstrong & Batiuk

© Field Enterprises, Inc., Batiuk and Shamray, 1981 by permission of North America Syndicate, Inc.

NOTES

1. For an extended discussion see Charles Press and Kenneth VerBurg, *States and Communities in a Federal System,* 2nd ed. (New York: John Wiley, 1983), Chapter 1, "The Study of State and Community Politics."
2. David Morgan, *The Capitol Press Corps, Newsmen and the Governing of New York State* (Westport, Conn: Greenwood Press, 1978), Chapter 4, "The Rockefeller Years," pp. 43–47.
3. Frederick Fico, "Legislative Structure and Reporting Style: Statehouse Coverage of Parttime vs. Fulltime Legislatures," paper delivered at the meetings of the Midwest Political Science Association, April 11–15, 1984 in Chicago.
4. Jerry Moskal, "Flacks Perpetrate a 'Blizzard'" *Lansing State Journal,* Feb. 7, 1982.
5. Tom Littlewood, "The Trials of Statehouse Journalism," *Saturday Review* (Dec. 10, 1966): 82–83.
6. Delmer D. Dunn, *Public Officials and the Press* (Reading, Mass.: Addison-Wesley, 1969), Chapter 4, "The Reporter's Work: Gathering and Writing Stories," pp. 37–58.
7. Joey Reagan and Richard V. Ducey, "Effects of News Measure on Selection of State Government News Sources," *Journalism Quarterly* 60 (Summer 1983): 211–217, and Margaret K. Latimer and Patrick R. Cotter, "Effects of News Measure on Selection of State Government News Sources," *Journalism Quarterly* 62 (Spring 1985): 31–36.
8. George Bullard, "Underneath the Flash, They May Look Alike but Detroit's Nightly News Shows Offer a Surprising Diversity," *Detroit News,* April 1, 1984, p. E–1.
9. Lee B. Becker and Sharon Dunwoody, "Media Use, Public Affairs Knowledge and Voting in a Local Election," *Journalism Quarterly* 59 (Summer 1982): 212–218.
10. Doris A. Graber, "Candidate Images in a Mayoral Race of Racism, Feminism, and Ghosts of the Past." Paper delivered at the American Political Science Association meetings, Chicago, Sept. 1–4, 1983.
11. John D. Abel and Michael O. Wirth, "Newspaper vs. TV Credibility for Local News," *Journalism Quarterly* 54 (Summer 1977): 371–374.
12. David Weaver and Swanzy Nimley Elliott, "Who Sets the Agenda for the Media? A Study of Local Agenda-Building," *Journalism Quarterly* 62 (Spring 1985): 87–94.
13. Edward C. Banfield and James Q. Wilson, *City Politics* (Cambridge: Harvard University Press and M.I.T. Press, 1963), pp. 313–325.

Index